THE

Bible in the Counting-House:

A COURSE OF

LECTURES

TO

MERCHANTS.

BY

H. A. BOARDMAN, D.D.

PHILADELPHIA:
LIPPINCOTT, GRAMBO & CO.
1853.

STEREOTYPED BY J. FAGAN. T. K. AND P. G. COLLINS, PRINTERS.

TO THE

Merchants of Philadelphia,

THESE LECTURES

ARE RESPECTFULLY INSCRIBED,

BY THEIR FRIEND

AND FELLOW-CITIZEN,

H. A. BOARDMAN.

PREFACE.

MERCHANTS have had too little help from the Pulpit. They have been left, very much, to frame their own ethics, and to grapple, as they might, with the temptations and trials of business. There is no lack of sermons and books on the vices of great cities. Able treatises on the formation of character, enter largely into the conservative literature of the age. But an adequate Hand-book on the moralities of Commerce, is yet to be supplied. The present volume does not aspire to this elevated function: it is merely an humble essay in that direction. It has been prepared as a companion to the "BIBLE IN THE FAMILY"; and is offered to the Mercantile classes with the hope, that, through the Divine blessing, its suggestions may afford them some assistance in adjusting the casuistries of trade, and subordinating its aims and implements to the higher ends of life.

To the ten Lectures comprised in the series, there is appended a discourse delivered on a funeral occasion, before the Young Men attached to the "Jobbing-Houses" in this city.

PHILADELPHIA, *May*, 1853.

CONTENTS.

LECTURE I.

THE CLAIMS OF THE MERCANTILE PROFESSION UPON THE PULPIT.

LECTURE II.

THE RULE OF COMMERCIAL RECTITUDE.

LECTURE III.

THE TRUE MERCANTILE CHARACTER.

LECTURE IV.

HASTING TO BE RICH.

LECTURE V.

SPECULATING.

LECTURE VI.

BANKRUPTCY.

LECTURE VII.

PRINCIPALS AND CLERKS.

LECTURE VIII.

DOMESTIC LIFE, AND LITERARY CULTURE, OF THE MAN OF BUSINESS.

LECTURE IX.

THE CLAIMS OF THE SABBATH UPON MERCHANTS.

LECTURE X.

THE TRUE RICHES. — LIVING TO DO GOOD.

LECTURE XI.

SUGGESTIONS TO YOUNG MEN ENGAGED IN MERCANTILE BUSINESS.

Lecture First.

THE CLAIMS OF THE MERCANTILE PROFESSION UPON THE PULPIT.

An intelligent gentleman, a partner in an opulent commercial house, once said to me — "We could, without the least difficulty, increase our annual profits to the extent of several thousand dollars, if we were willing to conform to usages which are practised by many firms around us." This observation made the deeper impression upon me, because I had just been reading a small volume,* the object of which was, not precisely to discuss, but by means of a fictitious narrative to illustrate, the question — "Is it possible, in the present state of things, to do a mercantile business successfully, on Christian principles?" The author of this work, "A Counting-House Man," without replying to the question categorically, incorporates his answer with the facts of the narrative. His hero, an incorruptible young merchant, after a

* Herbert Tracy.

brief commercial career in New York, fails; and the book leaves him driving his plough, a cheerful farmer, surrounded by a happy family, at Tarrytown.

Why are such books written? Why such observations made? If they were the fruit of pique, or sprang from mere transient impulses, they would merit little attention. But they have a different origin, and are clothed with a much deeper significance. They betray a pervading anxiety and dissatisfaction among the mercantile community. They disclose the workings of the conscience which underlies the commercial world. They show that men of principle are not at rest; that they distrust the received methods of business; that there are current frauds and dishonesties in the impetuous rivalries of trade, which it takes all their equanimity to keep them from denouncing in the market-places and at the corners of the streets; and that they themselves are often harassed with questions of casuistry, which it requires a mature skill in the ethics of the New Testament to bring to a ready solution. The change which has come over the world within the last half-century is felt in the thoroughfares of commerce even more than in legislative halls and ecclesiastical synods. The moderation, the composure, the gradual, spontaneous expansion of trade, the rational hours, and tranquil sleep, which belonged to a mercantile life fifty years since, have given place to universal and prolonged excitement, restless activity, a competition which would not have disgraced the Isthmian games, an unquenchable passion for wealth, a subjugation of all the achievements of science and all the implements of art to the purposes of traffic, and a sacrifice of personal ease and domestic comfort which our fathers would no more have dreamed of than they would of spending life in a railroad car. Whether this revolution could have been prevented, or whether it is not, on the whole, beneficial, is not a question now before us. We must take things as they are; and in this view, the perplexities and perils incident to a mercantile career are such as no intelligent and upright man can contemplate without emotion. The subject is certainly one of profound and growing interest to all who are concerned for the morals of the country. That it has a claim upon the sympathy and the friendly co-operation of the PULPIT, which has as yet been recognized only in a very inadequate degree, must be too apparent to require any special demonstration. It may be doubted whether there is any work more imperatively needed, or one which would be more useful, than an able, judicious, and popular treatise ON THE APPLICATION OF CHRISTIAN MORALITY TO THE AFFAIRS OF COMMERCE. The admirable volume on this subject by the late Dr. Chalmers can never become superannuated. But, luminous and eloquent as it is, like every thing which bears the impress of his great mind, it needs to be supplemented by a corresponding work, devoted to certain topics which it did not fall in his way to discuss, and adjusted to the modern usages of the trading world. It may require another Chalmers to supply this desideratum, but whoever shall furnish it will confer a lasting obligation, not only on the commercial classes, but on society at large. For, in truth, under our institutions, we are all implicated in the character of that profession. Reticulated as they are, from their numbers, their intelligence, their wealth and enterprise, with every political and every ecclesiastical institute, it is impossible to segregate them from the mass of the people — to put the merchants on one side and "society" on the other. In the United States, society must be virtually what the merchants are. It reflects their morality, and uses their axioms in working out its cases of conscience. Every community has a stake in keeping up the barometers in its Counting-houses to the highest possible point. A downward tendency there is certain to be felt in every limb of the social structure; and whenever the mercury, by a simultaneous and rapid depression, indicates a general deterioration of commercial integrity, ten thousand secret sluices begin to discharge their deadly poison around the roots of all public and all private virtue.)

Allusion has been made to the difficulty of maintaining an inflexible honesty in mercantile pursuits. This is no imaginary difficulty. The business of buying and selling involves a constant appeal to the principle of self-interest. There is danger in this even under propitious circumstances, as in the simple barter which is carried on amongst the inhabitants of pastoral districts; and the temptations to dishonesty are indefinitely multiplied in large manufacturing or trafficking towns. Not to expatiate now on a topic which will frequently recur as we proceed, let it suffice to refer to the intense competition which prevails in every branch of business; to the number of unprincipled persons who betake themselves to merchandise for a livelihood; to the inexperience of multitudes who embark in trade; to the common effect of interest in misleading the conscience; and to the facile subserviency with which most individuals acquiesce in existing customs, without stopping to inquire whether they are sanctioned by the morality of the Scriptures. The dangers flowing from these and other sources are thickly strewn in the paths of commerce. They are subtle and imminent. They are permanent and cumulative. They are aggravated by the risks and hazards from without, which are bound up in a business-life. The merchant's motto is, and must be, "Nothing venture, nothing win." He must trust his property in the hands of others, who are often strangers to him and living hundreds or thousands of miles off. He must send his ships to explore distant oceans, and to seek out untried markets. He must expose his goods to the perils of land and sea, and to the capricious changes of winds and climates. A political revolution abroad may fall with crushing force upon his house. A popular tumult, or a hasty act of legislation, at home, may thwart his plans and blast his prospects. And, amidst these varied hazards — under the pressure of reverses, successes, disappointments, unlooked-for contingencies, fluctuating markets, and fluctuating hopes — he is all the while dealing with questions not merely of loss and gain, but of *right and wrong* — questions frequently of an intricate nature, and really demanding mature study, but which he is obliged to dispose of on the spur of the moment.— Do we err then, when we say that the Counting-room is a crucible to character? Or, are we at fault in contending that the great and influential class who are cast into this fierce alembic, are entitled to the sympathy of all who can lend them a helping hand? To relieve them of their anxieties, to exonerate them from all their risks, to transform the rugged path they are treading, into a broad, smooth, level causeway, is of course impracticable. The primeval curse is not to be annulled, and man must still live by the sweat of his brow. But the case of the merchant is not, therefore, a hopeless one. If we cannot remove all the obstructions from his path, we may a part. If we cannot shield him from every danger, we may from some. If we cannot clothe him with infallibility in resolving questions of duty, we may place in his hands a standard to which he can refer such questions with the confidence that it will not deceive him. The equipment he needs, the only equipment which will at all meet the exigencies of his position, is true religion. The chart he requires, the only chart which defines with accuracy the reefs and quicksands, the treacherous shoals and vagrant currents of the sea which he is traversing, is, the word of God. THE BIBLE IN THE COUNTING-HOUSE: — this is the only specific which will at all meet the moral necessities of the business-world, or which can make it expedient for men to plunge into the perilous excitements of a life of traffic, who have any serious purpose of ever getting to heaven. To bring about this end, to inaugurate the BIBLE as the controlling authority in the marts of commerce, the acknowledged arbiter in matters of casuistry, and the test by which every usage is to stand or fall, this, surely, is an object worthy of the best exertions of all who desire the prosperity of religion and the welfare of their fellow-men. The humblest effort in this cause may claim to be received with indulgence; nor will it have been put forth in vain, should it serve only to call the attention of abler moralists to this luxuriant and neglected field of practical Christianity.

There may be those who will regard this as delicate ground. The pulpit has itself moulded a public sentiment by which it is watched with a jealous eye, lest it should venture upon themes that lie beyond its jurisdiction. Curiously enough, the territory which it is sought to sequester from all the aggressions of the sanctuary, is that which embraces the actual application of the Gospel to no small portion of the daily avocations of men. Upon the paths which men are treading for six days out of every seven, upon their husbandry and their handicraft, their shops and their warehouses, their hoarding and their disbursing, their legislation and their jurisprudence, there is impressed the brand of a secularity so flagrant that the pulpit cannot venture into this arena, without contracting the taint of a grievous defilement! A pastor may, indeed, so far approach the boundary of this quarantined region, as to lanch the denunciations of the violated law against all and singular of its busy tribes who transgress its high requisitions; but he must not go to them, to explain what the law demands of them, and how they are to keep within the line of its prescriptions. He may arraign the manufacturer or the trader on the broad score of dishonesty, and set forth the penalty a retributive justice has attached to his misdeeds; but the sacredness of his office forbids him to take the Gospel and go with it into their mills and their counting-rooms, and aid them in applying its divine precepts to their respective avocations. And so it comes to pass, that when a Christian minister propounds for discussion one of these *tabooed* topics, he is quite likely, on the one hand, to wound the sensibilities of certain sincere and excellent people, who tremble to think of his degrading the Gospel into a mere scheme of morals; and, on the other, to disturb the equanimity of certain careless and somewhat unscrupulous devotees of mammon, who think he had better confine himself to his own sphere and leave them to theirs.

Now, if the occasion called for it, it would be easy to show that these views proceed upon a radical misconception of the functions of the ministry. Undoubtedly, the main office of the pulpit is to illustrate and enforce the great doctrines of revelation, and the duties of repentance towards God and faith in the

Lord Jesus Christ. There is a pregnant meaning in that declaration of the apostle, "I determined not to know anything among you save Jesus Christ and him crucified." A crucified Saviour — redemption by the blood of Christ, and regeneration by the Holy Spirit — as it is the grand, central theme of the New Testament, so it must be the burden of every preacher who would save the souls of men. Nor is this essential only in respect to its connexion with forgiveness and spiritual renewal. It is no less indispensable as supplying the only solid basis and effectual guarantee of a holy life. Those persons who, in their prejudice against theological disquisitions, would restrict the pulpit to the inculcation of charity, forget that you cannot build a house without a foundation, or that if you do, it will as certainly tumble down as do so many of the fragile structures which cupidity and recklessness run up in our cities. The χαριτας of the Bible — that divine love which clasps the whole human family in its embrace, and would wellnigh emulate the Saviour's benevolence and "lay down its life for the brethren" — draws its being from the TRUTH, lives upon the truth, rejoices in the truth, conquers by the truth, and will yet bring the nations back to their allegiance to Christ through the truth. To attempt to array it against the truth, to argue in favour of preaching love as contrasted with preaching doctrine, is as preposterous as it would be to contrast a stream with its fountain, or the fruit of a tree with its roots and sap. You may garnish over a bad character, or embellish an amiable one, by inculcating charity; but to expect in this way to transform a man into "a new creature," is as unphilosophical as it is contrary to Scripture. There can be no intelligent piety where the understanding does not lead the way. *Believe*, and thou shalt be saved.

But if morality is not to be preached without theology, neither is theology without morality. If Christianity makes its first appeal to the understanding, it does not rest there. If it reveals a heaven, it does not, like the god of the Epicureans, hold itself aloof from all fellowship with earth. It is a religion to live by, as well as to die by. As it challenges the homage of all mankind, so it exerts its prerogative over all human pursuits, and proffers its benign assistance to men of every character and occupation. The New Testament is one of the most *practical* of all works. Those who are so zealous for confining the pulpit to a stereotype round of subjects, to what may be defined as religious subjects, would do well to consider the generous commingling of moral precepts with the doctrinal utterances of the Saviour and his apostles. It may be worthy of their inquiry whether the Sermon on the Mount would fall within the sweep of that canon which they are anxious to impose on the ministrations of the sanctuary; and whether the closing portions of the Epistles, in the directory they present for the conduct of persons in the different relations of society, might not, under the same canon, lie open to a charge of legalism. Without illustrating this point in detail, take the following citations by way of example:

Render therefore to all their dues: tribute to whom tribute is due; custom to whom custom; fear to whom fear; honour to whom honour. Owe no man anything but to love one another.

We beseech you that ye study to be quiet, and to do your own business, and to work with your own hands, as we commanded you; that ye may walk honestly toward them that are without, and that ye may have lack of nothing.

See that none render evil for evil unto any man; but ever follow that which is good, both among yourselves, and to all men.

For even when we were with you, this we commanded you, that if any would not work, neither should he eat. For we hear that there are some which walk among you disorderly, working not at all, but are busy-bodies. Now them that are such, we command and exhort by our Lord Jesus Christ, that with quietness they work and eat their own bread.

Behold, the hire of the laborers who have reaped down your fields, which is of you kept back by fraud, crieth: and the cries of them which have reaped, are entered into the ears of the Lord of Sabaoth.

Charge them that are rich in this world, that they be not high-minded, nor trust in uncertain riches, but in the living God, who giveth us richly all things to enjoy.

In this way the principles of religion are carried out and applied to the affairs of every-day life. Men are not only exhorted in general terms to honesty, sobriety, and industry, but there is a specific adjustment of the perfect morality of the decalogue to their several relations and employments. It is reasonable to presume that if the world had been as *commercial* then as it is now, or if any large portion of those to whom the Saviour and his apostles immediately addressed themselves had been engaged in trade, the New Testament would have abounded still more than it does, in counsels, cautions, admonitions, and encouragements, appropriate to mercantile matters. As it is, there is prominence enough assigned to this subject to warrant, and even enjoin, the ministers of religion to go directly into the abodes of Commerce, and publish to the great army of traffickers, the high requisitions of Christianity. This, indeed, is no less a work of philanthropy than a work of professional duty; for the field here contemplated has been a most disastrous one to human virtue. If its chronicles could be written, they would furnish as well some of the saddest, as some of the brightest, chapters in the annals of the race. To an eye gifted with spiritual discernment, it is a field strewn with memorials of the dead, surpassing as much in their sorrowful significance as in their numbers, the bones which have whitened the soil of Leipsic or of Waterloo. Where War has slain its thousands, Commerce has slain its ten thousands: — with other weapons, indeed, and with a more terrible and far-reaching mortality. It presents to us no batteries and bayonets, no blood and carnage. It strikes not at the body, although this sometimes falls, but at the soul. It smites with a secret leprosy, which spreads its fatal virus through the arteries, even where there is every outward indication of health and happiness. The victims it has sealed for destruction are, by turns, young men who constitute the flower of society; capitalists who are conspicuous in the circles of fashion; merchants whose names are a synonym on 'Change for intelligence and efficiency; financiers who are treated with deference, because by their tact and shrewdness they have amassed a sudden fortune. These, and such as these, not unfrequently carry about with them the seeds of this moral plague, when they are for years together priding themselves on their good estate, and elated with the flatteries the world is so ready to bestow upon its successful votaries. Is it *not* a work of philanthropy to go and apprize them of their danger? Are these appliances and symbols of prosperity, which not only blind them to their real condition, but serve as inlets to the noxious *malaria* that is consuming them, to deprive them of the succour we would extend to sick or suffering poverty? And is the Christian ministry, whose express mission it is to do good to all men, to withhold its salutary counsels from the multitudes, who, though not yet seized by these insidious maladies, are breathing an infected atmosphere and in jeopardy every hour? You cannot take the affirmative of these questions, without virtually impeaching the conduct and teachings of the inspired penmen. If we would tread in their steps, we must lend a helping hand to all who are making their way through the dense, *chapperel*-like temptations of a commercial life; and the very best thing we can do for them, the thing which they all need, the shrewdest and thriftiest even more than the dullest, is to aid them in installing the BIBLE IN THEIR COUNTING-HOUSES. There is no talismanic power in this to charm away temptation; no "Open Sesame," to disclose subterranean vaults of bullion which may be had for the asking; but there is a repository from which they may draw light and strength and patience and hope, to fit them for their duties, and bring them through all changes with a conscience void of offence towards God and towards man.

It may give weight to these suggestions to reflect on the strong predilection for a mercantile life by which our countrymen are distinguished. To no people has so fine a field been presented for the culture of rural tastes, nor such opportunities for enjoying the substantial comforts of a country-life: but this is not to their liking. Agriculture is tame and passionless. Our young men must have more scope for ambition, more society, and, above all, employments which will bring in quicker and ampler profits. It is no objection with them that the hazards of commerce are far greater and its temptations more insidious; that they may drudge like slaves, and have little or nothing to show for it; that a very large proportion of the merchants in every city fail, and *they* may fail too. They admit all this, but it is more than counterpoised by the spectacle of huge fortunes made in a day. The tales of sudden wealth, which go out from our Atlantic cities, are rehearsed in the hamlets of the interior with something of the fascination excited in the olden time by the feats of crusaders and knights-errant. The brilliant speculations we so often see chronicled in the newspapers, have, no doubt, decided the question of duty with many a youth, who was considering to what occupation he should devote himself. In any event, there is no village in the land which does not contribute its recruits to that vast array of clerks and junior partners which constitutes so important a part of the effective force of commerce. If a foreigner, curious in such matters, wished to compare the natives of the different portions of the Republic, down to the remotest savannas and the most secluded valleys, the best thing he could do, would be to attend a general meeting of one of our "Mercantile Library Associations." From every quarter the tide sets with a steady flow towards the depôts of commerce. And so powerful is this current, that we must make up our minds, for the present, to see the greater part of our children drawn into it. Here and there a young man of metropolitan birth astonishes his friends by turning farmer. And it is gratifying to see that retired merchants are beginning to wake up to the fact that the globe is not *all* covered with rows of houses and stores, and that there are some sources of rational enjoyment *beyond the pavement.* This feeling ought to be fostered. It will promote that attention to husbandry which is already elevating agriculture amongst us from the debasement of a mere handicraft to the dignity of a science. It will develop our resources. It will embellish the country with those well-tilled farms and tasteful homes, which make the rural districts of England so delightful to the traveller. It will help to correct the earthly and sordid tendencies in our national character. It will give position and stability to our farming population, and invigorate those virtues on which the prosperity of States mainly depends, and which have usually found their most genial home among the cultivators of the soil.

> "Ill fares the land, to hast'ning ills a prey,
> Where wealth accumulates, and men decay:
> Princes and lords may flourish, or may fade:
> A breath can make them, as a breath has made:
> But a bold peasantry, their country's pride,
> When once destroyed, can never be supply'd."

We are not in immediate danger, certainly, from this source; but it will be of no ultimate advantage to the country, if our children are trained, whether by precept or example, to disparage agricultural pursuits as inferior in respectability, in usefulness, or in true independence, to a life of traffic. And every indication of an opposite kind is to be hailed as a conservative and patriotic movement in the right direction. — Still, commerce will continue to assert its claims, and they will be acknowledged. Merchants may become bankrupt; banks and insurance companies may fail; financial crisès may ever and anon spread disaster and ruin through all the world of trade; capitalists may remonstrate, and moralists admonish; but the mass of our young men will flock, as they have done, to the marts of business. And, dealing with this as a practical question, we are not merely to inquire into the wisdom and expediency of their course, but to lend them such help as we may in meeting the perils and difficulties before them.

These considerations may suffice to show that the mercantile body have a real and urgent claim upon the pulpit for all the assistance it can render them — a claim based upon their numbers, their dangers, and the essential difficulty of applying the principles of Christian morals to the endless and abrupt contingencies of a life of traffic. But it must further be taken into the account, as already hinted, that this is not a mere class-question, a matter affecting simply the commercial interest. The whole country has a deep stake in the character of its merchants. It is they who regulate in a great measure the current morality of our cities, and our cities in turn make their mark upon the nation at large. How potent this must be, may be seen by any one who will reflect upon the boundless resources of every kind, physical, financial, and intellectual, which are employed in mercantile business. Look at the imposing array of banks, insurance companies, loan offices, and general agencies, concentrated in every large city; look at the daily newspaper press; look at the fleets of ships and steamers at the wharves, the railroads clasping distant States together with bands of iron, the telegraphic wires along which the subjugated lightning, "tamed by one of our countrymen, and *taught to speak* by another," flies with its news, outstripping time itself: — all these are the implements of commerce, and have their share in giving tone and direction to the moral sentiment of the country. To this must be superadded the entire mercantile transactions of a nation like ours — the exchanges, the credits, the buying and selling, the contracts of every type and grade, involving the daily transfer from hand to hand of millions of dollars — all which goes, however imperceptibly, to fix the general standard of morals. And this view derives additional force from the reflection, that the people are identified with the government. The agency which fashions their morality, decides the moral tone of our legislation. Comparatively few mercantile men are seen in our legislative assemblies: they are otherwise employed, and cheerfully relinquish to others the honour of making and administering the laws. But their influence is there, and tells, often with a plenary, though noiseless, influence, upon the general course of administration. The purity of our government could not long survive the extinction or radical decay of commercial integrity throughout the Union.

We may take still another step. The character

of our merchants is so far from being a mere question of *caste*, that it involves our national reputation for probity, all over the globe. The Imports of the United States for the last fiscal year amounted to $207,000,000, and the Exports to $150,000,000; to which must be added, foreign merchandise re-exported $17,000,000, and $42,000,000 of specie. This enormous traffic was, of course, in the hands of our merchants. It carried them, or their deputies, to every accessible country. It brought them in contact with people of every government and religion, from Norway to the Cape of Good Hope, from Turkey, through the Pillars of Hercules, to Cape Horn and China. Our flag floated from the masts of their majestic clippers, in the harbours of Sydney and Valparaiso, of Macao and Monrovia, of Trieste and Tahiti, of Bombay and Archangel. In these, and hundreds of ports besides, they were the chief, not to say the only, representatives of our great confederation. By them were we to stand or fall, in the judgment of these numerous tribes and governments, as an honourable or a profligate nation. What we might be as to our political institutions, our schools and our churches; how opulent we might be in material or in intellectual wealth; who were our leading statesmen and jurists, our physicians and divines, our manufacturers and agriculturists; these were points about which they would give themselves little concern. But could they rely upon the men they were trafficking with? Did their goods answer to the labels? Were their bills of exchange genuine? Were they men of substance, trading on an actual capital, or men of straw, trading on craft and effrontery? These are the questions that would interest them, and by the solutions to which they were brought, would the sentiment go forth through their respective communities and countries, that the nation to which it is your boast and mine to belong, was a fraternity of sharpers, or a fraternity of high-minded men. It were idle to protest against such conclusions. Sweeping they may be, and unwarranted by the premises; but to so lofty a pitch of dignity and power has commerce attained in the progress of modern civilization, that every trading nation must count upon being judged by its merchants. The world is ruled by money. The real Colossus that presides over Cabinets, and sways the fleets and armies of the world, is GOLD. The gravest questions of state in European diplomacy, are not unfrequently determined by private capitalists. Many a Cabinet has been obliged to postpone favourite measures, until they had been canvassed in a certain small parlour at Frankfort-on-the-Maine, by a firm, the heads of which belong to a proscribed religion. The spectacle of Kings and their ministers awaiting the nod of a Jewish Banker, presents us with the finest possible illustration of that gradual, but mighty, revolution which has taken the SPIRIT OF TRADE out of the mire, and enthroned it over crowns and sceptres. The sun and the moon and the stars of the political firmament, doing obeisance to a subject who has neither political place nor power! Who can wonder, after this, that nations should be gauged by what they are in the market? That the inquiry should be, not, "Have they a fruitful soil, populous cities, ample wealth — are they brave and enterprising, intelligent and efficient, polite and refined?" but, "Do they pay their debts? Can you trust them? When you sell them a bill of goods, will you ever see the money for it?" These are the probes which are now used by the commercial nations; implements somewhat coarse, it may be, and not always handled with the delicate manipulation of scientific surgery, but likely, after all, to reach the vital parts, and detect the actual state of things there. And, whether we relish it or not, we must acknowledge that this ordeal is the natural appendage of a system which has substituted cotton-mills for cannon-foundries, school-houses for barracks, and the autocracy of the purse for the despotism of the sword.

The inference to be drawn from the fact here stated, is a very obvious one. You have, I believe, as a common medium of trade, what are called *Pattern-cards*, by which you buy and sell large quantities of goods, without ever seeing the goods themselves. Our importers, with their army of mercantile and nautical subalterns, are our Pattern-cards. It matters not that they may not bear our brand, and that, as to some of them, we might scruple a long while before we could consent to stamp them. They will be accredited abroad in the function they have assumed, and we shall be bought and sold by them, whether the samples happen to accord with the goods in bulk or not. We have, therefore, a broad, national interest in their character. It behooves us, as we value our good name as a people, or as we wish to propagate the principles of republican freedom, to look well to the training and conduct of our merchants. If we can maintain a universal and unsullied reputation for commercial integrity, it will not only be deemed by the nations to compensate for our admitted frailties, but go far to retrieve the prejudices which might be excited against our institutions by the occasional mal-administration of our public affairs.

Such are some of the grounds which seem to entitle Commercial topics to a place in the ministrations of the sanctuary. It would be the height of presumption in me to undertake a comprehensive and thorough exposition of the morals of trade. It is with no affected humility I say it, I have no capacity for that task. But having lived now for many years in the bosom of a mercantile community, I wish to acquit myself of an obligation to you which has long pressed upon my conscience. Without essaying any elaborate discussion of principles, there are various matters lying on the surface of the subject, which it may serve a useful purpose to consider. I aspire to nothing beyond hints and suggestions. On some points, it may devolve upon me to express opinions at variance with the received doctrines in the walks of commerce. But it will be my aim to test every sentiment and usage by "the law and the testimony." And I shall esteem myself amply rewarded, if these Lectures should be at all instrumental in fostering a healthy moral sentiment in our business circles, or in assisting you to establish THE BIBLE IN YOUR COUNTING-HOUSES.

A single word in conclusion. I have just spoken of installing the Bible in your Counting-Houses. There is but one method in which this can be done effectually. It must first be enthroned in your hearts. If you do not love its morality, you will not practise it. And to love its morality, you must first love its SAVIOUR. If you trust in Him as your Redeemer, you will cheerfully serve Him as your King. Loyalty to Christ flows from faith and love, as naturally as light from the sun. And all who are united to Him, not in the way of a mere formal profession, but with a true and constant affiance, are certain to have his own gracious words verified to them, "My yoke is easy, and my burden is light."

Lecture Second.

THE STANDARD OF COMMERCIAL RECTITUDE.

PEOPLE who frequent the Philadelphia market, are in the habit of meeting there an important personage, who passes from stall to stall and waggon to waggon, and with a magisterial air, casts certain of the products of the dairy into his scales, which, if they be found wanting, he confiscates to the public treasury. What would be the result, if an official, clothed with the authority of the government, and supernaturally endowed with the requisite penetration and firmness, could go through all the haunts of commerce, equipped with the balances of the sanctuary, the WORD OF GOD, and subject every fabric and every usage of the trading world to this unerring test? Is it possible to conceive of any greater revolution in the wide realm of merchandise, than that which would be involved in adjusting the totality of its customs and its transactions to this, the only righteous, standard? What reformations would there be in weights and measures and labels, in service and in salaries, in the stereotype dialect of trafficking, in the endless expedients for entrapping the ignorant and misleading the unwary, for injuring rival houses, for depreciating goods in the buying of them and enhancing them in the selling, for creating a factitious credit and oppressing upright insolvents! What activity would there be in extricating trust-funds from illegal and perilous investments! What revisions of invoices! What remodelled instructions to captains and supercargoes! What retractions of custom-house oaths! What an augmentation of duties! What commotion at the stock-exchange! What a gathering up of bank-capital, to restore it to its legitimate channels!

This is not to say that truth and honesty have been ostracised out of the domain of commerce. It is not to admit that the Roman mythology assigned Mercury his proper place in making him the god of merchants, orators, and *thieves*. This may have been apposite enough among them; and the merchants of Rome doubtless had their own reasons for observing an annual festival in honour of their patron, on which occasion they offered sacrifices in his temple, and besought him to forgive whatever artful measures, false oaths, or falsehoods, they had used or uttered in the pursuit of gain. But the imaginary scene just sketched, carries with it no impeachment of the general integrity of the commercial classes: that, happily, is beyond the reach of suspicion. It recognizes, however, the prevalence, more or less extensive, of practices which are as freely admitted as they are deeply deplored, by upright and intelligent merchants. These practices are not covertly hinted at, or talked of in a whisper. They are among the common-places of the street and the Exchange, too notorious to be denied, and too mischievous not to be felt. That they are not met with a more decisive reprobation, and scourged out of the arena of honourable traffic, as the buyers and sellers were driven out of the temple, is to be ascribed, in some measure, to that lax morality which has so entrenched itself in the business-world as to hamper the freedom even of those who abhor it. And this, in turn, is to be traced to the substitution of false standards of virtue, for the law of God. This law has suffered no abatement in consequence of the coming of Christ. It is as much a rule of duty to us as it was to the generations that lived before the advent. He came, not to destroy, but to fulfil it. And, in his exposition of it, he has not only ratified every jot and tittle of the decalogue, but added a "new commandment." "Thou shalt love the Lord thy God with all thy heart and with all thy soul and with all thy strength and with all thy mind; and thy neighbour as thyself." "All things whatsoever ye would that men should do to you, do ye even to them: for this is the law and the prophets." This is the Scripture code. It is no local or temporary enactment. It extends to all times, all countries, all classes, all transactions. It is no chameleon-like scheme, which takes its hue from the interests with which it may happen to come in contact. It knows no variableness, nor shadow of turning. It speaks the same language in the palace as in the cottage, on the banks of the Ganges as on the banks of the Delaware. It is a stranger alike to fear and favour, to pity and resentment. Creation has not wealth enough to bribe it. The most evanescent emotion that flits across the human breast, is not subtle enough to elude it. The threats of power and revenge, are shivered upon it, like spears upon a granite rock. The appeals of interest and affection recoil from it, like the waves which break and die at the base of Carmel.

This is the august and immutable standard of morality, which demands the homage of the eager tribes of commerce, of whatever clime, or tongue, or occupation. Impressed with the image and superscription of the only Lord of the conscience, it claims to be installed in every counting-room, and wheresoever men may meet for traffic. And if the claim were as universally conceded as it is urged, that auspicious transformation would pass over the wide domain of Commerce, which was described in the opening of this Lecture. But this code is too pure and too just to suit the masses in any country. And there is a constant disposition to substitute for it some other, which will bend to men's passions and interests.

There are, for example, in every great trading community, individuals whose only rule of conduct is *Expediency*. Right and wrong are with them mere professional technicalities. Questions of casuistry are as regularly ciphered out as the details of a balance-sheet. If a transaction promises to promote their interest, it is right; if not, it is wrong. If a lie will answer a better purpose than the truth, it would be effeminate not to use it. If they can take the advantage of a customer, without being detected, they would be faithless to themselves to let the opportunity slip. I say, "without being detected:" for it must not be supposed that this class of persons have cast off all outward decorum. Far from it. It is one of the elements which enter into their current calculations, how far they can go in this or that direction without being exposed, and whether any proposed measure can be adopted without a sacrifice of their reputation. They are so graphically delineated by the great Coryphæus of the school to which they belong, that I am tempted to quote his own words. In considering the question, "whether Princes ought to be faithful to their engagements," Machiavelli observes, "It is not necessary for a Prince to possess all the good qualities I have enumerated, but it is indispensable that he should appear to have them. He should earnestly endeavour to gain the reputation of kindness, clemency, piety, justice, and fidelity to his engagements. He ought to possess all these good qualities, but still retain such power over himself as to display their opposites whenever it may be expedient. He should habituate himself to bend easily to the various circumstances which may from time to time surround him. In a word, it will be as useful to him to persevere in the path of rectitude, while he feels no inconvenience in doing so, as to know how to deviate from it when circumstances dictate such a course. He should make it a rule, above all things, never to utter anything which does not breathe of kindness, justice, good faith, and piety: this last quality it is most important for him to appear to possess, as men in general judge more from appearances than from reality."*

---

* The Prince, chap. xviii.

The cool atrocity of this deliverance may at first suggest a doubt, whether the system it defines really has its disciples as well among merchants as politicians. But the distinctive characteristic of the system, is, policy as opposed to principle. In this view there are, it is to be feared, as many Machiavellian merchants as politicians. They are men who, at heart, sneer at the "precision" and "scrupulosity" of firms which are controlled by Christian integrity. They have no conception of a virtue which brings no cash with it. "Honesty, like every other commodity, has its market value. 'Too much honesty won't pay.' What reason is there in being so very 'upright,' when your neighbours are all outstripping you? If it is lawful to traffic at all, it must be proper to resort to such expedients as will insure you success in your operations. The main thing at present is to 'make money.' The sooner that is accomplished the better. And then it will do to talk of 'doing to others as you wish others to do to you.'" — These are the maxims,

——— "uttered or unexpressed,"

of the class of men we are speaking of. The only authority of which they have any dread, is the statute-book. If they can keep out of the hands of the Grand Jury, and carry a fair exterior among men of honourable sentiments, they are satisfied. And this they are frequently able to do, by means of proxies. The machinery of commerce and finance is now so complete, that the mechanism itself is all that appears: the power that moves it is out of sight. You may stand behind the curtain, nay, you may even sit among the audience, and work the ropes and pullies that control the shifting panorama, without seeming to have any more agency in the exhibition than the spectators around you. This is constantly done by men of integrity: it promotes despatch, convenience, and efficiency. But of course, it is very liable to abuse. Unprincipled operators wield it to good purpose. Many a Shylock sits in his quiet office, during business-hours, with his hands upon the lever which is crushing his neighbours' hearts. They writhe under the terrific engine, and look one way and another for help. But no help comes. The fatal hour of *three* draws on, and another turn of the thumb-screw tells them what mercy they are to expect. "Mercy?"

> "You might as well go stand upon the beach,
> And bid the main flood bate his usual height;
> You might as well use question with the wolf,
> Why he hath made the ewe bleat for the lamb;
> You might as well forbid the mountain pines
> To wag their high tops, and to make no noise,
> When they are fretted with the gusts of heaven;

You might as well do anything most hard,
As seek to soften that, (than which what's harder?)
His mercenary heart."

He has but one passion, one principle, one end, one god, HIMSELF. What is it to him that hearts *are* crushed; that deserving men have in desperation thrown themselves into his machine of torture, and that with every turn of the wheel, not only they, but a wife and children, are wrenched and racked. This is their misfortune, but not his fault. He is no more to blame for it, than is the fire or the water which drives the enginery, for the death of the man who is drawn into the whirling mass and killed. They were seeking their own advantage. He is doing no more. Their reverses cannot be charged upon him. The propositions he now makes, they are not bound to accede to; nor can he be required to forego an opportunity for a profitable bargain. It is an every-day transaction, too simple and too common to raise scruples or excite feeling in any quarter.

If this is a strong case, it is none the less apposite for illustrating the true working of the principle of Expediency, when thoroughly carried out as a rule of conduct in commercial life. It may be hoped that the number of individuals who have wedded themselves to it with all this recklessness of moral obligation, is very small: but whether few or many, they must be regarded, whenever known, as the opprobrium of the mercantile profession. They prove, at least, that Commerce has its racks and inquisitors, no less than the Church.

If an illustration of this topic on a broader scale be needed, there is one at hand, which has too often engaged the attention of the Christian world not to be familiar to you all. I refer not to the slave-trade, but to a traffic which is second only to that in atrocity, to wit: the British opium-trade in China. "In putting down the slave-trade," says a very intelligent English writer, "it was not considered too much to maintain a naval force on the coast of Africa; and, to abolish slavery in the British dominions, the sum of twenty millions was willingly sacrificed; yet slavery was not productive of more misery and death than the opium traffic, nor were Britons more implicated in the former than in the latter."*—The facts are in a nutshell. The Chinese are passionately fond of opium. It is at once the most fascinating and the most destructive poison they could use, greatly surpassing intoxicating spirits in both these respects. "In proportion," says Mr. Medhurst, "as the wretched victim comes under the power of the infatuating drug,

---

* Medhurst's China.

so is his ability to resist temptation less strong; and, debilitated in body as well as in mind, he is unable to earn his usual pittance, and not unfrequently sinks under the cravings of an appetite which he is unable to gratify. Thus they may be seen, hanging their heads by the doors of the opium shops, which the hard-hearted keepers, having fleeced them of their all, will not permit them to enter; and shut out from their own dwellings, either by angry relatives or ruthless creditors, they die in the streets, unpitied and despised." "Every opium-smoker may calculate upon shortening his life ten years from the time when he commences the practice: one-half of his physical energies are soon gone; one-third of his scanty earnings are soon absorbed; and, feeling strength and income both diminishing, while the demands upon his resources are increased, he seeks to obtain by duplicity what he cannot earn by labour; and thus his moral sense becomes blunted and his heart hardened, while he plunges into the vortex of ruin, dragging with him his dependent relatives and all within the sphere of his influence. Calculating, therefore, the shortened lives, the frequent diseases, and the actual starvation, which are the result of opium-smoking in China, we may venture to assert that this pernicious drug annually destroys myriads of individuals." The Emperors have steadily refused to legalize the traffic.

Animated by a paternal regard for their subjects and an enlightened estimate of the true prosperity of the realm, they have by repeated edicts prohibited its introduction into the country, under the most rigorous penalties. Bribery, however, nullifies these edicts; and the infamous traffic goes on under the very eyes of the government officials around Canton. The extent to which the nation is becoming debauched by this poison, may be inferred from the rapid increase in the trade, as appears from the following statement: —

1816	Chests,	3,210	Value,	$3,657,000
1825	"	9,621	"	7,608,206
1836	"	27,111	"	17,904,248
1850	"	60,000	"	40,000,000

It has now reached, it will be seen, the enormous sum of $40,000,000 (of which $15,000,000 goes into the British Exchequer), and this amount is annually withdrawn from China in solid silver. The opium is raised in India, where the natives in certain districts are compelled, under pains and penalties, by their British rulers, to cultivate the poppy for the sole benefit of the government. The government sells it to merchants, at a large profit, who, in turn, ship it to China. The most urgent remonstrances have been from time to time addressed to the East India Company, the India Government, and the British Parliament, against the traffic, but without the least avail. So little sympathy, indeed, have the imperial authorities with these remonstrances, that they actually engaged in a war with the Chinese, some years since, because the latter undertook to enforce their own ordinances against the opium-trade; and several millions of dollars were wrested from them, at the cannon's mouth, in payment for opium they had caused to be destroyed. Here is Christianity on one side, and Paganism on the other. Paganism is trying to shelter its subjects from one of the worst curses which can light upon a nation, and Christianity insists upon blasting and destroying them, even though it cost a war to accomplish its purpose. This is an edifying spectacle to the unevangelized world—and happily a unique one. With a single exception, no similar example of rapacity disgraces the history of modern commerce. That exception was the magnanimous attempt made by the Cabinet of the late Louis Philippe to force French brandies and Popish missionaries upon the poor Sandwich Islanders, by means of powder and ball. This was not much out of character for a government which was covertly swayed by the Jesuits. But surely something better might have been expected of a great Protestant nation, which boasts of its Christianity, and rebukes with so magisterial an air, the real or supposed delinquencies of other nations.

This case is a pertinent one, in illustration of the topic we are considering. The sole principle recognized in this contraband traffic, is expediency. The question of its moral rectitude, seems not to have disturbed the complacency either of the merchants engaged in it, the East India Company, or the British government. It is "expedient" that they should get thirty or forty millions of dollars annually out of the Chinese, over and above the liberal profits on their lawful trade; and the right or wrong of the thing is not to be listened to. If the Chinese were a powerful nation, it might be "inexpedient" to press this traffic upon them. England very well knows what would follow, if a French fleet should enter the Thames and demand a free ingress yearly for several millions of French wines and laces. But China is very weak, and England is very strong; and as England wants the silver, this settles the morality of the question. The sufferings inflicted upon the wretched natives, are nothing to the purpose. Poverty, emaciation, starvation of families, premature and horrible death, wide-spread misery and ruin — these are no more to the dealers in the pestiferous poison, than are the anguish and desperation of the unfortunate debtor to the relentless creditor, who is resolved upon his "pound of flesh." Their standard is expediency; and expediency is as much a stranger to sensibility as to true integrity. It has no heart, as it has no conscience. And, whether you encounter it in Cabinets or in individuals, it will facilitate your negotiations with it to remember, that it has but one sense, recognizes but one standard, aims at but one end, and is swayed by one motive — self-interest. — Beware of the morality which has policy, not principle, for its foundation.

Your great danger, however, lies in another direction. The social element in our nature occasions more or less of mutual assimilation in every organized community, from the family to the commonwealth. No sooner are we brought into intimate fellowship with other persons than we begin reciprocally to mould each other's characters. A variety of collateral agencies may contribute to retard or accelerate this process: where self-interest comes to reinforce it, it is usually carried forward with energy. The beneficial results of this principle are numerous and decisive. Providence employs it in many ways for the well-being of individuals and the general improvement of society. But it has also its adverse results. And among these must be reckoned, the disposition to make the community itself the arbiter in questions of morals. This is not done of deliberate and set

5 *

purpose. It is the spontaneous effect of the assimilating element in humanity — the tendency to do what others do, and to take it for granted that what has the general sanction must be allowable. Considering what man is, it would be a marvel, if codes of morals formed in this way were not radically defective: for the stream cannot rise higher than its fountain. In some communities they are, of course, better than in others. There is scarcely any class or association which is without its peculiar code, its body of unwritten maxims and usages, which, like the common law, has been handed down from one generation to another, and is clothed with all the authority of regular statutory enactments. Even among thieves there is a law of honour. And Mr. Borrow tells us of a gipsy mother, who said to her child, "Now that you have said your prayers, you may go and steal." The Spartan code made the sin to consist, not in the stealing, but in the detection. The gipsy-code made the sin to consist in stealing without prayer. Some Diogenes might be cynical enough to insinuate, that there are civilized people who act upon the maxim, "Say your prayers, and then steal." Schools have *their* decalogue. It is apt to be one which is very tolerant of idleness and of equivocation. Straightforward honesty in dealing with a master, is not one of its provisions. In many schools, if a boy is skilful in deceiving his teacher, he is applauded for his tact and smartness. If they acknowledged the Bible-code, such a boy would lose caste: as it is, the youth may lose caste who rigidly conforms to that code. The flexible morality of *politics* has passed into a proverb, which is used to sanctify all sorts of craft and falsehood. The man who in the midst of an exciting canvass, should insist upon a literal adherence to the high morality of the Scriptures, in all the details and with all the agents of the contest, would be regarded very much as a guest who should appear at a social entertainment in the costume of the age of Queen Elizabeth. "All's fair in politics:" how preposterous, then, to bring out the antiquated ethics of Moses, to control the elections of a great nation in the nineteenth century! The *Bar*, it is alleged, has a traditionary code not coincident in all respects with the Sermon on the Mount, and tolerant of some customs which an advocate like Paul would hardly have resorted to, either before the Sanhedrim or the Areopagus. That this standard should be frowned upon by the better portion of the Profession, is honourable to them and conducive to the ends of justice. But there are many things nestling under its shade, which, if the BIBLE could be brought to bear upon them, would speed away like a fleet of Malay pirates on the approach of a steam-frigate.

In asserting that Commerce also has its conventional standards of morality, it is not meant that there are no merchants who adhere to the true standard. This would be a gross calumny. But merchants who bear this character, will be the last to deny the fact (for they feel the pressure of it in maintaining their own principles), that the "custom of trade" goes far in every business-community to supersede the law of God. Every man who embarks in business, encounters, at the outset, a most insidious temptation "to put his conscience in commission." He finds various practices, more or less current, which, if tested by "the law and the testimony," must be condemned. But they have the sanction of the commercial body; and does it become him, a tyro in trade, to set himself up as more righteous than his neighbours, and to censure usages which are interlaced with the whole modern system of merchandize? This question meets him under the most unpropitious circumstances. For, in the first place, the party concerned will, not improbably, have become familiarized with these usages in his previous training. His clerkship brought him into contact with them; and he will still recall at times the feeling of astonishment and revulsion excited in his mind when, fresh from his father's house, with all the ingenuousness of a virtuous youth, his employer first laid some service upon him which he felt to be an infraction of the Divine law. The mental struggles of his novitiate may have been painful and protracted; but in the end, he will be apt to regard these early misgivings as the promptings of a too scrupulous conscientiousness, and to acquiesce in the customs which awakened them as, on the whole, indispensable to the prosecution of business. And, then, in the second place, his stand-point is one of the worst he could occupy for looking at the question in all its bearings. The demon of self-interest is at his elbow,

—— "well stor'd with subtle wiles,"

and plying him with such arguments as the Serpent used when,

"With burnish'd neck of verdant gold, erect
Amidst his circling spires, that on the grass
Floated redundant,"

he whispered in the ear of our first mother, "Ye shall not surely die." It takes a clear-sighted man to see that his duty lies one way when his interest seems to point another. And this difficulty is increased with merchants, not only by reason of the haze which the "custom of trade" has thrown around such questions, but by the necessity they are often under of deciding them without time for deliberation. It is not surprising, therefore, that so many should content themselves with taking business as they find it, and falling in with the established routine of traffic, without going to the trouble of investigating the morality of every practice.

To illustrate the working of the artificial code thus quietly inaugurated over the realm of commerce, would be to anticipate topics which may come up in future Lectures. But, by way of example, does not the *established phraseology* of the trading classes betray the existence and the potential efficacy of such a code? That trade should have its peculiar dialect, is perfectly natural. But how different it is in its principles from the dialect of social life! There is, it is true, a language prevalent in fashionable circles, which may be traced to a similar origin. It deals largely in compliments and flatteries, aims to make you think well of yourself by assuring you of the esteem your shining virtues have awakened in the bosoms of others, and abounds in generous promises and proffers of service. But no one is so simple as to interpret it literally. It is well understood that these fine phrases mean no more than is conveyed by the expressions of courtesy, in the winding up of a letter. Aside, however, from the mere complimentary intercourse of society, we are accustomed to take people at their word. We confide in one another's veracity and candour as a matter of course. For mutual confidence is no less the cement which holds society together, than the bond of friendship. But how is it when you enter the arena of business? Will the same dictionary answer, or is it like going from London into Yorkshire? Does the endless small-talk of "shopping" keep within the broad domain of truth, or has it the equivocal reputation of a border-tenantry, who do not scruple, as occasion serves, to make forays into the adjacent territory? That there are in our own city and elsewhere many retail stores where you may rely upon every word spoken, as safely as you can upon the conversation in your own parlour, is most certain. But, allowing for all just exceptions, is there not, the world over, a facility and a latitude of expression indulged in the matter of buying and selling, which requires every one to be on his guard against deception? In some countries this is carried to a provoking extent. You do not expect an Italian shopkeeper to tell you the truth. The received code, in that country, sanctions the most wholesale lying; and no man forfeits the esteem of his fellows for using truth or falsehood indifferently, on Machiavelli's plan, according as the one or the other will best serve his turn. And there are lands this side of Italy where a person may spend a day in shopping, and on sitting down to review its incidents at evening, feel a considerable degree of uncertainty as to whether every fluent and graceful utterance heard across the counter, was framed with legal precision, and whether every purchase is exactly what it was taken to be. If you were simply thrown upon your own resources, and left to judge of the quality of goods for yourself, there might, as to many articles, be little reason to complain on finding that you had made a poor bargain. But it is the ready endorsement of the goods as reaching a certain standard, and the concealment of defects which must elude the sagacity of the purchaser, that impress so disagreeable a character upon this minor trafficking. Let an example illustrate this, and, with it, the factitious rule of morals on which we are commenting: —

A gentleman from the country placed his son with a merchant in our sister-metropolis. A lady came one day to the store, and having agreed with the young man for a silk dress, he was about cutting it off when he discovered a flaw in the silk. "Madam," said he, pointing to the place, "I deem it my duty to tell you there is a fracture in this silk." She declined taking it. His employer, having overheard what passed, immediately wrote to the young man's father, to come and take him home, as "he would never make a merchant." Hastening to the city, he called at the store, and begged to be informed of his son's delinquencies. "Why will he not make a merchant?" "Because he has no tact," was the reply. "Only a day or two ago, he told a lady *voluntarily*, who was buying silk of him, that the goods were damaged; and I lost the bargain. Purchasers must look out for themselves. If they cannot discover flaws, it would be foolish in me to point them out." "And is that all his fault?" "Yes." "Then," said the father, with a glow of parental pride, "I love my son better than ever; and I would not have him another day in your store for the world."

Now, I shall not stop here to define the limitations of the principle which requires a man to specify to a buyer the defects in his goods, nor to enlarge on the idea that room must be left, in the prosecution of commerce, for the exercise of skill and sagacity. The case just stated is clearly one where the clerk was right and the principal wrong. And yet the merchant himself had been trained to think otherwise. The "custom of trade" had, with him, supplanted the Scriptures. He could set his foot upon the morality of the Bible without compunction; and, what is still more to the purpose, without the slightest prejudice to his mercantile standing. There would be nothing in this transaction repeated from day to day, as it is daily repeated in thousands of stores, to damage him as an honourable and upright man. He has kept within the sweep of that conventional virtue which presides in the thoroughfares of commerce, and his integrity is not to be gainsayed. — Have we not here a proof that there *is* a morality of trade, which differs essentially from the morality of the Bible?

And on what principle, but the "custom of trade," can we explain the use of fictitious labels, and, in general, the habit of selling things for what they are not? I have no wish to explore the workshops and laboratories of commerce. I lay claim to no special familiarity with the mysteries of trade. But if merchants themselves are to be believed, there are inexhaustible quantities of *European* goods manufactured in this country. It is deemed no ground of reproach to a manufacturer to furnish such goods, nor to merchants to deal in them. If a customer prefers French broadcloths to American, what harm is there in calling your cloths French, especially if you know them to be a good article? If he wants wines in the original casks, why should you hint to him your suspicions that the casks are more genuine than the liquor? If he wants some patent drug from Boston, why should you not supply him with a better article from nearer home, with all the requisite vouchers and certificates under the proper New England imprint?

You must know better than I do, whether practices like these are passively acquiesced in by the mercantile body. Appearances warrant the conviction that they are; that while there are many houses which have no fellowship with them, the public sentiment of the profession extenuates and shelters them; and that the numerous respectable firms which give them their immediate and efficient sanction, do it without feeling that they are traversing any rule of morality. Assuming, then, what may safely be assumed in *this* place — what, indeed, it would be very ominous not to be able to assume — that all usages of this description are in contravention of the law of God, we are furnished with another decisive proof of the repugnance between this law and the "custom of trade," another illustration of the lengths to which commerce has gone in substituting its own theories of virtue for the only legitimate standard.

There may be those who will deem it a very superfluous and a very puritanical procedure to undertake to set up the BIBLE as the grand regulator of commerce. But how is commerce to be exempted from its jurisdiction? Who is empowered to say, "We will have the Bible in our houses, our schools, our churches, our charities, but it shall not come into our stores. We are quite willing to live by it, and to die by it, and to go to heaven by it, but as to trafficking by it, that is out of the question." It may well happen that to subject the entire business-world to this regimen, to replace prescription, usage, expediency, and every spurious rule, with the precepts of Scripture, would lead to inconveniences and losses. It might require some persons to abandon the business they are engaged in, and abridge the profits of others. But what alternative is there? "I had rather be right," said one of our great statesmen a few years since, and the remark is quoted oftener than anything he ever said — "I had rather be RIGHT, than be President." You all applaud the sentiment. You honour the memory of Henry Clay, because he uttered it. We do but apply it to your own profession, when we insist upon your enthroning THE BIBLE IN YOUR COUNTING-HOUSES. We press it upon you as the one controlling, unalterable, indispensable, rule of life, that you do RIGHT. It may demand sacrifices; it may cost you many a trial of feeling; it may separate you from friends; it may expose you to reproach. These are serious evils. They are to be shunned, if they can be, with a good conscience. But if you have to choose between them and a good conscience, you cannot be at a loss where truth and duty lie. It is not necessary that you should escape trouble, but it is necessary that you should do right.

This may seem to imply a doubt as to the *profitableness* of high-toned integrity. It is put in this form only to give the statement the greater strength. A host of merchants could be cited to show from their own books that honesty is, in the long run, the best policy, and that godliness hath the promise of the life that now is, as well as of that which is to come. But waiving this, the question of right must always take precedence of the question of interest: and the Bible is, therefore, just as much entitled to be heard in the Exchange as in the Sanctuary, in the manufactory and the warehouse as in the nursery and the library.

It may well impress this conviction upon your minds, and abate any disposition you may have felt to make expediency or the custom of trade your rule of conduct, to reflect that neither these nor any other earth-born codes will be recognised in the final judgment. It may serve the purpose of men to mix themselves up in the crowd here, and to merge their individuality in professions and corporations. But there will be no professions and corporations at the bar of Christ. These alliances will be dissolved. The parties that constitute them will be arraigned singly and individually. The criminality of those numerous transactions which even "men of character" so frequently sanction in their corporate or collective capacity, while as private persons they would scorn them, will then be traced to its sources, and charged upon their active originators and their passive abettors, according to a just rule. No one before that tribunal will be so foolish as to imagine that he can transfer his own responsibility to his neighbours, or vindicate his delinquencies by pleading general connivance and example. To his own Master, he must stand or fall. And the LAW OF GOD is the inflexible rule by which he must be judged.

The sooner, therefore, we get rid of all hallucination on this subject, and admit into our hearts the full, strong, abiding sense of our personal accountability, the better for our business and the better for our souls. Because the world is full of people who are selling their souls for a mess of pottage, that is no reason why we should do it. They are no law to us, as they certainly will be able to extend us no relief, if we find ourselves ruined by following their example. The chart prescribed to us is not, it is true, a scheme of salvation, in the sense of making our own obedience the meritorious ground of our acceptance with God. That way to heaven was for ever barred up when our first parents were driven out of Paradise. If saved at all, we must be saved through the atonement of Christ. But an upright and useful life, a life conformed in its aims and motives and habitual endeavours, to the Divine law, is no less indispensable, as a part of our personal meetness for heaven, than is genuine faith as the bond of our union with the Redeemer. God has joined faith and works together, and we put them asunder at our peril. Nor will any other scheme of morals besides this, meet the exigencies of the commercial body. Whatever name they may bear, all other codes are radically deficient in precision, in comprehension, and in authority. They have no solid basis, no uniformity, no adequate sanctions. They tolerate in one place what they prohibit in another. What they concede to-day they withdraw to-morrow. By sending every man to his own interest, or to the custom of his neighbours, for his rule of conduct, they sap the foundations of integrity, and make the morals of commerce as variable and capricious as the waves which float its ships.

In majestic contrast with these fluctuating and arbitrary codes, the morality of the Bible asserts its sovereignty, and challenges the homage of the world. Emanating from the throne of the Deity, and radiant with supernal splendours, it demands the obedience of every human being, in every act and moment of his life. It waits upon us with the first dawn of moral agency, and cleaves to the disembodied spirit as it wings its way up to the throne of God and onward into the unknown depths of eternity. Endowed with the ubiquity of its Author, if we ascend up into heaven, it is there; if we make our bed in hell, behold it is there; if we take the wings of the morning, and dwell in the uttermost parts of the sea, even there will it lay its immutable behests upon us, and sit in judgment on our most unguarded actions and our most subtle thoughts. There is no spot in the universe, where we can elude its jurisdiction: no finite arm, which can shelter from its anathema the man who fails in the least jot or tittle of its requirements. But there *is* a spot where we can learn to love this sublime and holy law, even while it condemns us; and a Power which can absolve us from its curse and enfranchise us with its rewards, without abetting disloyalty or encouraging ingratitude. That spot is Calvary. That Power is the God and Father of our Lord Jesus Christ, who "so loved the world that he gave his only-begotten Son, that whosoever believeth in him should not perish, but have everlasting life." The blood of the cross is the only safe-guard against the penalty of the law. And it is the mysterious property of that blood, when sprinkled upon the heart, not only to avert from it the descending bolt of Divine justice, but to inspire it with the same affectionate veneration for the holiness, which it has for the mercy, of God. This truth, which we are all so slow to understand, it is the gracious office of the SPIRIT to impress upon the conscience. Under

His administration, we gratefully receive the Gospel as our ground of hope, and the law as our rule of duty. Let it be your care to invoke, with earnestness and importunity, that help which He alone can afford you. Transformed by Him into the Divine image, you will view even your secular employments in their higher relations, and endeavour to conduct them on Christian principles. It will be no irksome task to set up the Bible in your Counting-Houses, when the God of the Bible is once admitted to his rightful place in your hearts.

Lecture Third.

THE TRUE MERCANTILE CHARACTER.

As I was about writing the closing paragraphs of my last Lecture, I received a letter from a gentleman of the highest social and commercial standing in one of our principal cities, which contained the following paragraph: —

"It gives me pain to inform you that our friend, Mr. ——, is in a very critical state of health: he is confined to his house, and forbidden even to see his intimate friends. No man could be taken from this community, whose loss would be more severely felt: for everywhere his influence has been exerted for good. Such a liberal outlay of money, combined with unwearied personal exertions, in the cause of benevolence, we have never seen here — the whole directed by intelligence and sound judgment. In the mercantile community, he stands without a peer, while he is the delight of the social circle, in which, however, he mingles with great moderation. Added to all, he is a conscientious Christian. He observed to a friend of ours, a few days since, that he regarded his present illness as a blessing that had been sent to snatch him from the whirlwind of a life he was leading, and afford him the opportunity of paying some attention to his more important interests."

Sad as this intelligence was, I felt that there was a providence in its reaching me at the moment when I was casting about for some method of bringing before you a suitable exemplar of the TRUE MERCANTILE CHARACTER. The gentleman referred to in this extract, is at the head of a house which is known in every leading port of the globe. No wind can blow which will not waft one of their ships homeward. Their counting-rooms have more the aspect of a great banking establishment than a mercantile house. The administrative capacity requisite to conduct their affairs, would be more than sufficient to endow the entire cabinet of many a European principality. But the business is in the hands of one who is quite equal to the position. Possessing a ready and sagacious mind, stored with ample professional knowledge and embellished with general reading, energetic, prudent, systematic, conscious of his own resources, and thoroughly conversant with every department of their operations, his whole character reposes on a basis of inflexible integrity, is pervaded with a spirit of enlightened piety, and garnished with a serene and cheerful temper, which sparkles like a fountain in the sunshine. Enter his private office when you may, be it "Steamer-day," "Packet-day," or any other "day," be it when he is surrounded by the captains and super-cargoes of their fleet, or absorbed with negotiations involving a half-million of money, you are certain to be met with a manly smile. Despatch, you will find, and promptitude: but no flurry, no imperiousness, no gruffness. Refinement and courtesy preside there as visibly as in his private mansion. And if your errand be one of philanthropy, you are quite as sure of a cordial greeting as though you called to charter a ship for Canton or to buy a thousand bales of cotton. Indeed, it is one of the singular excellencies of this accomplished merchant, that while conducting an extended commerce with every part of the globe, he is known as one of the most efficient managers in various charitable institutions, and devotes a large amount of time to *personal exertions* for the relief of the suffering poor.

Having hung up this portrait, crudely sketched as it is, where we can all see it, we are prepared to say that the true mercantile character comprises, as one of its essential elements, *a comprehensive and liberal conception of the dignity and utility of commercial pursuits.*

Boswell relates that he one day asked Dr. Johnson, "What is the reason that we are angry at a trader's having opulence?" "Why, sir," he replied, "the reason is (though I don't undertake to prove that there is a reason), we see no qualities in trade that should entitle a man to superiority. We are not angry at a soldier's getting riches, because we see that he possesses qualities which we have not. If a man returns from a battle, having lost one hand, and with the other full of gold, we feel that he deserves the gold; but we cannot think that a fellow by sitting all day at a desk, is entitled to get above us." *Boswell.* "But, sir, may we not suppose a merchant to be a man of an enlarged mind, such as Addison in the Spectator describes Sir Andrew Freeport to have been?" *Johnson.* "Why, sir, we may suppose any fictitious character. We may suppose a philosophical day-labourer, who is happy in reflecting that by his labour he contributes to the fertility of the earth, and to the support of his fellow-creatures; but we find no such philosophical day-labourer. A merchant may, perhaps, be a man of an enlarged mind; but there is nothing in trade connected with an enlarged mind."

This is a very characteristic growl; but even Johnson would hardly have emitted it, had he lived a half century later. Commerce has fought its way (if this phrase may be used of a pursuit which is proverbially the patron of peace) to a position in which it can afford to treat cynical sneers, from whatever quarter, with contempt. And yet, with all the opulence and power it has attained, there is still but too much occasion given for strictures like those we have quoted. Crowded to repletion as the mercantile profession is in this and some other countries, it is not surprising that there should be found in its ranks a large commixture of the precious and the vile. No inconsiderable portion of the traffickers of our land have gone into business, without the slightest preparation. The high reputation of the merchants of Great Britain throughout the globe, is to be ascribed in a great measure to the thorough training involved in their *novitiate.* The long and rigorous apprenticeship to which they are subjected corrects their extravagances, disciplines their powers, and forms them to habits of caution and to principles of integrity, before they have a counting-room of their own. And then, the whole spirit of their institutions, not to say the very genius of the nation, coalescing with this system of tutelage, goes to foster the various practical virtues for which the commercial body in England is so honourably distinguished.

This wise and salutary process is as much in conflict with the genius of our people, as it is in harmony with that of our respected relatives across the water. While the substance of it is retained by our leading commercial houses, it is quite too tedious to suit the temper of the trading classes generally. They cannot brook its restraints. Preparation for business, is not what our young men want: they must have business itself. Why waste their time in learning in the abstract, what they could so much sooner and better learn from actual practice? While they are getting ready to do something, they might be making a fortune. Plodding and moiling may do "in an old country:" the only motto which befits an American, is, "*Go ahead!*"

Such is the feeling which hurries multitudes into the various branches of trade, or starts them on bold and hazardous speculations. To say that their theory of mercantile life is a very erroneous one, would be doing them too much honour. You might as well talk of the geological theory of the China-man who is flourishing his pick in a California ravine. The only "theory" they have, is, that they want a fortune, and that "*merchandizing*" is the way to get it. What they mean by "merchandizing" is not particularly clear to their own minds; but they have a vague notion that the whole scheme of trade is a sort of scramble, where every man is to clutch all he can, regardless of the rights and interests of other people. Taking their departure from this point, one of two results is apt to follow: they are either "lucky" enough (Luck and Mammon are the only gods in their mythology) to capture some rich prizes, or, missing their reckoning, they run upon the rocks and founder—if, indeed, that can be called "foundering," which admits of a speedy refitting, and a fresh start, as often as the disaster occurs.

It would be a mistake, however, to attribute this view of mercantile pursuits to those only who embark in trade without any experience. It unhappily enters into the creed of too many persons who have served at least a partial apprenticeship, and acquired considerable tact in the management of business. Proceeding on the maxim that "each man must take care of himself," they see nothing, and care for nothing, beyond their own immediate interest. They want customers: why should they not decoy into their warehouse, men who have for years been dealing with their neighbours? Their neighbours can do the same, if they choose, with other people's customers. They have goods to sell: why should they expose their defects to buyers, when every buyer is presumed to be able to judge for himself? They have goods to purchase: why should they not avail themselves of the known or suspected embarrassments of the seller, to force him to part with his commodities below the market price? They have a bill of merchandize to pay: why should they use good money when they can, with a little legerdemain, induce their correspondent to take "country paper" or depreciated bank-notes? They require a book-keeper, and one offers whose qualifications are of the highest grade; but his family are in distress, and they know he will sooner take a meagre compensation than miss the place: why should they tender him the usual salary? — These hints will suffice to identify the class of dealers I have in view, and who are cited here for a single object. I would have you note the low, sordid, pitiful conception which these men must have of a mercantile life. They may, if you will, be rich men, successful men, men who have a potential influence in bank-parlours, and who are treated with great outward respect on 'Change. But if your profession were made up of such men, it would concentrate within itself more meanness than could now be sifted out of all the other trades and callings put together.

Commerce, as it lies before the mind of a true merchant — like him described in the opening of this Lecture, and like others we could all name, if required — has no affinity with these base principles. They see in it a system of interchanges founded on the organic structure of the globe, and mercifully designed by the Author of our being, to subserve the most salutary ends in our physical and moral training. Not, indeed, that they discard the ideas of profit and accumulation, or disparage prudence and energy in the buying and selling of goods, and in every other department of business; or deem it amiable and exemplary to let themselves be imposed upon by unprincipled rivals or adventurers. There are very few such transcendentalists in the walks of traffic. But they are men who believe in the homely maxim, "LIVE, AND LET LIVE." Instead of grasping at every thing within their reach, on the mercenary principle that "to the victor belong the spoils of the vanquished," they would not that there should be any "vanquished," but that all should receive a fair remuneration for their skill, their risks, their enterprise, or whatever they may have brought into the teeming arena of traffic. They welcome the propitious venture which fills their own lap with ingots; but they also rejoice in the prosperity which reaches their neighbours, and spreads over the whole community the ensigns of thrift and happiness. Aiming, as they are, to make a fortune, they are far from dwarfing a commercial life into this as its only or its highest function. They see it also in its nobler aspects, as looking to the well-being of individuals, the improvement of States, and the diffusion of Christianity. It supplies, in their view, one of the best of all schools for the culture of integrity, candour, moderation, decision, generosity, and other elevated qualities. These qualities are not the growth of a day. Luther specified *temptation* as one of the three things requisite to make a minister. It is equally indispensable to make a merchant; and a business-life involves a perpetual trial of one's principles. It furnishes incessant openings for the suggestions of avarice, falsehood, extortion, and jealousy. It daily invites to indolence or to rashness. And no man can, year after year, repel the Protean-like enticements to wrong-doing, which lurk along the avenues of trade and make their way into every counting-room and insinuate themselves into every business-transaction, without becoming both a wiser and a better man. His virtue will grow apace. His probity will strike its roots deeper and deeper into the foundations of his character. And he will be garnering up strength to resist future assaults of a similar kind.

The very errors and reverses of commerce conduce to the same end. One of the proper fruits of indiscretion and disaster, is, to make men prudent. A little experience of the fluctuations of mercantile affairs, may teach an impetuous temper the value of that wholesome maxim, "Hasten slowly." A careful observation of the causes which have produced the downfall of others, may prompt to a cautious and moderate policy. The disappointments to which even the most sagacious are liable, are adapted to impress the mind with a becoming sense of God's universal

Providence and our absolute dependence upon Him for success in every undertaking. In fine, even the ordinary events of a commercial life are fraught with moral lessons, no less instructive than those our Saviour has taught us to gather from the fowls of the air and the lilies of the field.

Looking at the subject in another of its aspects, whatever promotes the physical or the moral well-being of individuals, is a substantial benefit to society: so that the salutary discipline just described, to which so many characters are constantly subjected, is enlarging the moral wealth of a country, as really as the processes of trade are contributing to its material resources. If commerce multiplies our wants, it augments both our capacity and our opportunity for useful labour. It encourages industry, stimulates skill, rewards enterprise, diffuses knowledge, and developes those capabilities of exertion which slumber in the bosom of every community.

There is a still higher view than this — that which affiliates a commercial life with the welfare of Christianity. This connection may be seen in that process of *self-discipline*, already adverted to, which is going forward in the shop of many an humble tradesman. In the tedious toil with which he enlarges his scanty stock of goods, in the vigilance with which he watches for opportunities of traffic, in the firmness with which he repels the suggestions of fraud and covetousness, in the patience with which he submits to his privations, in the alternate hopes and fears, the mingled cheerfulness and anxiety, which fill up his days and too often his watchful nights, there is a gradual maturing of his character in integrity, self-command, contentment, and trust in Providence. And when we consider upon what masses of population, distributed among the various grades of mercantile life, this training is brought to bear, it can excite no surprise that we find numerous examples of a perennial and robust Christianity along the thoroughfares of trade.

On a broader scale, commerce proves itself the friend and ally of true religion, by supplying means and opening channels for its diffusion. To this result, indeed, it unconsciously contributes, even while contemplating only pecuniary gains. This was once beautifully expressed by a late illustrious advocate and statesman, who was justly esteemed as one of the chief ornaments of our city, and whose death has been felt as a national bereavement:*—"The ship which, in quest of profitable traffic, seeks out the abode of barbarian ignorance, covered with the thick darkness of inhuman superstition, is *like the first ray*

---

* The Hon. John Sergeant.

of the morning upon creation. Feeble it may be, and insufficient of itself, but it is the earnest of approaching day, growing and growing, until at length the message of piety is borne by the winds in the same ship upon the unfurrowed bosom of the ocean, and the Missionary of the Gospel comes to plant the Tree of Life in the wilderness, humbly trusting to his Almighty Master to give the increase." In this way, it may be added, Commerce has conveyed the Book of Life to many a pagan land, the harbinger of peace and freedom to the benighted nations, the emblem of approaching amity among all the tribes of earth.

These are topics which can only be glanced at here. They open to the eye a very inviting field, but we cannot enter it. The end I have in view is simply to illustrate by these hints, the elevated and generous conception of a commercial life, entertained by a true merchant, as distinguished from the narrow and debasing notions of the mere adventurer. It is satisfactory to know that in all our great centres of business, there are influential men who have formed this liberal estimate of their profession, and who habitually contemplate it in its powerful and beneficent bearings upon the best interests of individuals, and the improvement of nations in intelligence, virtue, and rational happiness. It will commonly be found that merchants of this stamp, are no strangers to the BIBLE. It is from the study of the sacred records, that they have come to regard business, not as a mere matter of personal subsistence or of political economy, but as an essential part of that great scheme of Providence by which men are to be trained to the practice of virtue, and the remotest nations drawn to each other in the bonds of a common brotherhood.

With these views of a commercial life, there are associated *certain virtues which may be regarded as indispensable to the true mercantile character.* On this point, an eminent authority* has said: "Analyze the true qualities of a man of business, and you will find them reduce themselves to fairness, vigilance, and steadiness: fairness, exemplified in declaring his terms at once, and in never deviating from an engagement; vigilance, in superintending his assistants, his clerks, and his workmen; and steadiness, in following up his proper line, year after year, without turning to the right or left in pursuit of mere speculative advantages. These, plain as they are, form the true virtues of mercantile life: the man who is known to possess them will be at no loss for connections, and may safely leave to others the task of seeking a reputation for hospitality by their mode of living, of

* The Encyc. Brit.

activity by the frequency of their solicitations, or of liberality by an unusual prolongation of credit."

No one could be disposed to abridge this catalogue of the radical mercantile virtues: many would enlarge it. But all parties would unite in assigning the first place to what this writer terms "fairness," meaning, no doubt, INTEGRITY. It is proper here to be more specific. There are higher and lower grades of this as of the other virtues. The integrity which belongs to the best type of mercantile character, is evangelical integrity; that which is based upon an intelligent and hearty reception of Scripture truth, nurtured by Divine influences, and swayed by motives drawn from revealed religion. I utter not one word in disparagement of the honesty which is so often found apart from personal godliness. It is well for the world that men *are* honest from interest, from habit, from general custom, from a sense of future accountability, from what is called "goodness of heart," and from various other motives. But it will not be denied that the integrity which springs from religious principle, is in all respects a nobler and a more reliable virtue, and that this constitutes, in fact, the only adequate panoply for a man who means to expose himself to the perils and hazards of a commercial life.

The integrity of a merchant, to be of any avail, must have some well-known, immutable, and readily accessible standard. Christian integrity has such a standard, clear, precise, authoritative, and always at hand — the WORD OF GOD. His integrity must be, not a matter of calculation, of constraint, of appearances, but a matter of principle and of disposition. He must be resolved to do right; and he must find his happiness in doing right. He must do right as well in the smallest matters as in the greatest. He must do right where there is a moral certainty that by some slight deviation from the line of rectitude, he could add to his immediate gains without the least hazard of detection. He must do right when pressed on every side by an eager competition, and when a refusal to conform to the equivocal expedients which his neighbours employ to increase their business, promises to involve him in losses. He must do right in those junctures when he is tempted by an inviting combination of circumstances, to embark in schemes which neither the amount of his capital nor his existing financial obligations would warrant him to meddle with. He must do right in those fearful crises when the omens of ruin are gathering thick and fast around him, and his breast is haunted day and night with the horrible spectre of bankruptcy. *This* is the integrity you need. And if there be any virtue which is equal to these requisitions, it can be no earth-born endowment. It would be going quite too far to say that even men of undoubted *Christian* integrity never fail in these scenes of peril. They have often fallen; and truth and righteousness have fallen with them. But Christian integrity is, under God, the best possible protection you can have against these insidious and serried dangers. No other equipment could do so much to shield you. If you are without it, you cannot escape the moral contamination so incident to a business-life. You certainly will not attain to the dignity and purity of the true mercantile character.

We must go further still. There is a style of excellence in the world of commerce, beyond that we have described. The merchant referred to in the opening of this Lecture, is a man of scrupulous integrity; but if this were all, he would not fill the place he does now in the affectionate regards of that community. I have known men — you must have known men — whose rectitude was without a stain; men rigidly punctual and exact in all their transactions; whom you would not have hesitated to entrust with all your property or to name as your executors: and yet men in whom there was a something wanting to awaken in the breast emotions of reverence and affection. The truth is, a man may *do right*, and yet come far short of his duty. We are not satisfied, and the Bible is not satisfied, with a man's "doing justly." He may "do justly," according to the letter of the law, and yet do some very unamiable things. He may abstain from the slightest invasion of the rights of others, and "render to all their dues," and still leave *undone* many offices of kindness which it was in his power, and he should have felt it to be his pleasure, to do. The true merchant will not only "do justly," but "love mercy." The realm he lives in is one where Mercy has the amplest opportunities to exert her mild prerogative. Such are its uncertainties, its fluctuations, its hidden dangers, its frequent disasters, that its busy tenantry are all liable to need, and should therefore all be ready to perform, offices of sympathy and kindness. It will not answer for one of them to go to his fellows indiscriminately, and take them by the throat and say, "Pay me what thou owest!" There may be those among them who richly deserve this treatment. But for the mass, he must remember who has said, "He shall have judgment without mercy, that hath shewed no mercy." He must consider — and if he is what a merchant should be, he will consider—that he may perpetrate grievous wrongs in the name of law and justice. He will never strike until he has heard. He will reflect, that the being who stands before him, deprecating his severity, is not simply his debtor, but his fellow-creature, his brother; that his inability to meet his engagements may be the effect of unavoidable misfortunes; and that even if they are attributable to rashness or improvidence, it does not become *him* to visit these infirmities with a too rigorous retribution — "considering himself, lest he also be tempted."— Nor is it in this way only that his kindness of heart will show itself. A merely just man may isolate himself from the community around him. He is among them, but he is not of them. He buys and sells with them, pays them their dues and requires them to pay his; and this is all. He is not an excrescence. He is not an incumbrance. His capital is an advantage to the common traffic. His example is useful in so far forth as he is an upright man. But he is bound to the community by no ties of sympathy. He takes no interest in anything outside of his own warehouse. He is not the man, if he hears of a worthy neighbour who has been overtaken by some sudden emergency, to go to him and say, "Here are funds: take them until you have weathered this cape!" He is not the man to turn business he does not want or cannot do, into the hands of a young firm across the way, who, commercially speaking, might be glad to get the crumbs from his table. If men want counsel, his counting-room is not the one where they will instinctively go to seek it. Every one confides in his fairness, and respects him for his skill and capacity; but the general feeling about him will be, that he is a *cold* man; that without being a miser, he is still a selfish man, who has no generous impulses; and that to ask a favour of him is too disagreeable a service to be undertaken, except under a stringent necessity.— This is not a type of character peculiar to mercantile life. Men of this description are to be found in the learned professions and among civilians. Great men they may be, erudite scholars, eloquent, judicious, influential, and quite accessible where they are consulted *officially;* but in their ordinary bearing, wrapped in a cloak of dignified selfishness, which makes you feel that their proper place would be in the Armory of the Tower of London, or with some other collection of *mailed* heroes of the Middle Ages.

The true merchant is cast in a very different mould. His bosom is the home no less of genuine sensibility than of inflexible justice. He understands that his relations to his fellow-men are not all summed up in buying and selling with them. He remembers that life has other and higher ends than the mere exchanges of commerce and the profits which accrue from them. He esteems it as his privilege to do good according as God may have given him the ability. He will be found among the supporters of those noble religious institutions which constitute the brightest ornaments of our age, and are doing more for the amelioration of the race than all other agencies combined. But his benevolence will not begin and *end* in the sanctuary. It will be his pleasure to help forward every prudent scheme, which promises to contribute to the general welfare. He will be ready to assist with his advice, and as far as circumstances may warrant it, with his means, firms of tried character which need succour. He will have his eye upon young men of real merit, and at the proper time put them in the way of doing something for themselves. If a vacancy is about to occur in a bank or an insurance office, he will have some unfortunate, but deserving and competent, man to nominate for the place. If he sees the affairs of some remote firm going to ruin through the dissipation or dishonesty of their agent in his own city, he will in a delicate way cause a hint of it to be given them. If a widowed mother invokes his aid in behalf of her sons, he will do what he can to obtain situations for them. In a word, a merchant of this sort will make it the guiding principle of his life, to endeavour to do unto others as he would have others do to him; he will cultivate no less in his business, than in his social intercourse and his religious duties, the spirit of Christian candour and Christian kindness; and the whole texture of his life will go to illustrate the benefits which would accrue to Commerce, if the BIBLE could once be fairly established in all her COUNTING-HOUSES.

Let it not be inferred from these remarks that the merchant who draws his ethics from the Scriptures, and carries the benevolent spirit of Christianity into his business, must expose himself to imposition, or, in any event, will be likely to forego frequent advantages of which he might fairly avail himself in prosecuting his plans. There is nothing in the Bible to discountenance that "*vigilance*" which the writer we have quoted, specifies as one of the essential mercantile virtues. Its whole tenor, on the contrary, goes to make men earnest, watchful, and sagacious, in their secular callings. It were, indeed, an ill omen for Christianity, if a faithful adherence to its precepts should reduce men to a state of amiable imbecility, and make them, according to the Italian proverb, "so good that they would be good for nothing." Religious principle is of somewhat sterner stuff than this. A Christian merchant is even under special obligation not to be remiss in any appropriate means for promoting his business. He will shrink from no honourable competition. He will put forth all his powers in deciding how he may best apply his resources. He will be as resolute as his neighbours in getting up new fabrics, in cheapening the cost of production, in seeking out fresh markets, in calculating the contingencies which may affect prices at future periods or in distant ports, and turning these to some useful account, in guarding against accidents and losses, in meeting the convenience of his customers, and, generally, in devising measures which, without involving unwarrantable risks, may enlarge his business and his profits. He will resist to the utmost, the schemes and tricks of unprincipled traders, who may essay to make capital out of his good nature. He will show himself as resolute in bringing knaves and sharpers to justice, as he is lenient to those whose only crime consists in their having been unfortunate. Nor will his moral courage exhaust itself in meting out a righteous retribution to piratical adventurers from the interior. If there are firms in his own line of business, however wealthy and prosperous, which set at defiance the common maxims of integrity and the established courtesies of commerce, which circulate slanders against their neighbours, inveigle away their customers, and do other things which no honourable merchant would do, he will, on all fitting occasions, manifest his abhorrence of their conduct. He will unite with his brethren in suspending all professional intercourse with such firms, and treating them as marauders, who have no legitimate place within the domain of commerce. It is the opprobrium of the mercantile class that there should be men of this description among them. If new men rise up along the street, who simply excel them in enterprise and skill, who beat them in energy and tact, and through these means outstrip them in business, they cannot complain. But there can be few things more trying to a mercantile body than to have an establishment planted among them which thrives at their expense, on principles that ought never to be found outside of a Penitentiary. The craft with which these concerns are managed, is a great aggravation of the evil. Like other free-booters, they sail under false colours. They bear all the outward emblems of respectability and integrity. Here is the warehouse, stocked from basement to attic with seasonable goods. The principals and clerks are as bland and polite as possible. There are porters and draymen and packers and piles of boxes and the usual *paraphernalia* of a driving business. But the honeyed words which are spoken there in the ears of the country merchant, who has just been enticed from the firm he has always traded with, are words of falsehood. The sly insinuations he hears about "other houses" are calumnies. The alleged superior facilities for making purchases, enjoyed by his new friends, are a sheer fabrication. The extremely liberal terms on which they are willing to sell to "a gentleman of his standing," are a decoy for the time being, or, if anything more, will be found no more liberal than he could obtain elsewhere. And the voluble commendations lavished upon the goods, are reliable just so far as his own experience and tact will enable him to verify them, and no further. For *the whole establishment is a deception and a lie.* There is no moral principle there, except that shallow, thriftless, counterfeit integrity, which is based on policy. From the cellar to the dome, truth and falsehood are used indifferently. The very invoices and labels are taught to lie. Where it will serve a purpose, a neighbouring firm is largely complimented; and where it will serve a purpose, the same firm is prodigally abused. Character has no intrinsic value there. Virtue is nothing. Honour is nothing. The esteem of the community is nothing. Religion, as a system of practical godliness, is less than nothing. MONEY is everything. The one paramount aim of the concern, its only code, its only care, is, to make money. And if in prosecuting this object, it seem expedient to repudiate the recognized comities of trade, and to make open or secret war upon other houses, why the end will justify the means — for money must be made at all hazards!

Now it is not only compatible with religious duty, but every merchant of true Christian integrity is bound to unite with his neighbours in treating establishments of this sort as beyond the pale of honourable traffic. This is precisely a case for the application of the apostolic injunction, "Have no fellowship with the unfruitful works of darkness, but rather *reprove* them: for it is a shame even to speak of those things which are done of them in secret." And this is important, as on other and lower grounds, so because it ought to be seen in the realm of trade, what the genius of Christianity is. It should be seen that the Bible, though the friend of meekness, is not the patron of pusillanimity; that in fostering benevolence, it no where inculcates acquiescence in fraud and falsehood; and that while it bids us forgive an erring brother, on his repenting, to the extent of "seventy times seven," it requires us to withstand and rebuke obdurate offenders, who are trampling truth and righteousness under their feet.

It would exhaust your patience to delineate the other mercantile virtues with the same detail. And it will be both a more summary and a more satisfactory expedient to lay before you, in concluding this Lecture, a sample of the teachings of the Bible on this subject. You may judge for yourselves, whether Commerce would not be the gainer by having enthroned in its expanded empire, and over every, even the minutest, of its traffickings, an authority which abounds in utterances like these: —

He that loveth pleasure shall be a poor man.

Love not sleep, lest thou come to poverty.

He that is slothful in his work, is brother to him that is a great waster.

He that trusteth in his own heart is a fool.

Be patient toward all men.

The meek will He guide in judgment.

Before honour is humility.

A man's pride shall bring him low.

Ye shall do no unrighteousness in judgment, in meteyard, in weight, or in measure.

Just balances, just weights, and a just ephah, and a just line, shall ye have.

This is the will of God, that no man go beyond or defraud his brother in any matter; because that the Lord is the avenger of all such.

He that oppresseth the poor to increase his riches, shall surely come to want.

He that maketh haste to be rich shall not be innocent.

Trust not in uncertain riches, but in the living God, who giveth us richly all things to enjoy.

He that giveth to the poor shall not lack.

Say not to thy neighbour, "Go, and come again," when thou hast it by thee.

Putting away lying, speak every man truth with his neighbour.

A poor man is better than a liar.

Seest thou a man hasty in his words? there is more hope of a fool than of him.

Meddle not with him that flattereth with his lips.

"It is naught, it is naught," saith the buyer; but when he is gone his way, then he boasteth.

There is that maketh himself rich, yet hath nothing: there is that maketh himself poor, yet hath great riches.

By humility and the fear of the Lord, are riches and honour and life.

A man void of understanding striketh hands, and becometh surety in the presence of his friend.

He that is surety for a stranger shall smart for it: and he that hateth suretyship is sure.

If any of you lack wisdom, let him ask of God, that giveth to all men liberally, and upbraideth not; and it shall be given him.

Follow after righteousness, godliness, faith, love, patience, meekness.

All things whatsoever ye would that men should do to you, do ye even so to them.

Call upon me in the day of trouble, and I will deliver thee, and thou shalt glorify me.

Let your conversation be without covetousness; and be content with such things as ye have; for He hath said, I will never leave thee nor forsake thee.

Such are the counsels of inspired wisdom; such the ethics of the Word of God. It is a safe and reliable guide. It meets all the exigencies of your profession. It provides for every duty and every danger. Its principles are as immutable as the throne of the Deity. Its precepts are written as with a sunbeam. Its promises breathe the benevolence of heaven. The character which is formed upon its model, will command universal homage. The life that draws from it its inspiration, will enrich and bless the community which embosoms it. Let Commerce take the BIBLE as its chart, and throughout all its teeming thoroughfares, the primeval curse of labour will be despoiled of half its severity. Enthrone the BIBLE in your COUNTING-HOUSES, and the God of the Bible will bless you and make you a blessing.

Lecture Fourth.

HASTING TO BE RICH.

SOME few years since an ingenious manufacturer of porcelain, in Persia, acquired a celebrity which reached the court, and brought him a message from the Shah, that he might make china for the royal household. Under any constitutional or just government, such an intimation would have been a fortune to a man. But what did the artisan do? Mustering all the money he could, he took it to the prime minister, and bribed him to report to the king, that he was not the person who made the china, and that the real workman had run away, nobody knew whither. The ruse succeeded. The man was discharged, and vowed that he would never make a bit of china, nor attempt any other improvement, as long as he lived.

How is this conduct to be explained? The government of Persia is a pure autocracy, and the kings are for the most part insatiate tyrants. They have the absolute control of life, liberty, and property, throughout the empire. They can degrade, and even decapitate, the highest nobles, at pleasure. They can seize and confiscate any estate. For a mechanic to display any remarkable ingenuity, is only to expose himself to be coerced into the service of the crown without compensation. For a merchant to accumulate property, is to invite the most merciless exactions from the myrmidons of the throne. The mechanic just mentioned, knew that he would be compelled to spend the rest of his life in working for the king and his court, without requital; and not relishing the prospect, devised the scheme I have described to escape from it. The necessary tendency of this despotic system, is, not only to foster deceit and falsehood among the people, but to repress the efforts of industry and paralyze the powers of invention; for no man will sow where he has no prospect of reaping. Security of life and property is one of the essential elements which distinguish true civilization from a state of barbarism. There can be no real liberty in a country, the inhabitants of which are debarred from the legitimate exertion of their powers, or not protected in the possession of the property they have fairly acquired.

And if these things are so, then the agrarian

reformers of our day, who declaim against the accumulation of fortunes, and demand a distribution of all large estates among the poor, have mistaken their country. They are the types and representatives of barbarism, a foul excrescence on the fair face of Christian civilization; and their proper place is with the horde of extortioners who do the bidding of the Shah of Persia or the Grand Mogul. The attempts which men of this stamp put forth, to array the poor against the rich, to make them feel that the rich are their oppressors and the enemies of society, are of such flagitious wickedness, that any legislature would be warranted in making them a penitentiary offence. The interests of a community, certainly of any community in this country, are too firmly interlaced to be torn asunder, without inflicting irreparable injury upon the body politic. There is a reciprocal interdependence of the various classes and professions upon one another. The same principles which guard the ample wealth of the capitalist from invasion, secure to the weaver his loom, to the shoemaker his bench, to the drayman his cart, to the labourer his dollar-a-day and the little furniture which adorns his attic. The very capitalist, whom some blustering Fourierite may stigmatize in his harangues as a useless and rapacious leech whose resources ought to be thrown into a common stock, once sat, perhaps, at his loom, or hammered at the anvil, or served as proof-boy in a printer's office. Living in a land of law, where the strongest motives impelled him to exertion, and the whole power of the State guarded his humble earnings, he has risen, by the favour of Providence, to his present honourable position. Is there an honest weaver or blacksmith or printer to be found, who will say that his fellow-craftsman is to be blamed, or that our institutions are to be denounced as unjust and oppressive, because they admit of such results as this? Unjust to whom? Oppressive to whom? Surely not to the poor. They, of all classes, have the least reason to complain of a system which makes it practicable for them, which even makes it an every-day thing with them, to emerge from their condition of dependence, surround themselves with the comforts of life, and bestow upon their families the advantages which a competence can always command.

This, however, is not all. The capitalist is so far from being an incubus, that he is quite indispensable to the vigorous and healthy working of the great social machine. Let the entire property of Philadelphia be thrown into a common stock, and divided *pro rata* among its population: and what would be the effect? At one blow, the banks, insurance offices, savings-funds, and other financial institutions, would tumble to the ground. The large mercantile houses, which give employment to so many clerks, porters, draymen, coopers, carpenters, and the like, would dwindle into small retail shops. All the business which now rests on a credit-basis would cease. Not a hammer would be heard in the ship-yards. The silence of death would replace the intolerable, but productive, clatter of the foundries and machine-shops. All the spindles in the factories would stop at once, and those in private tenements would soon follow them. Dismantled ships would deform the wharves. Idlers and vagabonds would throng the streets. Fresh prisons and alms-houses would be needed, and there would be neither funds nor credit to build them. Our noble array of religious and charitable associations would be shorn of their efficiency, if not annihilated. And, in fine, this proud metropolis would disclose the symptoms of a universal and remediless decay, and the multitudes, as they passed by, "would say, every man to his neighbour, 'Wherefore hath the Lord done thus unto this great city?'"

While, however, this prejudice against capital, whether personal or associated, is a shallow and hateful feeling, and while the absolute security of property and the accumulation of riches are admitted to be essential to the prosperity of States and the diffusion of Christianity, it is quite possible for individuals to aspire after wealth with an inordinate passion, and to pursue it by unwarrantable and pernicious methods. In vindicating the established institutions of society against the revolutionary doctrines of pseudo-reformers, we by no means assume the championship of the commercial classes, in respect either to all their usages, or to the *animus* by which they are so largely controlled. In particular, if the BIBLE is to be recognized as an authority in the COUNTING-HOUSE, the stamp of a stern and decisive reprobation must be put upon that PASSION FOR SUDDEN WEALTH which has long been one of our prominent national characteristics. This, indeed, is no new sin in the world. It is, in any event, as old as the time of Solomon. And it is curious to trace its *diagnosis* in his day. Thus he says, "He that maketh haste to be rich, shall not be innocent." Again: "An inheritance may be gotten hastily at the beginning; but the end thereof shall not be blessed." And again: "He that hasteth to be rich, hath an evil eye, and considereth not that poverty shall come upon him." (Proverbs, 28: 20, 22. 20: 21.) This appears to be the identical disease which has come down to our day — identical, even if we combine with the symptoms noted by Solomon, the consequences pointed out by the apostle a thousand years later: — "But they that will be rich, fall into temptation and a snare, and into many foolish and hurtful lusts, which drown men in destruction and perdition. For the love of money is the root of all evil: which, while some coveted after, they have erred from the faith and pierced themselves through with many sorrows." (I. Tim. 6: 9, 10.) The malady and its effects are the same now as of old, and it is at least as common and as malignant in this country as in any other.

I am aware with what jealousy remarks from the pulpit on this subject are likely to be listened to. You are apt to feel that when the pulpit denounces the lust of prompt and eager accumulation, it touches upon ground beyond its jurisdiction, and betrays an ignorance of the legitimate ends and methods of traffic. You are ready to ask, somewhat tartly, "Whether it is not one of the proper objects of trade to make money?" and "Whether there is any more sin in clearing five hundred dollars a day, than fifty?" But these are mere cavils. They are rarely uttered in good faith, and therefore they require no answer. Every merchant worthy of the name, understands the nature and the pernicious working of the passion I have spoken of, as distinguished from the genuine commercial spirit. The strength and prevalence of it in this country, are to be ascribed to a variety of causes, among which may be enumerated, the genius and tendency of our liberal institutions, the extent and variety of our physical resources, the absence of all aristocratic distinctions and the consequent social importance and influence which follow the distribution of wealth, the enterprise and ambition developed by the peculiar circumstances of our country, and the momentum impressed upon the age by the discovery of new mechanical powers, fresh inventions in the arts, and the unexampled concentration of the talent and the science of the world, upon matters pertaining to the practical improvement of society and the economical well-being of the individual man. These and other agencies have combined to stimulate the love of money to a very unhealthy degree, and to inoculate the nation at large (it may almost be said) with a restless hankering after wealth.

In the Counting-room, this passion displays itself in *an intense eagerness for large and quick profits.* The ordinary profits of business are neither very quick nor very large. It is one of the most common of all errors with young merchants to over-estimate them. The prospective results they cipher out, with all imaginable skill and pains-taking, are rarely, if ever, realized. Many a man of undoubted sagacity and tact, has been astounded with the retrospect of his first year's business. Such an excess of personal and domestic expenses above his calculations — such remissness or dishonesty among his customers — such unforeseen vicissitudes in the markets — so many incidental chinks and crevices through which his profits have percolated, — he can scarcely credit his own senses, when he lays his truth-telling Balance-sheet along-side of the magnificent scheme he adjusted with so much precision a twelve-month before. The appropriate remedy in a case of this kind, any prudent merchant could suggest: but prudence is not a favourite counsellor with ardent and ambitious men in any department of life. And the too common effect is, to put the disappointed parties upon a course of policy, which may enlarge their sales, indeed, but will in a greater degree multiply their perils. Traders in these circumstances not only, but others who are more advantageously situated, are apt to revolt at the idea of spending a long series of years in the "drudgery" of business. Their profits *must* in some way be increased. This may be tried by taking advantage of the distance or the ignorance of customers, and selling them goods above the market value, or antiquated goods for fresh ones. Firms that attempt this, may succeed in it for a while; but it is preposterous to suppose they can carry it on long. Buyers are of course on the alert to learn the actual state of the market; and whenever they discover that their confidence has been abused, they will feel no scruple in stigmatising the offending house far and near as as a dishonourable concern.—*This* expedient for securing large profits is not to be commended.

As little can be said in favour of selling to parties without due inquiry as to their commercial standing. It might be supposed that self-interest would be a sufficient restraint on this point, but the fact is quite otherwise. Such are the zealous rivalries of trade, that goods enough to stock a score or two of small towns, are annually sold to men of no responsibility. The embarrassment and difficulty inseparable from investigations on this point, must constitute one of the chief trials of a mercantile life, a source of anxiety akin to that of the paying-teller of a bank, who must be all day haunted with apprehension lest some of the checks received at his counter may be forgeries. But no desire for business will justify recklesness in trafficking with men who are without satisfactory credentials. It will not do to say, that if you are willing to assume the risk, no one else can have any reason to complain. There is a question of morals here as well as a question of dollars and cents. The ethics of the BIBLE certainly will not sanction your running this hazard. Imprudence may amount to a sin. And what *right* have you, even though you might afford to lose your whole venture, to set an example of rashness, which can hardly fail to have a hurtful influence upon other houses? What right have you to put your *imprimatur* upon shiftless adventurers, who will make the bill of goods you have sold them a passport to the confidence of the firms around you? The body to which you belong, has a common interest in shutting out from the walks of trade all unsound and fraudulent dealers. Many of this description must come up with the spring and fall *freshets* from the South and West, which pour themselves into our large cities. To countenance them, is to inflict a double wrong: it is a wrong to the metropolitan merchant, and an equal wrong to their customers from the country. The buyers are no less concerned than the sellers, in having their ranks purged of unreliable men: for the misdemeanors of these men operate to the disadvantage of the body at large, by raising the market and impairing that confidence which lies at the basis of successful commerce. On these grounds we affirm the immorality of that facility in trusting parties of no ascertained responsibility, which so often goes along with a craving for sudden wealth.

On the same principles, it may be observed here in passing, every community is liable to suffer more or less from instances of fraudulent bankruptcy. If one wished to select an emblem of timidity from the commercial world, he would fix upon *credit*. Nothing is more easily frightened; nothing so keen in scenting danger. To its ear the world is a great whispering-gallery, which transmits every note of alarm, whether emanating from the council-chamber of a distant cabinet, the cotton-fields of Mississippi, the gold mines of California, or the crash of a mercantile establishment. Every example of this latter kind, especially if stamped with dishonesty, creates distrust, sets capital upon demanding fresh securities, increases the difficulty of getting discounts, occasions mischievous conjectures as to the stability of other houses, and in various ways damages the whole trading interest. On the low ground of self-protection, therefore, every merchant has a stake in keeping up the morals of trade to the highest standard, and in setting his face as a flint against every form of dishonesty.

It is a natural transition from the topics with which we have been occupied, to *over-trading*. And it will not be inappropriate to consider in this connexion, the subject of *contracting debts*, whether with or without a morbid passion for exorbitant and speedy gains. The word "over-trading" has a vagueness of meaning for which some persons may like it all the better. The lexicographers do not recognize it; and if they should, they would be obliged to substitute a periphrasis for a definition. And yet for all practical purposes it is sufficient to say, that it denotes the doing a business disproportionate to one's capital.

The just relation, it is true, between capital and business, is not immutable. The same capital would perhaps warrant a business of a half-million now, which would not have warranted a quarter of a million a few years ago — such is the general prosperity of the country, and so favourable, in a commercial view, the condition of the world at large. These, however, are the seasons when men are tempted to be imprudent. Disregarding the contingencies involved in so auspicious a state of things, and borne onward upon the current of a redundant success, they are induced to assume new engagements and to extend their transactions, until it would startle them, could they pause long enough to see upon how slender and fragile a base they have reared their imposing superstructure. They did not *mean* to be imprudent. But it requires a more than Fabian virtue for a merchant to be moderate and tranquil when all his neighbours are flying towards the goal of Fortune with a telegraphic velocity. Few men can, in these circumstances, resist the tendency to do indiscreet things. Not only is the dividing line between prudence and imprudence obscured, but the landmarks of right and wrong glimmer before them as they would if their eyes were smitten with the cataract. They do not see — they are not anxious to see — where they ought to stop buying goods, nor where they should stop selling. They are not in a mood for examining Ledgers and Bank-books. Figures have lost their fixed, mathematical significance. They look at them through a combination of cross-lights, which makes another thing of them. All their estimates and calculations tend in one direction, because they exclude from them any proper consideration of the hazards and uncertainties incident to their extravagant operations. And if ever some experienced friend ventures to hint that they may be going too fast, the monition is treated as the well-meant, but womanish, fear of one whose ideas quite antedate this sublime era of locomotives and electric telegraphs.—This imperial style of doing business might answer, if it were not for one trifling consideration, to wit, the necessity, so much insisted upon, of a man's paying his debts; for "creditors are a superstitious sect, great observers of set days and times." Absolution from this practice, would put it in the power of our adventurous traffickers to replenish their warehouses with an inexhaustible stock of goods, and to do an amount of business commensurate with their largest ambition. But in default of such exemption, the period of settlement will by and by come round, when the cataracts will be removed, and the figures will stand out in all their colossal proportions, and nothing will answer, in place of the profound calculations and brilliant day-dreams of the business-season, but vulgar cash — sober, substantial money, that can be weighed like lead, and with as little poetry in it. The scenes which are apt to follow, need not be described : there will be occasion to refer to them hereafter. Enough for the present, to have glanced at the usual winding-up of a career of over-trading.

Improvidence in contracting debts, is but a part of the same system. An excessive business demands excessive means, and these means can be obtained only by borrowing. Borrowing, again, requires *endorsing*, and endorsing becomes a reciprocal thing. A. endorses for B., and B. endorses for A.; and, keeping their accounts in different banks, to say nothing of loans from private bankers, they are able to get all the money they want, and, possibly, a great deal more than they ought to have. It may seem presumptuous to impugn a principle which has the general sanction of the commercial world; but no one can deny that the practice of endorsing is peculiarly liable to abuse. In the first place, the security it affords is very often of no real value. Such are the mutual responsibilities of endorsers, that the failure of one is the failure of all: when one link gives way, the chain is gone. In the second place, the custom encourages imprudence. It is hazardous to put a man in a position to feel that if his plans succeed, all the gains will be his own, and if they fail, he can share the loss with his neighbours. Why should you lend your name to a man to do that which he would not feel it safe to do if he were going to risk only his own capital? This, I am aware, is not always the case in endorsing, but it is frequently the case. And the conviction that an endorser is at hand, will bring up questions before the mind in a very specious and illusive aspect. To contract a debt is a serious matter; but it loses half its gravity when half its responsibility is cancelled. The feeling is, "I will go into this operation if you will stand by me; if not, I will let it alone." To say that this is necessarily a wrong feeling, or that the transaction must be an unwise one, would be going too far. But will it be denied that very many of the transactions undertaken in this spirit, might better be let alone? that they even trench on the line of strict honesty? Honesty forbids that we should assume obligations without having, on a fair and reasonable estimate of things, the ability to discharge them. The moment a man is assured of an endorser, he is in danger of over-estimating his resources. Mistaking the nature of the arrangement, he even regards the endorsement as *pro tanto* an accession to his *capital;* whereas not one dollar is added to his capital, but his liabilities are increased to the full amount of the sum borrowed. I say "*his* liabilities," because in morals they are his in a sense in which they are not his endorser's. The law may hold them to a joint responsibility; and integrity will exact payment of the endorser if the drawer fails. But the drawer is bound to the endorser. He has no more moral right to procure an endorsement without adequate means of protecting it, than he has to order a bill of goods without the means of paying it. Just in proportion, however, to the facility with which endorsements can be obtained, will men of limited capital, who are impatient for the profits or the honour of a large business, be tempted to use them. It is on this ground — as an enticement to rashness and a bait to dishonesty — that a teacher of morals is authorized to remonstrate against the prevalent abuse of this principle of endorsing in the commercial world.

There is a third objection, viz.: that it is a fruitful source of financial disaster and ruin. It ruins, frequently, the very parties who resort to it, by seducing them, in the way just specified, into mercantile extravagances wholly incommensurate with their means. It ruins endorsers. And among these, too often, are men whose improvident kindness reduces their families to penury. Inquire of the decayed merchants of any city, go through the teeming ranks of seamstresses, school-mistresses, and boarding-house keepers, go to the widows' asylums and other kindred institutions, and see what an amount of suffering and sorrow you can trace to this vicious principle of endorsing. It is a perennial fountain of trouble, the bitter streams of which have desolated thousands of once happy homes. One is sometimes almost ready, in surveying a wreck of this kind, to denounce the principle itself, which has been the occasion of the disaster, as unworthy of a place among the implements of honourable commerce. Nor is this feeling abated by the suggestion, that no one is compelled to endorse for his friend, and that it is wrong for men to assume responsibilities of this sort disproportioned to their property. It *is* wrong. No man has a *right* to imperil the comfort and earthly happiness of his family for the sake of accommodating his neighbour. Good neighbourhood has its claims, but this is not one of them. And it is a sad thing that men should so often lack the firmness to refuse favours which they cannot grant without jeoparding the interests of their own households. Still, men *will* do these things. They will put their names on paper which they ought no more to touch than they would dally with a rattle-snake. And the process will go on as it has gone; other families will be ruined, and widows and orphans without number will continue to swell the ranks of the unfortunate victims of endorsing.

It should not, therefore, excite surprise that persons who look at the working of the principle from a distance, take up the conviction that there is something wrong in it; that the alleged commercial necessity for retaining it, if not of the most stringent character, ought to give way to the numberless social and moral evils it produces; and that, in any event, some further efforts should be made in the way of legislative enactments or otherwise, to abate the intolerable abuses now incident to the system.

These observations can scarcely be deemed out of place in treating of the contracting of debts. Unhappily, the laxness which prevails on the subject of endorsing, is not confined to that mode of running in debt. The current tone of the business-world on this point, is quite below the proper standard. No one would wish to see all the trafficking of the world reduced to cash payments. Credit is one of the beneficent fruits of Christian civilization, and, though itself an effect, is in turn a most powerful agent in developing the resources of nations and accelerating their progress. But to contract debts without a reasonable prospect of being able to pay them when they become due, is both a sin and a sure source of perplexity and trouble. That is a very pregnant aphorism, "the borrower is servant to the lender." Dr. Franklin has expanded this thought in one of his pithy essays. "Think what you do when you run in debt: you give to another power over your liberty. If you cannot pay at the time, you will be ashamed to see your creditor, you will be in fear when you speak to him, when you will make poor, pitiful excuses, and by degrees come to lose your veracity and sink into base, downright lying: for 'the second vice is lying, the *first* is running in debt,' as poor Richard says; and again, to the same purpose, 'Lying rides upon debt's back:' whereas a free-born Englishman* ought not to be ashamed nor afraid to see or speak to any man living." These are among the ordinary effects of recklessness in contracting debts. It puts a man in bondage to his creditors, and makes him shun them. It drives peace from his bosom, and brings down a cloud upon his brow. It fills him with harrowing apprehensions of disaster. It puts him, or may put him, upon shifts and expedients for averting the dreaded storm which he once would not have resorted to, and which the Bible in his counting-room (if he have one there) will not sanction. Understand — this is not said indiscriminately of men in debt, but of those who have been culpably improvident in contracting debts. There is no necessary disgrace attached to being in debt, nor to being unable to

* Written before the Revolution.

meet one's engagements. Such are the contingencies of commerce that the most honourable and prudent men may find themselves in this situation; and they have no cause to feel abashed, no reason to shrink from meeting their creditors as freely as they have always met them. The creditor who in a case of this sort would not treat his unfortunate neighbour or correspondent with courtesy and kindness, is unworthy of a place among upright merchants. But these examples, it is to be feared, are the exceptions. A large portion of the debts which involve mercantile houses in embarrassment, are to be traced to a grasping after sudden wealth, to the ambition of doing a great business, or to extravagance in living. Impelled by these causes, men of moderate means commit themselves to the resistless current which sweeps through the channels of commerce, and are too much regaled with the omens of an opulent prosperity to observe whither it is bearing them. When the enchantment is at length dissolved, they learn how much easier it is to contract liabilities than to meet them. And they have ample opportunity to consider whether a transient eclât for enterprise, or an evanescent notoriety for splendid entertainments, is any adequate recompense for a ruined business, the displeasure of creditors, and a wounded conscience.

I am acquainted with an estimable young man who

remarked one day, "If I cannot make money enough by the time I am thirty years old, I don't wish to do business." What would his grandfather have thought of a youth who had made that observation in his day? What would our senior merchants have thought, forty years ago, of a system of business which contemplated a man's *retiring* on a fortune at thirty! This, to be sure, may not prove that the feeling is a wrong one. Nor, as a matter of fact, is the plan without some actual examples to illustrate it. But the sentiment I have quoted, is useful as showing the ideas of business which prevail in our day. It was the view my young friend had imbibed while a clerk in Market street, and which, it must be conceded, fairly reflects the spirit of the times. It is the identical spirit I have been combating in this Lecture, and which every one must resist, who would have the BIBLE established in our COUNTING-HOUSES. It is, in a word, a craving after sudden wealth. It ignores all the moral uses of a frugal and industrious *life*. It overlooks all the contingencies of trade. It proceeds on the assumption that "a fortune" can certainly be made within a specified period. So visionary a theory might at first be deemed very harmless; but while it is powerless for good, it has a great capacity for evil. Aspiring to the fulfilment of its own prophecy, it must predispose those who embrace it, to adopt the very measures we have been reprobating as devices for rapid and excessive accumulation. It is a dangerous thing for a man to set out in business with the feeling, that his work is to be done in at most ten years, and then he is to *enjoy* his wealth for the rest of his days. He will need, on this plan, to insure something besides his property. For it will be a miracle if he runs through his brief, but tumultuous, circuit, without compromising his integrity and debasing his conscience. And aside from this, whence comes the vagrant notion that you can "enjoy" life only when you shall have earned a discharge from business? Business certainly has its cares and its anxieties; but it were a curious classification of things, to array business and happiness against each other — to assign business to one portion of life, and enjoyment to another. Good and evil are not arranged in these massive strata, but intermixed throughout the whole of life. There are no happier men than some whom you could find among the busiest of our busy merchants; there are none more miserable than some whose ample patrimony or acquired wealth has exonerated them from the necessity of labour, and left them to die of *ennui*. Viewed as classes, the balance is strongly in favour of the working, as distinguished from the retired, men. The latter not unfrequently find the vacuity of a leisure life so intolerable, that after a few years they put on the harness again, and go back to the counting-room.* You must have observed how much deeper and more enduring is the interest your children take in a toy or play-thing which is to be thrown or turned or *worked* in some way, than in one which is simply to stand under a glass vase and be looked at. We are but grown children. You may renounce Market street at thirty, and build your elegant mansion and adorn it with objects of luxury and taste, but unless you have some *employment* with it, you will soon tire of looking at the beautiful toy, and long for something on which your powers can exert themselves. I need not dwell upon a topic which will recur again; but rely upon it, any theory of life must be wrong which disparages

* "Every one knows the story of the tallow-chandler, who, having amassed a fortune, disposed of his business, and taken a house in the country, not far from London, that he might enjoy himself, after a few months' trial of a holiday-life, requested permission of his successor, to come into town and assist him on *melting* days. I have heard of one who kept a retail spirit-shop, and having in like manner retired from trade, used to employ himself by having one puncheon filled with water, and measuring it by pints into another. I have also heard of a butcher in a small country-town, who, some little time after he had left off business, informed his old customers that he meant to kill a lamb once a-week, just for his amusement!" — THE DOCTOR.

reputable labour, or neglects the sources of present enjoyment in visionary anticipations of future good.

"All earthly comforts vanish thus;
So little hold of them have we,
That we from them, or they from us,
May in a moment ravished be.
Yet we are neither just nor wise,
If present mercies we despise;
Or mind not how there may be made
A thankful use of what we have."

The future is not ours; and should it ever become ours, it will bring its own cares more certainly than its own pleasures. What we are concerned with is present duty. It is a sad and foolish mistake to spend life in getting ready to live. There is a sense in which the famous Epicurean apothegm, "Dum vivimus vivamus," "Whilst we live, let us live," expresses a wholesome truth. Dr. Doddridge, whose family motto it was, has paraphrased it in what Dr. Johnson justly terms "one of the finest epigrams in the English language."

"Live while you live, the *Epicure* would say,
And seize the pleasures of the present day.
Live while you live, the sacred *Preacher* cries,
And give to God each moment as it flies.
Lord, in my views let both united be;
I live in pleasure while I live to thee."

If you cultivate this spirit, making the Bible your

daily chart and text-book, and trusting in Christ for pardon while you walk in the way of his precepts, you will neither find a business-life such hopeless drudgery, nor be impatient of the day when you are to exchange the bondage of the Counting-room for an Elysium of idleness.

Nor let it be supposed that a retirement from business will necessarily deaden that excessive passion for wealth, which has been rebuked in this Lecture. The Ethiopian does not so readily change his skin, nor the leopard his spots. The covetousness which has ruled a man through all the activities of his working days, will not let go its mastery on his ceasing to work. It may assume a new form. The essential principle or core of avarice, is selfishness. And no man need bless himself that he is a stranger to the worship of Mammon, who is spending all his revenues in self-indulgence. "His hand, like a channel, may be ever open; and because his income may be perpetually flowing through it, the unreflecting world, taken with appearances, may hold him up as a pattern of generosity; but the entire current is absorbed by his own selfishness. That others are indirectly benefited by his profusion, does not enter into his calculations; he thinks only of his own gratification. It is true, his mode of living may employ others; but he is the idol of the temple — they are only priests in his service; and the prodigality they are empowered to indulge in, is only intended to decorate and do honour to his altar. To maintain an extensive establishment, to carry it high before the world, to settle his children *respectably* in life, to maintain a system of costly self-indulgence, — these are the objects which swallow up all his gains, and keep him in a constant fever of ill-concealed anxiety; filling his heart with envy and covetousness at the sight of others' prosperity; rendering him loath to part with a fraction of his property to benevolent purposes; and making him feel as if every farthing of his money so employed were a diversion of that farthing from the great ends of life. New channels of benevolence may open around him in all directions; but as far as he is concerned, those channels must remain dry; for, like the sands of the desert, he absorbs all the bounty which Heaven rains on him, and still craves for more. What but this is commonly meant by the expression concerning such a man, that 'he is living up to his income'?"*

This is one type of covetousness among the men who have given up business. Its more vulgar form, that of hoarding, is no less familiar. It is a curious and instructive fact, that rich men are usually more

* Harris.

disposed to hoard after relinquishing business than before. What with the constant handling of money, the ceaseless barter of commerce, and the excitement kept up in a career of trafficking, their hearts have little opportunity to get steeled against all generous impulses. But when they exchange the counting-room for the snug domestic office or the library, and have nothing to do but receive their rents and interest and dividends, every dollar stands out in its own importance, and it becomes a serious matter to divert this money from new investments. To contribute a hundred dollars to a charity, would be to "lose" or "throw away" the interest on more than sixteen hundred! A donation of a thousand dollars, would swallow up the interest of nearly seventeen thousand! If they had less leisure, they might consent. But to look such "sacrifices" deliberately in the face, and *then* submit to them, is more than their virtue is equal to. This revenue too, once in hand, is no longer, in their view, of the nature of interest; it belongs to their principal; and they have a profound reverence for the maxim which requires a man to keep his principal intact under all circumstances. Thus they reason: the swelling income passes, from one six-months to another, into the body of the estate: and the love of money grows apace with every fresh investment. Most other vices find a partial corrective in the gradual decay of the physical powers; but avarice is proverbially the vice of old age, and

> —— "rarely venturing in the van of life,
> While nobler passions wage their heated strife,
> Comes skulking last, with Selfishness and Fear,
> And dies collecting lumber in the rear!"

Worse than "lumber" it is apt to prove—worse for themselves and for their heirs. For what can be more adverse to a man's spiritual good, more unfavourable to serious thought, more hostile to all adequate preparation for eternity, than to sell himself, as he is growing old, to Mammon? Those are very solemn words, "No covetous man, who is an idolater, hath any inheritance in the kingdom of Christ and of God." The "covetous shall not inherit the kingdom of God." How is it possible for men to elude this doom who are basely betraying their stewardship, and making it the chief end of life to enlarge an already overgrown fortune?—And, then, as to their children, for whose "benefit" they are denying themselves the true enjoyment of this life and hazarding all prospect of the life to come, what is more common than to see such a property become a curse to its inheritors?

But, happily, among those who retire from business, there are men who have no affinity with either of the classes that have been mentioned. They are among the brightest ornaments of our social state, and worthy of all the honour which is so uniformly accorded to them. It is one of their principles that accumulation has its moral limits, and that beyond these (varying, however, with men's circumstances) a fortune ought not to be increased. It is another principle with them, that wealth has its duties no less than its privileges. It is a third principle with them, that in managing and disposing of an estate, every man is bound to govern himself by the teachings of the BIBLE.—I can picture to myself a merchant, who, having relinquished business after a long and honourable career, has addressed himself to the remaining duties of his stewardship, under the guidance of these elevated principles. I see him the tenant of a stately and beautiful mansion, furnished in a manner suitable to his fortune and position. I censure not the works of art I find there. As long as Jubal's skill is perpetuated in "such as handle the harp and the organ," I dare not proscribe these instruments of music. While God continues to raise up Bezaleels and Aholiabs, and to "fill them with wisdom and knowledge to devise cunning works, to work in gold, and in silver, and in brass, and in cutting of stones, to set them, and in carving of timber, to work in all manner of workmanship," I dare not say, these sculptures and paintings and porcelains and mosaics are prohibited indulgences, and should have no place here. Still less should I presume to ask, Why is not this needless conservatory sold, and the proceeds given to the poor? The proprietor of this mansion has, in my view, a *right* to indulge himself in these elegant tastes: and it is pleasant to meet them, combined with sterling religious principle and Christian refinement. If this scene defined the sum of his being, the case were different. But he is one with whom these studies and objects are the mere fringe and ornament of life, not its end or substance. Remembering his stewardship, he cares not to augment his ample estate. No dollar of interest with him ever petrifies into principal. His entire income, after deducting personal and household expenses, goes to promote the happiness of his fellow-creatures and the prosperity of religion. He exercises a sound discrimination in his benefactions. The poor have in him a liberal and judicious friend. He is wont to aid deserving young men in obtaining an education. He secretly assists meritorious families that have experienced reverses, and struggling individuals whom most persons would pass by as being too well off to be entitled to help. He keeps his eye upon the progress of Christianity at home and abroad, and a munificent, though unostentatious, benevolence attests his cordial interest in whatever pertains to the kingdom of Christ and the salvation of men. And, to his other offices of kindness, he superadds such personal services as it may be in his power to render to useful public institutions, or to individuals requiring counsel or succour.

Men of this sort there are among our retired merchants. You will not be long in forming your estimate of them, as contrasted either with those who are consuming all their income in a lavish self-indulgence, or with their compeers whose hoarding propensities increase with their gold and their years. Let it be your care, should Providence ever place you among them, to shun the extremes of prodigality and penuriousness; to dedicate yourselves and your property to the service of God and the good of mankind; and to illustrate the excellence of that practical godliness which fits men to enjoy their earthly riches, and secures to them an inalienable portion beyond the grave.

Lecture Fifth.

SPECULATING.

An impression prevailed in England a century and a half ago, that the wealth of South America was inexhaustible. This led to the chartering, in the year 1711, of the famous "South-Sea Company," on which was conferred the exclusive right of trading with that country, together with other important privileges. Visionary as were the professed objects of this association, the most extravagant statements were circulated respecting its prospects. The managers declared enormous dividends from their alleged profits, and by this and other means not unknown in the financial world, the scheme was crowned with unparalleled success. The stock rose until in the year 1720, it was eagerly bought at 1000 *per cent,* premium. As the natural effect of this gigantic experiment, the country was soon filled with speculating projects of all sorts. Innumerable joint-stock companies started up everywhere. Every day brought its fresh "bubble." Some of these were of so preposterous a character that their titles could not be recited here without exciting an unbecoming merriment. One of them was styled, "A company for carrying on an undertaking of great advantage, but nobody to know what it is." The projector of this bold appeal to the public credulity, required a deposit of £2 on each share of £100 each, and engaged to each depositor a return of £100 per annum. He opened his office, and the first day received subscriptions for 1000 shares, with the requisite deposit of £2000. With this sum, he quietly withdrew that evening to the continent, and was never heard of again. This well-authenticated transaction may illustrate the mania which had seized upon the public mind. "From morning until evening, Change Alley was filled to overflowing with one dense moving mass of living beings, composed of the most incongruous materials, and in all things, save the mad pursuit wherein they were employed, utterly opposed in their principles and feelings, and far asunder in their stations in life and the professions they followed. Statesmen and clergymen deserted their high stations to enter upon this grand theatre of speculation and gambling; and churchmen and dissenters left their fierce disputes, and forgot their wranglings upon church-government, in the deep and hazardous game they were playing for worldly treasures, and for riches which, even if won, were liable to disappear within the hour of their creation. Whigs and tories buried their weapons of political warfare, discarded party animosities, and mingled together in kind and friendly intercourse, each exulting as their stocks advanced in price, and murmuring dissatisfaction and disappointment when fortune frowned upon their wild operations; and lawyers, physicians, merchants, and tradesmen, forsook their employments, neglected their business, and disregarded their engagements, to whirl giddily along with the swollen stream, to be at last engulphed in the wide sea of bankruptcy. Men of the highest rank were deeply engaged in stock-jobbing transactions; and investments in the most worthless bubbles of the age were made by them in heavy sums, and without the least hesitation or previous inquiry. Females mixed with the crowd; and forgetting the stations and employments which nature had fitted them to adorn, dealt boldly and extensively in the bubbles that rose before them, and like those by whom they were surrounded, rose from poverty to wealth, and from that were thrust down to beggary and want — and all in one short week, and perhaps before the evening which terminated the first day of their speculations. Ladies of high rank, regardless of every appearance of dignity, and blinded by the prevailing infatuation, drove to the shops of their milliners and haberdashers, and there met stock-brokers whom they regularly employed, and through whom extensive sales were daily negotiated. In the midst of the excitement, all distinctions of party and religion, circumstances and character, were swallowed up. Bubbles were blown into existence on every hand, and stocks of every conceivable name, nature, and description, were issued to an incredible extent."*

It is superfluous to add, that by and by the *crash* came — a crash which shook the land like an earth-quake. Some of the leaders of the South-Sea scheme fled the country, and others were thrown into prison: while tens of thousands of people sat them down in their poverty, to bemoan the quick and terrible retribution their folly had brought upon them.

This is a cursory glimpse of a nation bewildered with a spirit of SPECULATION. It is not, unfortunately, so remote from our own experience, that we shall find any difficulty in appreciating it. Similar crises occur at irregular intervals in the history of every commercial nation; and the mercantile men who listen to these Lectures, can recall a period when our own land reeled and staggered under one of these catastrophes, as if struck by the hand of Omnipotence.

---

* Hunt's Merchant's Magazine.

You have seen the whole process from beginning to end. A superfluity of capital — facile credits — inflated prices — all classes maddened with the lust of money — Mammon put in the place of God — new projects for sudden wealth broached every day — new banks, new land-companies, new railroads, new cities, new joint-stock associations of all sorts — over-trading — shrewd and successful operations — trust-funds invested in bubbles — banks covertly trafficking at the stock-board — fortunes made without time or trouble — splendid mansions, equipages, entertainments — bubbles bursting—banks breaking—merchants breaking — stagnation in the streets — silence among the spindles — ships rotting at the wharves — defalcations — forged certificates of stock — debtors absconding — States repudiating — sheriff's sales — crowded alms-houses — interminable dockets — impoverished widows — impoverished orphans — general despondency and wo! Such are the ensigns of one of these crises, which meet the eye: they have blacker shades, and more fearful results, which need not be indicated. Those who have seen for themselves, as you have, will require no daguerreotype sketch: the least outline will recall the whole.

And now, if I undertake to found upon facts like these, a remonstrance against unbridled speculation, you may try to parry it by reminding me that "all business is a speculation, so that you must either speculate or give up business altogether." This is not candid. There is no merchant here who does not know the difference between the usual workings of a speculating mania and the sober methods of legitimate commerce. Every one who is capable of moral distinctions, must perceive, that while these seasons of redundance and inflation last, wealth is taken out of its proper place, and invested with adventitious and illusive qualities. Men come insensibly to regard it as the chief good — as indispensable to the true enjoyment of life. It takes precedence with them of mental culture, social happiness, and even moral excellence. They will sacrifice to it comfort, health, books, domestic affection, and the very ordinances of religion. They hear more talk of money and fortunes than of all other topics together. The crowds that rush by them on the side-walks are fierce after money. They listen to the plaudits bestowed upon successful operators. They find that the world sets a much higher value upon wealth than upon merit. And they become possessed with the feeling, that whatever may be neglected, it will never do to incur the indignity of not being rich.

Of course in this eager race after wealth, there can be no proper recognition of an overruling Providence. There is the greatest possible incongruity between the reigning spirit at one of these periods, and that cordial, implicit, cheerful reliance upon God, which the Bible bids us cherish no less in all our secularities than in our spiritual services. The apostle has remonstrated with them on this point. "Go to now, ye that say, 'To-day or to-morrow we will go into such a city, and continue there a year, and buy, and sell, and get gain': whereas, ye know not what shall be on the morrow. For what is your life? It is even a vapour that appeareth for a little time and then vanisheth away. For that ye ought to say, 'If the Lord will, we shall live and do this or that.' But now ye rejoice in your boastings: all such rejoicing is evil." The temper of mind here inculcated, every consideration of modesty, of piety, and even of self-interest, bids us cherish: for how absolute is our dependence upon God; and what will all our tact and energy avail, without his blessing? But who among the hosts of speculators, thinks of God in framing his plans, or seeks his help in prosecuting them? Who would presume to invoke his aid in consummating schemes of which He has said, "He that maketh haste to be rich shall not be innocent." "Ye cannot serve God and mammon." It is not the least of the multitudinous evils bound up in these seasons of excitement, that they turn men into practical Atheists. They at least have the decency to abstain from a pretended reliance upon God, when their real feeling is that every thing depends, not upon his favour, but upon their own activity and skill in calculating chances and taking advantage of circumstances.

The antagonism of this passion to the genuine mercantile spirit has been adverted to. The end of honourable commerce is to exchange equivalents for mutual advantage. Speculation (using the term in its technical sense) looks only to its own good. Like a rapacious military chieftain, it aims at self-aggrandizement; and this object it pursues, reckless of the consequences to others. In the view of a confirmed speculator, the aggregate property of a community is but the stake in a game of chance; the people at large are the players; and each man is to get what he can, without caring, or even asking, who loses. Such a man must necessarily regard every one around him with a jealous eye, especially those in his own profession. They are not *to him* associates and honourable competitors, whose generous rivalry is to stimulate their mutual sagacity and enterprise: they are his opposers, almost his enemies. What they gain, he loses; and he must lay his plans so as to make them lose, that he may pocket their losses. If an extreme type of his class, he will not confine his hostile demonstrations to his fellow-traders or co-financiers. Like Ishmael, his hand is against every man; and, worse than Ishmael, even against those whose hand is not against him. He would as soon speculate upon the property of the widow and the orphan, as upon any other. It is not a question with him in arranging his projects, "How will this affect the interests of others?" He does not, except on selfish grounds, even take the trouble to inquire whose interests his manœuvres are likely to damage. His motto is, "Each one for himself;" and if in carrying out this very honourable and humane principle, he happens to ruin a few families of females and children, he comforts himself with the reflection, that "he was not aiming at their ruin, but only at his own advantage; and that if they have lost their property, it is an incidental evil, for which their guardians are responsible, not himself."

The base sophistry taught in this school, is in keeping with its hardening effect upon the sensibilities of men. There are few more loathsome characters in society, than the shrewd, cold-blooded operator, who will speculate the fortune of an innocent family out of their possession into his own, and then have the audacity to attempt to soothe the victims of his villany by telling them that it was a "fair business-transaction." This is as though a highwayman should plunge his knife into you, and console you, while you were bleeding to death, by telling you that he had severed the arteries *scientifically*. The sort of operations in question may be styled "fair business-transations," but it can only be in deference to that flagitious code of morals already spoken of as having supplanted, in some business-circles, the law of God. Tried by the Scriptural standard of morality, there is nothing "fair" about them. That standard forbids covetousness; it prohibits the injuring of the property of others; it requires us to do as we would be done by. In each of these points, the speculator has contravened it. Possibly he has infringed no human law. But that must be a very lax integrity, which has no higher standard of right and wrong than the statute-book: for by far the greater part of the daily dishonesties of trade and finance, are too subtle to be caught by the meshes of any human legislation. And of what force can it be to allege that the sort of transactions he has been engaged in, are current in the business-world, and have the sanction of "men of character"? "Men of character" will sometimes do very strange things; and questions of morals are not to be decided by a show of hands. There is another tribunal by which these cases are to be adjudicated. Let the parties implicated consider, whether the paltry pleas by which they would gloss over their avarice and oppression, will avail them *there*.

The confidence with which the confirmed speculator adduces arguments of this kind, shows how callous his master-passion has made him to the claims of justice and humanity. And yet, inconsistent as it may seem, this same man may be found in private quite accessible to the appeals of misery. It is in his business that he is so unfeeling. Convinced by a vicious sophistry that his schemes are no more reprehensible than a staid and prudent traffic, he will strip a neighbour of his property by a few dexterous operations, without seeming to know that he is violating the plainest principles of integrity — that corresponding conduct in a prince, would make him a tyrant, and in a peasant, would make him a robber. And of the very fruits of this grasping covetousness, he will perhaps contribute to works of charity, while his bosom knows nothing beyond a transient feeling of regret for the individuals he has ruined. This, however, is really in keeping with his character. Professed gamblers are proverbially prodigal in dispensing their funds, though they are dead to the sufferings of their victims. The spirit of speculation is one type of the gambling-spirit. Like that, it grasps at sudden wealth; it aims to secure it, not by industry and legitimate traffic, but by sleight of hand; and it is indifferent as to who suffers, or to what extent, by its acquisitions. It is no strange thing, then, that it should also display a similar profusion in disposing of its gains.

It is too apparent to require argument, that wherever this spirit enters the walks of trade, it must tend to degrade commerce to a system of shuffling and trickery. All traffic carries with it some degree of insecurity. And yet the established laws of trade are on the whole so uniform in their operation, that where a community faithfully adhere to them, the hazards of business are comparatively small. Every intelligent merchant understands its chief contingencies; and if he takes these into the account in making his contracts, he will not ordinarily encounter any *great* losses. But impregnate this same community with the delirium of speculation, and it is like withdrawing the balance-wheel from a massive piece of machinery. Its movements, before harmonious and regular, become spasmodic and untractable, until in the end it may destroy itself and every thing within its reach. A people in this condition have lost their regulator. Their mutual confidence, the foundation of all healthful traffic, is supplanted by general suspicion and distrust. The unprincipled and the indiscreet plunge into one extravagant scheme after another; and thoughtful men prepare, as they may, for the fearful collapse which is so certain to follow one of these violent paroxysms.

The temptation with which merchants are beset in times like this (aside from over-trading), is, to engraft speculative projects upon their stated business. It would be going too far, to say that this ought never to be done. There are houses which have so ample a capital, that they can, without imprudence, employ a part of their means in *judicious* enterprises, collateral to their main business. But as a general rule, it is unwise and even unwarrantable — unwise, because the issue must in every case be doubtful, and, in any event, the practice fosters an evil habit of mind: unwarrantable, because it is unjust to creditors. It is a very specious bait which Satan throws in your way, when he invites you to put a few thousand dollars temporarily into some brilliant project, which is "certain to succeed" — when he whispers in your ear, "Why not accept the boon that Providence offers you, and make more money in a month than your broadcloths and muslins will bring you in years? Why surrender all these golden opportunities to your neighbours who are rapidly getting rich by them?"— But consider, have you a *right* to do this? You may purpose to use for it, instead of your own capital, certain *trust-funds* in your hands, which will not impair your mercantile resources. But whence do you derive your authority? Unless the terms of the trust clearly convey this power, you have no right to touch those funds. They are not yours. You cannot borrow them. You have bound yourself legally and morally, in accepting the trust, to hold them exclusively for certain specified objects. You could not take them even to keep yourself from breaking. You could not take them to supply your family with bread. Much less can you use them for a single day to carry on a speculation. It is a most dangerous thing to invade the sanctity of a trust. The man who does it, although from no unworthy motives and with the full intention of replacing soon the means he "borrows," has weakened his own sense of obligation and put his integrity in imminent jeopardy. He may even have in view the good of the party whose trustee he is, but if he acts without warrant, this will not exculpate him. "To obey is better than sacrifice, and to hearken, than the fat of rams." Our courts and those of England are justly rigorous in enforcing fidelity to trusts. And notwithstanding this, the inexperienced and the helpless are continually falling a prey to recklessness or cupidity on the part of their financial guardians. Times of speculation especially make sad havoc with the consciences of trustees. Thousands of widows and children have had reason to mourn these disastrous seasons, so fatal to the virtue or the prudence of the custodians of their little property.

But irrespective of trust-funds, a merchant, I have said, is not authorized, in ordinary circumstances, to employ his capital or credit in speculations aside from his proper business. The reason is, because this was not contemplated by his creditors in their transactions with him, and it would be unjust to them. They loaned him money, or sold him goods, with the clear understanding that he was to confine himself to the business he was engaged in. They knew the usual risks of trade, and were willing to trust him. Had he said to them, "I intend also to speculate in stocks," they might or might not have trusted him:—(somewhat remarkable men if they *had.*) In any event, they would have acted with their eyes open. But now that he has their property in his hands, he has no right to subject it to hazards which they never sanctioned. If you add a new flue to your store without notifying your insurers, it absolves them from all responsibility in case of loss. You are violating the same principle, and on a much broader scale, when you secretly embark in these foreign speculations. You are augmenting the risks of your creditors manifoldly, without increasing your *premium.* The original contract is vitiated by the introduction of a new element; and they might justly complain of you as deceivers and covenant-breakers. You certainly will not attempt to vindicate this conduct by the morality of the Bible: the very least of your children, if old enough to grasp the terms of the statement, would tell you that you had done wrong.

And morality aside, this is madness for a firm, even on the score of policy. A habit of this sort is pretty certain to become known; and this will give the death-blow to the credit of any house of limited means. Banks and importers will not trust a house which is known to be dabbling in stocks or other "extra-hazardous" commodities. A year or two since, one of the partners in a wealthy New-York firm lost a large sum of money at a watering-place by gambling. The newspapers reported the occurrence, and the firm was soon dissolved. This was their only alternative. Who would trust them, after it was known that they had a confirmed gambler among them? The same principle applies in the other case. Credit and responsibility are correlative terms. Where there is no presumed responsibility, there will be no credit. And the responsibility of a mercantile house, whose position is such that the daily bulletins of the Board of Brokers are of more interest to it than the "Price-Current," is like one of the unknown quantities in an algebraic formula. Such a house has no moral right to borrow money for pretended commercial purposes, and apply it to the purchase of fresh scrip or to the liquidation of its losses on previous speculations. This is practically conceded by the very men who are guilty of it. It is consciousness of wrong-doing which makes them conceal these things from their creditors: for they well know that on giving the least hint of them, the loans now so generously granted, would be as peremptorily refused.

It might abate the ardour of those financiers who are so eager to entice merchants (or their capital) into the Stock Exchange, to consider, that if a member of a firm embarks in these speculations without the knowledge of his partners, the firm is not bound by his engagements. "The legal authority of the partners" (I use the language of one of the first commercial lawyers in the United States*) "takes its form and shape from the ordinary scope and objects of the partnership-business, and is limited to their contracts; and acts done by each copartner in the ordinary or fair prosecution of the ostensible business of the firm, are obligatory on it; beyond this, they are not binding on the partnership; they are unauthorized, and can only be made to affect the copartnership by showing the actual consent of all its members. Thus, a house dealing in dry goods, would not ordinarily be bound by the purchase, by one of its partners, of a ship, unless the purchase were sanctioned by his co-

---

* Daniel Lord, Jun., Esquire, of New York.

partners. So, a house running a line of packets to another port, would not ordinarily be bound by a purchase of hardware by one of its partners. A house dealing in hardware would not be bound by a purchase of dry goods, nor would any mercantile firm be charged with stock-speculations. — The principle is, that by openly pursuing a specific kind of business, the copartnership limits are announced, and the copartners are not to be deemed authorized to transact other kinds on the credit of their firm. The common purpose of the union being specific, the acts and conduct of the parties having reference to this purpose, must conform to the contemplation of the parties; nor have the public reason to hold it otherwise."

The speculating eras of which we have been speaking, are so associated in the public mind with BANKS, that it may be proper to make a few observations at this point on the management of those institutions. Their vital connection with the general prosperity of nations, must be too apparent to admit of argument. The State has delegated to them one of its highest prerogatives, that of creating a currency. The course of events has made them not simply conveniences, but indispensable implements to the prosecution of commerce. Politicians may find it useful to decry the entire policy, but no man whose character and experience are such as to entitle his opinions to respect, would think it expedient to annihilate the present banking system of the world. Then, again, the extent of its operations shows how closely it is identified with all the substantive interests of commerce. The transactions of the fourteen banks in this city, amount, on the lowest estimate, to five hundred millions of dollars *per annum*, and may reach twice that sum. It will be seen at once, when the number of banks in the United States is taken into the account, that every citizen, however secluded his situation, has a stake in the proper management of this colossal enginery. That there is much misconception abroad respecting the legitimate functions of these corporations; that they are often expected to perform offices which have not been confided to them; that the jealousies and prejudices directed against them are frequently the fruit of private spleen or political craft—are points which do not admit of a question; but it is not my province to discuss them. There *are* things which the moralist may insist upon. And one of these, is, that the directors of a bank or other corporate institution, are obviously *bound to be faithful to their trust.*

This seems a mere truism. But there is a prevalent impression that as a practical matter, it is greatly neglected. It is alleged, that gentlemen are in the habit of seeking a place in the Direction of these institutions, whose qualifications are quite apocryphal, and whose aims are purely personal. It is further alleged, that many gentlemen holding these situations, take no pains to keep themselves informed of the actual state of the business entrusted to them; that they remit the whole control of things to the executive officers, with, perhaps, one or two of their own number; and that thus they are directors who direct nothing, or, as we say in the church of a certain class of the clergy, "ministers without charge." If these things are so, the parties implicated may well be admonished of their error. They are the administrators of a Trust. They have engaged to administer it wisely and faithfully, according to their ability. They stand before the stock-holders and before the public, as the guardians and sponsors of important vested rights. Their names inspire confidence in the trust, and invite operations based upon its presumed security. This responsibility cannot be transferred. They have no moral right, as they have no legal authority, to perform their duties by vicar. If they are not competent, or if they have not the time, to attend to these duties, let them resign. While they retain the office, they will be held accountable for diligence and fidelity in meeting its requisitions. This does not imply that they are to usurp the functions of presidents, cashiers, and secretaries.

Still less does it exact of them such a supervision as shall preclude all possible fraud and forgery on the part of unprincipled officials. No human sagacity can counterwork villany in all cases. But it does import that they shall know what their institution is doing, how its funds are employed, and whether it is honestly carrying out the ends contemplated in its charter. A little more fidelity on the part of Boards of Direction, would have prevented some of the worst financial "explosions" which have disgraced the country.

Another principle (just hinted at) which a teacher of morals may insist upon, is, that these institutions *shall confine themselves to the objects for which they were chartered, and prosecute these with integrity, prudence, and impartiality.* This they have agreed to do in accepting their charters; and it is an immorality, more or less marked, if they come short of it. Various questions might arise here, on which casuists, no less than financiers, would differ. Declining all debateable topics, it is evident that a corporation may contravene the spirit, if not the letter, of its charter, by wielding its power for political purposes. It is a supposable case, for example, that the railroad companies of a State might combine to effect a revolution in its politics: or that a bank might employ its funds in promoting the election of particular candidates to public offices. This would be a breach of trust: their charters were given for no such purposes as these.—Equally apparent is it, that an institution which loans its money at a usurious interest, is guilty of an immorality. Of the expediency of the usury laws, I am not called upon to speak. While they exist, all corporations are bound to respect them — bound, not simply by the obligation which rests upon private citizens, but by a specific compact which they have entered into with the Commonwealth, and the violation of which, directly or indirectly, is a crime against society.

There is an opinion somewhat prevalent, that banks ought to confine their loans to "business-men," and that, among these, they should rarely lend money to their own directors. We may dissent from this doctrine in both its parts, without sanctioning the acknowledged abuses from which it has sprung. The business-men of a community may in general be allowed a precedence in the way of bank-accommodation, but there seems no reason, in the nature of things, why all other classes should be excluded. If a physician requires a loan for the purchase of a horse, or a lawyer in buying a library, why should they be denied? And if a merchant becomes a bank-director, possibly at a sacrifice of his personal convenience, why should this circumstance deprive him of the aid the bank has been in the habit of according to him? But there are — at least there have been in former times — usages which are justly to be reprobated. In the annals of American finance, examples are not wanting of institutions which have employed their entire resources in illegitimate schemes. The capital which should have gone to the promotion of commerce, has gone into the hands of favourites, to be used in speculation, or in building up a few houses at the expense of their neighbours. Notes which have been refused at their counters, have been "done" with the identical means *elsewhere* and at usurious rates. Merchants who had an equitable claim upon their help, have been left to "make or break" as they might, while the funds they *should* have received, have been secretly used to carry on some magnificent operations on private account. What commerce has lost, the stock-exchange has gained. And however it may have fared with the plodding traffickers, the speculators have had no cause to complain.

It is pleasant to think that in so far as our own city is concerned, institutions of this sort, if they ever had a place amongst us, belong to the province of the historian;* and that if one of them should re-appear

* This opinion has been called in question. If it be erroneous, the compliment is of course cancelled. But I choose to hope for the best.

here, it would meet with no sympathy from the banks which now adorn our metropolis. Such an institution, wherever found, is, in fact, a nuisance. The men who control it, faithless to every trust, and swayed by the basest motives, are chargeable with a criminality so much the more flagrant than that of private offenders, as they have prostituted to a mercenary self-aggrandizement, a more generous confidence and more ample resources. They have used the seal of the government to sanctify their treachery, and abused the confidence of the commonwealth to aim a serious blow at its prosperity. To attempt to screen themselves behind the impersonality of "the bank," is only another proof that cupidity and cowardice are twin sisters. The "bank" is but an *alias* for themselves. Human jurisprudence may fail of establishing their identity; but it may be worth their while to consider, whether it is the "bank" that will be called upon to answer for these delinquencies at the *Great Assize.*

No crisis ever occurs in the money-market, that "the banks" do not come in for a lavish amount of censure. The usual assumption is, that they have had a controlling agency in inflating prices to a dangerous extent, and are therefore responsible for the reaction which follows. That this may have been so in any particular case, is quite certain. But it ought to be considered that banks, in their legitimate character, are not the regulators, but the implements of trade; and that while they may influence the tides which bear the great flotillas of commerce, they are themselves swayed by those tides. It is not their prerogative to decide whether a merchant shall extend his business beyond prudent limits or embark in an insane speculation. That is his concern. And if a community choose to do those things, and find themselves after a while, as the natural consequence, drifting towards the shoals of insolvency, they should at least suspend their maledictions against the banks, until they learn whether the fault may not lie nearer home. It is one of the invariable contingencies of business, that the financial institutions of a country *may* be obliged abruptly to reduce their discount-line, and, to borrow a nautical phrase, shorten sail in every practicable way. The money and the commerce, the husbandry and the politics, of the world, are so reticulated, that a failure of the crops in Turkey, or a civil revolution in Spain, might seriously affect the condition of every bank in Missouri or Iowa. A wise merchant will consider this in laying his plans, and beware of so entangling himself with banks that a change in their policy will subvert his foundations. The spirit of this observation is also applicable to the banks. Subordinate as they are to higher agencies in the trading and political world, it should be a point of morals with them, no less than a rule of practical wisdom, so to conduct their affairs as to reduce the amount of disturbance they may suffer from these extrinsic causes to the lowest possible degree. The very best quality in the working of a bank, next to inflexible honesty, is steadiness. If I may recur again to the sea for an illustration, when a vessel is in tempestuous weather, or traversing an intricate channel, one's ear is saluted with the constant iteration of the cry to the helmsman, "Steady!" "Steady!" I know not that there is any word in the language which better deserves to be hung up in large capitals in our bank-parlours, than this homely Saxon dissyllable, "STEADY!" "STEADY!" The crew that can keep a financial ship steady through all the conflicting winds and currents of the business-world, is deserving of as much honour as the intrepid navigators who thread their way in safety through the ice-fields of the Northern circle. And, it may be added, the crew that do not aim at this, and strain every nerve to accomplish it, should be discharged on the first opportunity.

I have not intended by any remarks which have been made, to exonerate banks from all responsibility in bringing about commercial panics. In too many instances they have had a leading part in producing these calamities. It may be unreasonable to require them to "regulate the trade" of a country, but they can abstain from a policy which will engender a speculating mania, and tempt houses to be imprudent. Indeed, there is a question of morals, as well as a question of expediency, involved in the loaning of their funds, whether with or without reference to a crisis. They are neither to feed the fever of speculation by "doing" the paper of firms already, as may be currently understood, beyond their depth in rash adventures; nor are they to abet dishonesty by sustaining men who have made a fortune by failing. Honourable men who have experienced misfortune, have a claim upon them. Nor is there among all their functions a single one more beneficent and praiseworthy, than that of assisting to set on their feet, individuals of tried integrity, whose disasters have only revealed to their creditors fresh grounds for respect and confidence. But they have no right to treat a swindler thus. A man who has notoriously defrauded his creditors, and is by common consent branded as a rogue, it is not their province to restore to his former standing. They might as well put their seal on a forged draft, and send it out as genuine. It matters not that the party concerned may tender them ample securities. His paper is tainted; and if they touch it, the profits they make upon it, go into their vaults as the "wages of unrighteousness." They are not a mere money-making corporation. They are trustees. They have no more right to debauch the morals of the community, than they have to circulate counterfeit notes. And they are doing this whenever they employ their great powers to reinstate an unprincipled man in the public confidence.

The only qualification to be appended to this statement, is, that the principle shall not be extended to cases of merely alleged fraud. Almost every failure brings out a charge of fraud from some quarter. And a majority of failures certainly involve indiscretions which cannot be deemed innocent. But these are usually treated with lenity, where a man bears himself frankly and ingenuously *at the time* of his catastrophe. Banks must beware how they allow themselves, in dealing with examples of this sort, to imbibe the resentments of creditors, and oppress firms which are trying to retrieve their former errors by a judicious and upright policy. It is one of the benign principles of the Divine government, "He that confesseth and forsaketh his sins shall find mercy." We are bound to adopt it in our intercourse with one another. But neither individuals nor corporations can be required to countenance those who, having defrauded their neighbours once, give no evidence that they will not, should occasion offer, do it again.

The bank which violates this rule for the sake of securing an advantageous account, invades the rights of society, and tramples the moral code of the Bible in the dust.

I have had repeated occasion to refer to STOCKS. To preclude any misapprehension in what I am about to say further on this subject, I wish to observe, that as stocks have become one of the essential means of commercial and political progress, so they are as legitimate an article of traffic as any other commodity. It is highly proper that there should be a distinct class of men devoted to this business. Nothing shall be uttered here in derogation of the respectability and utility of the profession as such. It comprises many gentlemen, in all our cities, of the highest standing for integrity. If it also embraces not a few individuals of equivocal honesty, this is no less the misfortune of other professions. Indiscriminate censures are always unjust. No profession is to be judged by its unworthy members, nor any usage by its abuses. But neither should the personal excellence of individuals, nor the honourable nature of their calling, prevent us from arraigning the abuses which may have crept in among them, and which they may be supposed to deplore equally with candid observers from without. It is, indeed, impossible to avoid this topic in the most cursory notice of a passion for speculation: for the stock-board is, more than any other point, the focus where this passion concentrates itself, and which has the chief agency in inflaming it.

If this business were confined to *bona fide* stocks and *bona fide* investments, the moralist might have little ground of complaint. But this is not so. Many of the stocks which are bought and sold, have no real value, and are thus excluded from the sphere of honourable commerce, which, as already observed, consists in "the exchange of equivalents for mutual advantage." What "exchange of equivalents" is there when you sell a man one of these "fancies" worth five dollars, for a hundred dollars? Have you given him the worth of his money? You will say, the man should know his own business, and if he chooses to buy a worthless article, it is no fault of yours. But have you a right to deal in "worthless articles"—that is, have you a right to set an exorbitant fictitious value upon them, and so put them off upon your neighbours, who, as you know, can make no use of them, and, to recover their outlay, must treat some one else as you have treated them? You will meet this by saying, that transactions of this kind are perfectly understood: no one is deceived by them: the stocks are neither sold nor bought for investments; they are not even transferred: the whole object with both parties is to make a profit on them. If you add, these contracts are usually *on time*, we shall have the whole case before us. And a very bad case it is.

For, in the first place, you are trafficking in a mere *fiction*. As this class of transactions is commonly managed, the scrip would answer your purpose just as well if it ostensibly represented so many lots at the North Pole or in the moon. It is no part of your real object to sell the stock at all, nor of the buyer's to purchase it. You do not, probably, own it: and he does not want it. And at the stipulated period for consummating the transaction, you will part with no stock, and he will receive none. You sell your neighbour, for example, 100 shares of some fancy stock, deliverable in thirty days, for $11,000. When the day arrives, you may be able to purchase the requisite amount of scrip for $10,000. Or, the market having advanced during the month, it may cost you $11,500. The other party does not want the scrip, and you never meant to buy it. All you were aiming at, was, the "differences." So the operation is closed, in the former case, by his handing you his check for a thousand dollars, and in the latter, by your handing him your check for five hundred dollars — the market-price on the day of settlement regulating the balances. This is substantially the nature of these transactions: with their endless modifications we are not concerned. The briefest possible glance at the thing will show that this is not commerce, but gambling—*sheer*, *downright*, *unmitigated* GAMBLING. If you sell a cargo of flour or of cotton, a case of merchandize or a dwelling-house, deliverable at the end of a month, you expect, as a matter of course, to transfer the property, and the other party expects to receive it and pay the money. This is legitimate commerce. There are responsible parties, a contract, and an actual exchange of equivalents. In the other case, the parties may be responsible men, or irresponsible. Any individual who is able to get together a few hundred dollars (if even this is necessary), can operate in these gambling stocks on a large scale. All he requires is cash or credit enough to meet the amount of his *bet*, in the event of his losing. For, stripped of its technicalities, this selling "on time" is simply a *wager* that the stock in question will be worth a certain sum on a specified day. The principle is identically the same with betting on a battle or a horse-race. So the laws of England and those of some of our own States regard it. In England, a penalty of £500 is laid upon every person who makes a "time-bargain," and the same penalty upon every one contracting for the sale of stock of which he is not possessed at the date of the contract. In Pennsylvania, all sales of stocks to be delivered more than five days after the contract, are prohibited, under a penalty of from one hundred to a thousand dollars; and the amount of the "differences" paid under any such contract, with an additional penalty of twenty per cent. on the said payment, may be recovered at law by the losing party, his heirs or assigns. In New York, the statute prohibits all contracts for the sale of stocks, and declares them absolutely void, unless the party contracting to sell or transfer the same, shall, at the making of such contract, be in the actual possession of the certificates thereof, or otherwise entitled in his own right, or acting for others so entitled, to sell or transfer the same. It also prohibits and declares void all *wagers* concerning the present or future price of stocks, and provides that money paid or goods delivered by way of premium or difference, in pursuance of contracts or wagers so made, may be recovered back from the party receiving the same and his personal representatives. — It is quite immaterial to our purpose, whether these laws are enforced or not. Enough that this sort of traffic is pronounced by the public authorities of different countries, to be an *immorality.* Like other kinds of gambling, it requires but little capital, and holds out great enticements to mere adventurers and fortune-hunters. The most honourable men may amass a sudden fortune by dealing in stocks. There is no reason why they should not employ their sagacity, experience, and capital, in watching for favourable investments and opportune transfers, in the Funds — provided only they shun contracts on time, and do a real, not a fictitious, business. But it *is* a great social evil that speculators who have neither means nor moral principle, should, by a few reckless wagers at the stock-board, roll up a princely estate, and then use it to dazzle the town with their extravagance. These examples are adapted to have a pernicious influence upon the tribes of young men who are engaged in mercantile and manufacturing occupations. They are apt to enkindle in the minds of clerks a disgust at the tedious processes of commerce, and to allure them from the solid paths of industry into the treacherous realm of speculation. Many of them venture upon this without counting the cost, and end by robbing their employers and blasting their own characters. Scarcely a year passes that does not bring to light some melancholy instances of this kind; and there are doubtless very many others which are never revealed to the public.

The whole evil has not been stated. It results from the nature of these transactions, that where any great amounts are pending, the market will not be left to the control of natural or legitimate causes. It is the interest of one party to enhance, and of the other to depress, it. Each, therefore, will employ all available agencies to accomplish his own end. Reports favourable or prejudicial to the stock; false rumours about public affairs; "money-articles" in venal newspapers; combinations and counter-combinations among the dealers; these are familiar implements in carrying forward the contests of the stock-exchange. Whatever generalship the operators may have, is sure to be put in requisition. No other form of gambling opens a wider field for strategy and deception, or one which is more thoroughly cultivated. To say that the necessary effect must be to sear their feelings and debauch their principles, is only to repeat what may be heard every day in the street. But the mischief is not confined to themselves. Such a system as this, is like a cancer at the heart of a community. Very many are drawn in and actually infected with the poison. Then, again, the enormity of the practice is lost sight of in the numbers and the respectability of the parties who countenance it. It goes to diffuse lax notions of moral obligation; to elevate craft and cunning to a level with integrity; to inspire the feeling that success will sanctify fraud; and to stimulate still more the predominant passion for speedy accumulation. This is not conjecture, but history. The public sentiment in all our great cities is so vitiated on this subject, that there is very little hope of correcting it. "Gambling in stocks" is as current a phrase, as gambling at cards or at billiards. But the public sentiment tolerates and shelters it. It even lavishes its respect and its honours upon the men who win the most bets and carry off the largest stakes. The moralist who ventures to point the maledictions of the decalogue against the system, is viewed as a well-meaning, but simple, man, who might as well spare his strength, or apply it to the removal of some more tractable evil. And neither the remonstrances of the pulpit, nor the frequent disasters which overwhelm men engaged in these pursuits, and leave them with blasted fortunes and characters and with ruined families, have hitherto sufficed to arouse the community to the demoralizing tendencies of this traffic. This is the more ominous, because there seems to be no theoretical difference of opinion on the subject. All persons not engaged in these speculative schemes, concur in branding them as immoral in their very principle. If the immorality lay in the adjuncts or incidents, the antidote would be, reformation. But it lies in the essence of the thing, and the only effectual remedy, therefore, is excision.

Every consideration of virtue and of social prosperity demands that the traffic in stocks should be regulated by the same general rules which govern the other branches of commerce. Why should it not be? What is there in the nature of the commodity itself which is bought and sold, or in its relations to the public interest, to entitle this traffic to an exemption from the established laws of trade? Yet such an exemption is conceded to it. Let an association of merchants attempt to introduce the usages of the stock-exchange into the business of Market street or Pearl street — to buy and sell "on time" worthless or fictitious fabrics — fabrics of which there was not, and never would be, a piece in their stores — for dealing in which neither clerks, nor porters, nor packing boxes, would be required — and which would only pass from hand to hand in a supposititious transfer, by the payment of "differences" on the prescribed day of delivery. Is there a city in the Union that would tolerate such a bare-faced system of gambling for a single month? Would there not be a universal burst of indignation, at the audacity and profligacy of the thing? Yet wherein would it differ from that class of transactions in stocks on which I am animadverting? The commodities are unlike, but that is all. The principle is the same. And the question for merchants and financiers to settle, is, why a practice should be openly fostered and encouraged in one department of commerce, which would be hooted from any other department of commerce as a disreputable immorality? This question derives increased significancy from the fact, already noted, that the true character of the practice is not denied. All men (those interested excepted) agree in pronouncing it, not only a violation of the Scripture code of morals, but a huge fountain of social corruption. Why, then, is it not suppressed? Why do not the large and influential body of upright men belonging to that profession, wipe off this stain from their escutcheon, and bring back at least the official business of the stock-board to its legitimate channels? Private transactions they cannot control, although by a moral influence they might reach even these. But their inability to prevent private gambling, does not absolve them from the obligation to discountenance, and, if possible, abolish, public gambling. If they have not the courage to attempt this, the officers of the law should supply their lack of service. And if these are disposed to wink at the evil, measures should be adopted to form a more healthful public sentiment, which might suppress this iniquity, and protect society from its multifarious mischiefs.

In dismissing this subject, I must once more disclaim any intention to impugn the ordinary traffic in public and corporate securities. The stock-broker is as indispensable as the merchant, and his legitimate business every way as respectable and useful. I will not say that there are no evils to be corrected within the sphere where his business lies, and to which, if he is a true man, he confines himself. But I have not chosen to speak of them in this Lecture. Every word of censure I have uttered, has had respect to a system which is beyond the pale of lawful commerce, the opprobrium of the stock-exchange, and a plague-spot upon the face of society.

Logical exactness might demand, in deference to the main design of this Lecture, some further notice of stock-jobbing in its connection with periods of excessive speculation. But the length of this discussion admonishes me to close — which I do by reminding you of a saying of our Lord's, which is extremely apposite to our own age and country. The motive power which propels the vast machinery of commerce, its iniquitous no less than its beneficent agencies, is the desire of wealth. This desire takes its moral hue from its motives and its implements. Its perpetual tendency is to excess; and we cannot, therefore, ponder too often or too seriously the admonition, "Take heed, and beware of covetousness: for a man's life consisteth not in the abundance of the things which he possesseth." You may accomplish all that you have set your hearts upon, and compass the utmost limits of accumulation with which your fancy has loved to decorate your future consequence, and still be without any solid happiness. Nay, the more you surrender yourselves to the mastery of this passion, the more certain are you to miss the true enjoyment of life. Nor is this all. Amidst the cares and aspirations of your Counting-rooms, there is a process going on which involves your profoundest interests. Business may thrive or languish, success or disappointment may attend your plans, wealth or poverty may be standing at your doors — it is all one as to your *future* destiny. Every hour is bearing you on towards the judgment-seat of Christ; every transaction in which you engage, every calamity that sweeps over you, every auspicious venture that helps to fill your coffers, is helping to mould your characters for endless blessedness or eternal wo. Whether you are oppressed by the leaden stagnation of trade, or elated by the ensigns of a luxuriant prosperity, there is *one* interest that never droops, one mighty Trafficker whose work never intermits. Invisible to mortal eyes, he is gliding about among you, alike active and unsparing in your seasons of depression, and in the palmiest days of your commercial triumph. While he keeps at a distance, you heed him not: he may mow down his victims by thousands without disturbing your composure. But sometimes he crosses your path so near you — he strikes down a partner, a neighbour, a friend, so dear to your heart or so closely affiliated with you in business, that you are startled: you feel like one who sees the ground torn up at his feet by a thunderbolt. For the time, you feel that life's misnamed realities are airy nothings. You are ready to exclaim, with the great British statesman, "What shadows we are! What shadows we pursue!" But how transient, too often, are these impressions! You miss that familiar form in your walks, but the crowd closes in, and, after a few days fills up the void produced by his removal; and though *he* may not be at once forgotten, the solemn and tender reflections awakened by his death, are soon merged in the absorbing secularities of your profession. — Is this to act as becomes your rational nature? Can you appeal, in its vindication, to those maxims of prudence which govern you in your business-arrangements. While you are contriving how you may increase your property, you may be summoned to that world where all the gold that was ever mined, could not purchase a drop of water to cool your parched tongues. While you are hanging with suspense upon the mails and the telegraph, for intelligence which is to consummate or blast your earthly hopes, the voice of God may fall upon your ear, "This night thy soul shall be required of thee!" — I speak as to wise men.

You need a portion which is satisfying and inalienable; which neither life with its temptations, nor death with its disruption of all mortal ties, can take from you. Such a portion is to be found only in the Gospel of Christ.

> "This is the field where hidden lies
> The pearl of price unknown;
> That merchant is divinely wise,
> Who makes the pearl his own."

To secure it, is to have God for your Father, Christ for your Saviour, and heaven for your heritage. To neglect it, is to peril your everlasting felicity on the uncertainties of every fleeting hour. Yield, while you may, to the strivings of the Spirit, and accept the proffered mercy: for "the redemption of the soul is precious, and it ceaseth for ever!"

Lecture Sixth.

BANKRUPTCY.

There is one invariable feature of a speculating era, which, though alluded to in previous Lectures, has not been set forth as its importance demands — I mean, *luxury and extravagance.* These are terms of variable import, and it is not always practicable to use them without the hazard of being misunderstood. Nor is it the easiest thing in the world for a Christian teacher to expound the utterances of the Bible on this subject, in a way which shall meet satisfactorily the exigencies of every case that may demand a solution. To say, for example, that the Bible prohibits all indulgence in luxuries, would be taking very ambiguous and very dangerous ground— ambiguous, because the term "luxuries" is of apocryphal and mutable signification; and dangerous, because, rigidly carried out, this rule might take the bread out of some millions of mouths. To our ancestors at different periods, most of the articles which we reckon among the indispensable conveniences, if not the necessaries of life, would have been luxuries — our houses, food, clothing, equipages, and the like. Down to the fourteenth century, houses were built without chimneys. Glazed windows were so rare in England, that so late as 1567 the glass casements at Alnwick Castle were taken down in the absence of the family, to guard them from accident. It is recorded as a special proof of the munificence of the pompous Thomas à Becket, when Lord Chancellor (A. D. 1154), that "he caused his servants to cover the floor of his dining-room with clean straw or hay every morning in winter, and green branches of trees in summer, that those guests who could not find room to sit at table, might sit on the ground without spoiling their fine clothes." The first watches were made in the fourteenth century. Linen and cotton and silk were luxuries among the Romans: and the families of tradesmen are now more finely attired than were the wives and daughters of the Cæsars.—And the thing that has been, is that which shall be. Many of our luxuries will in turn become commonplace comforts.

The term, too, has another relative meaning of more practical importance than this. The station and circumstances of individuals must be taken into the account. That may be a luxury, certainly an extravagance, to one family, which is not to another. It is not for a censor of morals to denounce every private picture-gallery, or every elegant mansion, as an extravagance, because these possessions are beyond the reach of most persons: "for why is my liberty judged of another man's conscience?" It is neither argument nor apology, to say, "My neighbour has done thus; therefore, I may do it." Where there is an element of right and wrong, questions cannot be settled in this way. There is another standard, "the law and the testimony."

In another view, the absolute prohibition of luxuries might have a most disastrous influence upon the well-being of mankind. The question of labour, it is often said, is the great question of this age. What shall be done with the masses? How employ them? How remunerate them? How elevate them? Idleness has always been fatal to them. And if they were restricted to the production of the mere conveniences of life, whether by agriculture or the mechanic arts, the great body of them would soon have to abandon their occupations, and either go into almshouses or betake themselves to hunting and fishing for a livelihood. Nothing is more certain than that the traffic in articles of taste and fancy, is one of the chief sources of support to the working population of the globe. How many deserving families would suffer by a sumptuary law forbidding the citizens of this country to use coaches, or gold watches, or books in costly binding; or by a statute like that of England in 1337, restricting even the wealthy to two courses at a meal and two dishes to a course; or like one in Ireland a century later, prohibiting gilt bridles and harness, under pain of confiscation. That cannot be a Scripture code of ethics which would turn thousands of industrious artisans adrift upon the world without occupation. Nor could society sustain itself under such a regimen. Its means of wealth and progress would be seriously abridged, and a general decline would ensue, no less in its intellectual and moral, than in its material interests.

The evil, however, is, that these principles are grossly abused and perverted in seasons of speculation. The money which is hurriedly made, is wastefully expended. The contest for gain in the arena of business, is carried forward as a race for ostentation in social life. Profusion becomes the order of the day with those who can, and those who cannot afford it. Luxury is made, not the exception, but the rule. Houses vieing with palaces in splendor, a style of dress suited to a Court, entertainments which would not discredit an imperial "Reception," day turned into night and night into day, artificial manners, artificial characters, and the endless trumpery which goes to make up a life of fashionable dissipation, — such are the familiar concomitants of one of these periods of commercial inflation. The entire social structure assumes by degrees a type corresponding with the prevailing idolatry of Mammon. The current talk is of money and fortunes. The flow of adulation is in the channels money has dug, and toward the points where new-made wealth holds its levees. People are gauged, not by their worth, but by what they *are* worth;* or rather by what they seem to be worth. For these are times of show more than of substance. It is one of the foolish and unwarrantable expedients for maintaining credit, to keep up an expensive domestic establishment; and you know not from any outward symbols, whether such an establishment is an evidence of wealth, or simply a device to preserve the appearance of wealth. We will put the most charitable construction, however, on all that meets the eye, and assume that the examples around us are those of men who have really amassed great riches by a brief career of earnest and daring speculation. Let us trace them a step or two further.

It is apparent (to repeat a thought already ex-

---

* "For what in worth is anything
But so much money as 'twill bring."—BUTLER.

pressed), that they have lost the advantages which are bound up in a business-*life*. They have reached the goal, but by a side-road. Their hopes are turned into golden fruition; but they have missed that personal training which would have outweighed all their gold.

> "What men most covet, wealth, distinction, power,
> Are baubles nothing worth, that only serve
> To rouse us up as children in the schools
> Are roused up to exertion. The reward
> Is in the *race* we run, not in the prize;
> And they, the few that have it ere they *earn* it,
> Know not, nor ever can, the generous pride
> That glows in him who on himself relies,
> Entering the lists of life."

The parties we are contemplating, are most happy to relinquish these advantages to others. The road to fortune by which they have travelled, has conducted them to the rewards of business without its cares and anxieties. Their garners are filled, without the trouble of sowing and reaping. What remains but to address themselves to the duties of their new position, and to *enjoy* the fruits of their good fortune?

One of the visions which flitted before them in their days of speculation, was a well-stocked *Library*. The vision is realized. *There* is the library, very rich and very beautiful — books, cases, lounges, pictures, all arranged with skill and splendour. One thing only is wanting — a taste for reading. They wonder that the great lights of literature should be so very dull. They pass from History to Philosophy, from Philosophy to Biography, and then to Politics, Travels, Divinity, Romance, Painting, but "'tis all barren." Paradise Lost is nothing to the "money article" in the morning paper.—Literature is taking its revenge. They discarded her for years, and now she discards them. They surrendered themselves to one passion. The chief end of man, in their creed, was to get rich. And they talked and planned and dreamed of money, until the world was, to them, nothing but a great money-shop. They won the race, but came out of it altered men. "Can a man take fire in his bosom, and his clothes not be burned? Can one go upon hot coals, and his feet not be burned?" Neither can a man sell himself to avarice, without having every refined and generous sentiment of his nature weakened by it. They may have the library; but it will be to them very much what the great libraries of the Dark Ages were to the monks who kept the keys of them.*

* Some other persons have bought literature "by measure," besides the English steward who wrote to a bookseller in London, for books to complete his master's library, in the following terms: — "In the first place, I want six feet of Theology, the same quantity of Metaphysics, and near a yard of old Civil Law, in folio."

Another of their visions was a quiet and elegant *Home*, with ample leisure for the training of their children and the fruition of domestic comfort. During their few years of business, their houses have been to them rather like taverns, where they have taken their meals and lodgings, than their homes. When ostensibly there, it has been their physical presence merely, their thoughts have been on 'Change or at the Board of Brokers, with a cotton speculation at Liverpool, or a land speculation in Illinois, or a flour speculation at San Francisco. As to educating their children, they have indeed transferred them to a larger house, and thrown around them the glare of luxury; but the whole responsibility of forming their principles has been left to other hands. This hard necessity has now passed away, and they will hasten back (so they think) to their firesides as a bird to its nest.

But home, somehow, is not what they expected to find it. They dispensed with it so long, that it ceased to be essential to them. The master-passion which consumed their early literary tastes, made sad inroads upon their domestic affections. They learn, to their surprise, that going abroad, which has ceased to be a necessity, has become a matter of choice, and that the financiers and traffickers of the town, are better company than that around their own hearth.

Their children they can instruct in the mysteries

of trade and finance, in the most lucrative kinds of traffic and the best investments; but they would be at some loss how to imbue them with enlarged views of their relations and duties, and to inspire them with those pure principles and exalted aims which are alone worthy of an intelligent and accountable race of creatures. In one aspect, they may have done more to educate them than they were aware of. A family of children accustomed to hear money made the standing theme of conversation, the gauge and measure of all other values, will be likely either to inherit the father's covetousness, or to plunge into the vortex of fashionable frivolity. And in the latter case, he may find it as hopeless to bring them back to the simple tastes and habits which preceded his first successful speculation, as he would to reduce a forest of giant oaks to a nursery.

Another duty which has been all along assigned to this golden era, is, *preparation for death and eternity*. But the same incapacity or indisposition waits upon them in this office as in the others. They discover that there are other obstacles between their souls and heaven, than "the claims of business." They have "made haste to be rich," and they must bear the consequences. A career of speculation has a peculiar tendency to make men both selfish and proud, not to speak of its searing the conscience and multiplying the cords which bind them to the world. And where covetousness and inordinate self-esteem join *together* in taking possession of a man, he is about as well fortified against religion as any character to be met with in society. "With God all things are possible," and such men are sometimes changed into humble and liberal Christians. But it is, unhappily, no fancy sketch which the poet has drawn of gold and its worshippers, who

—— "on its altar sacrificed ease, peace,
Truth, faith, integrity; good conscience, friends,
Love, charity, benevolence, and all
The sweet and tender sympathies of life;
And, to complete the horrid, murderous rite,
And signalize their folly, offered up
Their souls and an eternity of bliss,
To gain them — what? an hour of dreaming joy,
A feverish hour, that hasted to be done
And ended in the bitterness of wo."

The best side of this picture is not very promising. If such are the common issues of a career of *successful* speculation, what are its opposite issues? It would be useless to portray in its details the collapse which usually follows one of these eras of commercial bewilderment; but this seems a proper place to make a few observations on the general subject of mercantile EMBARRASSMENTS AND BANKRUPTCIES.

Nearly twenty years ago an aged gentleman of

large experience in business, said to me, "Almost every merchant fails." The remark startled me; and he immediately repeated it, with emphasis: "Almost every merchant fails once." Most persons might be disposed to qualify it. And yet there are some very striking statistics published on the subject. The testimony of the late General Dearborn, who was for twenty years Collector of the Port of Boston, must be familiar to most merchants. In the course of an agricultural address delivered in 1840, he said—"After an extensive acquaintance with business men, and having long been an attentive observer of the course of events in the mercantile community, I am satisfied that among one hundred merchants and traders in this city (Boston), not more than three ever acquired an independence. It was with great distrust that I came to this conclusion; but, after consulting with an experienced merchant he fully admitted its truth."

The following communication subsequently appeared in the "Farmer's Library:"—

"The statement made by General Dearborn appeared to me so startling, so appalling, that I was induced to examine it with much care, and, I regret to say, I found it true. I then called upon a friend, a great antiquarian, a gentleman always referred to in all matters relating to the city of Boston, and he told me that in the year 1800, he took a memorandum of every person on Long Wharf, and that in 1840 — which is as long as a merchant continues in business — only five in one hundred remained. They had all, in that time, *failed*, or died *destitute of property*. I then went to a very intelligent director of the Union Bank, a very strong bank. He told me that the bank commenced business in 1798; that there was then but one other bank in Boston, the Massachusetts Bank, and that the bank was so overrun with business that the clerks and officers were obliged to work until twelve o'clock at night and all Sundays: that they had occasion to look back, a year or two ago, and they found, that of the one thousand accounts which were opened with them in starting, only *six* remained: they had, in the forty years, either failed or died destitute of property. Houses whose paper had passed without a question, had all gone in that time. 'Bankruptcy,' said he, 'is like death, and almost as certain; they fall single and alone, and are thus forgotten: but there is no escape from it, and he is a fortunate man who fails *young*.'

"Another friend told me that he had occasion to look through the Probate Office a few years since, and he was surprised to find that over *ninety per cent.* of all the estates settled there were insolvent. And within a few days, I have gone back to the incorporation of our banks in Boston. I have a list of the directors since they started. This is, however, a very unfair way of testing the rule, for bank-directors are the most substantial men in the community. In the old bank, over *one-third* had failed in forty years, and in the new bank, a much larger proportion."

Allowing that these facts represent even approximately the general course of things in our great cities, there is matter in them for serious consideration on the part of young men who are about selecting their occupation for life. Those who have inherited an ample patrimony especially, may well ponder them; for it has come to be an axiom, that if a young man of fortune goes into business, he will fail of course. Our present concern, however, is with the moral, not the economical, aspects of this subject. And on this point, it is proper to observe that there are many failures which involve no dereliction of principle, and leave no stain upon the character. The most upright men sometimes fail. Men of tried prudence and of great experience fail. Although no man of proper sensibility can fail without feeling deeply concerned on account of the losses others may suffer by him, the circumstances of the disaster may be such as to remove all ground for self-reproach.

But, on the other hand, we must except from this category, bankruptcies brought about by causes like those we have been dwelling upon in this and the previous Lectures. A merchant who would recognize the authority of the Bible in his Counting-House, must consider carefully the proper *tendencies* of his measures. Habits and usages which *have usually led to bankruptcy*, have a taint of immorality. There is a line beyond which firms have no moral *right* to extend their business. It may not always be easy to adjust this line, but no house will get far beyond it without some misgivings; and when these begin, they had better retrace their steps. Failures may be brought about by sheer neglect and self-indulgence. A prosperous trader may grow weary of the routine of his warehouse. His clerks are competent and faithful: there is no necessity for confining himself as closely now as he did for the first year or two of his business: why should he not devote a portion of every pleasant day to sporting, or driving out, or some other recreation? He tries it — and fails. Is there no delinquency here? The case is still stronger with the insolvencies occasioned by rash speculations and domestic extravagance. A late eminent jurist of our city has expressed himself on this point in terms of eloquent indignation. "Money so easily got is as lightly spent, and brings us to another dark and deep stain on our commercial reputation. The proud splendour, the reckless extravagance, the boundless luxury, in which these ephemeral princes indulge themselves, is shockingly immoral, when, at the conclusion of the pageant, it appears that it was got up at the expense, perhaps on the ruin, of their creditors. Magnificent mansions in town and country, gorgeous furniture, shining equipages, costly entertainments at which five hundred or a thousand dollars are squandered in an evening; in short, a style of living, an exuberance of expenditure, which would be unwise in our country with any amount of fortune, and is absolutely criminal in the actual circumstances of the spendthrift. When the blow falls that prostrates this grandeur, what efforts are made upon the good-nature of the creditors, to retain as much as possible of these gaudy trappings for the family, instead of casting them away as the badges and testimonies of deception and dishonour! Little sympathy is shown for the injuries and losses of those who have fed with their substance the bloated folly of the delinquent; little regard to public opinion is manifested by him, and scarcely a sense of decorum or shame: but every thing is hurried to a conclusion, that he may resume what he calls his business, be trusted, and — betray again." *

It needs to be more deeply impressed upon the conscience of the commercial world, that *improvidence in contracting debts*, especially where this is associated with speculations and luxurious living, is itself a palpable violation of the law of God. And the question, whether a failure involves immorality, will admit of a speedy solution, if it can be shown that this was the cause of it. The statistics on this point

---

* The Hon. Joseph Hopkinson.

relating to our last commercial crisis, are frightful—as will be seen by the following table:—

Number of applicants for relief under the general Bankrupt law, 1841	33,739
Number of creditors returned	1,049,603
Amount of debts stated	$440,934,615
Valuation of property surrendered	$43,697,307

According to these returns, a capital of forty-three millions was made to sustain an indebtedness of four hundred and forty millions! And the real facts were much worse. The dividends actually paid were, in the Southern District of New York, one cent on the dollar; in the Northern District, thirteen and one-third cents; in Connecticut, a half cent; in Mississippi, six cents to one thousand dollars; in Maine, a half cent, in Michigan and Iowa, a quarter cent, in New Jersey, four cents, to the hundred dollars—and so on, throughout the Union. These figures are pregnant with meaning. And they concern the moralist, no less than statesmen and legislators. They display, as in a mirror, the reckless mania for speculation and prodigality, which brought about the crash of '37. Four hundred millions of dollars swallowed up, and nothing to show for it! Nothing? Alas, there was too much to show for it. A paralyzed commerce—stagnation in all the marts of business—

thousands of families ruined — comfort and opulence succeeded by penury and suffering — wrecks of fortunes and, far worse, wrecks of character, strewn all over the land — faithlessness, dishonesty, treachery, in every direction — crime enough to blast a nation for this world and ruin them for the next: *these* were the avails of that four hundred millions wasted in riotous and wicked speculation. I mean what I say — "*wicked* speculation." It was wicked, inexcusably, flagrantly wicked. And its criminality is not extenuated by the fact that through the favour of a benign Providence, the recuperative energy of the country has in a measure retrieved our pecuniary losses. The most revolting features of that period are ineradicable. History has engraved them upon her tablets, and will hand them down to all coming generations, as an illustration of the profound moral debasement to which an unbridled passion for wealth will reduce even the most powerful and prosperous nation.

It has been aptly observed, that "directly above the great cataract of insolvency, lie most dangerous rapids." A boatman whose shallop has been drawn into the whirling tide above Niagara, would supply no inapposite exemplar of an embarrassed merchant sweeping on towards the final catastrophe. Those who have seen and shuddered over the spectacle, tell us that the struggles of a waterman caught in the "Rapids," the superhuman energy with which he tugs at his oars, the spasmodic grasp with which he snatches at every projecting rock, the frenzy with which he flies from one end of his frail skiff to the other, and the commingled horror and despair depicted in his countenance, as the remorseless waves hurry him on to the verge of the cataract, constitute a scene which neither pen nor pencil could delineate. You have its archetype among you, too often presented amidst the fluctuations of commerce not to be familiar to every merchant. For who has not seen the corresponding process enacted over and over again in the walks of trade — an embarrassed house striving to elude the demon of bankruptcy, which is hovering over them,

> "Fierce as ten furies, terrible as hell."

With what anxiety and desperation do they labour to stave off the impending calamity, which they see, and yet will not see. What a rallying of their resources! What skilful and rapid transmutations of their precarious credit into successive shapes, adjusted to fresh exigencies! New purchases and forced sales — usurious loans — notes offered at untried banks — fresh drafts upon neighbouring houses — proceeds which should have been remitted to their principals, applied to cancel paper — one piece of property after another sacrificed — urgent appeals to private friends for succour — money raised on borrowed securities — and all this while, appearances kept up — mind and body on the rack — candour giving way to concealment — integrity breaking down — earnest and unsuccessful efforts to regard wrong actions as right, and to believe there is no real danger — conscience reclaiming — the whole character deteriorating — and the house driving on toward the abyss, until, at length,

> —— "all unawares,
> Fluttering their pennons vain, plumb down they drop
> Ten thousand fathom deep."

This is no picture of the imagination. There is not a large city in Europe or America where it has not been realized in all its fulness, too often to attract attention any longer by its novelty. All failures are not of this kind, but so many are — this is so much the usual course of things — that every merchant ought to make up his mind as to its policy and its morality. Viewing it from the stand-point we *now* occupy, and testing it by the morality of the BIBLE, there can be but one estimate formed of it. Its rashness, its folly, its (must I say it?) immorality, must be known and read of all men. We may sympathize with men who are brought into these most trying circumstances; we may honour their deep solicitude to save themselves and their creditors: but we cannot, as Scripture casuists, nor even as upright men, commend the course they have pursued. The universal feeling will be, that *they ought to have stopped* SOONER. They should not have shut their eyes to their real condition. However painful the conviction, they ought to have yielded to it, that their resources were inadequate to carry them through the storm, and that it would be far better to succumb at once than to consume their remaining assets in waging so hopeless a contest. These assets, they should have remembered, were not theirs. They belonged to their creditors. And it was a double wrong, not only to withhold from them what they had already in hand, but to procure of them or of others, fresh loans to be absorbed in paying off third parties. There can be few things in mercantile experience more vexatious, than to find that the paper your neighbour obtained from you, was used by him, as he was about breaking, to liquidate the claim of some other house; or to see the iron or the produce you sold him on credit last week, on the eve of his bankruptcy, stored away in the lofts of another firm, who were as clamorous in demanding their money, as you were generous in lending yours. It is too much to expect that transactions of this kind should be borne with equanimity. They are of a class of provocations which will set a passionate man on fire, and stir up the displeasure of the very meekest spirits.

When the blow has fallen, other errors are frequently committed no less serious. If the property of the bankrupt belongs to his creditors, it should be handed over to them — promptly, entirely, without concealment, without unjust preferences. It is not for him to say how it shall be disposed of, nor to divide it at his discretion. The least he can in reason or justice do, is, to surrender it to them, and let them say what shall be done with it. If he does this, he will have his reward. His own conscience will ratify it, and his creditors, if they are high-minded men, will be indulgent to his mistakes, and aid him, in so far as he is worthy of their help, in resuscitating his business. But instead of this honourable conduct, many a bankrupt conceals a portion of his property, submits a deceptive statement to his creditors, clogs his surrender with unwarrantable conditions, compromises on terms much below his true capacity, or otherwise contravenes the first principles of morality. You may even find men who grow rich by failing. They have the tact and the audacity to regain confidence in financial circles, break as often as they may. Every body believes them to be rogues, but they have money, and "money answereth all things." They are trusted, therefore; and when the most eligible moment in their stock-jobbing or other speculations arrives, they "stop." And the oftener they stop, the wealthier they get. If they were poor, the law might notice them.

> —— "Plate sin with gold,
> And the strong lance of justice hurtless breaks;
> Arm it in rags, a pigmy's straw doth pierce it."

This surely is the reason — there can be no other — why every great community embraces more or less of these unprincipled bankrupts, who look out superciliously from their ceiled houses or their gorgeous equipages, upon scores of industrious men whose property their pretended "failures" have absorbed into their estates.* "This is a sore evil under the sun:" happily for the mercantile body, it is less common among them than in the ranks of professed

---

* These men belong to the class for whom bankrupt laws were originally designed. "The first bankrupt statute, 34 & 35 Hen. VIII., c. 4, begins with this preamble: 'Whereas divers and sundry persons, craftily obtaining into their hands great substance of other men's goods, do suddenly flee to parts unknown, or keep their houses, not minding to pay or restore to any their creditors their debts and duties, but at their own wills and pleasures consume the substance obtained by credit of other men, for their own pleasure and delicate living, against all reason, equity, and good conscience." — CHRISTIAN'S BLACKSTONE.

financiers. But the baseness of such a career, may well admonish every merchant of the importance, should misfortune overtake him, of avoiding the remotest appearance of equivocation or dishonesty. Bankruptcy is not necessarily linked with disgrace. It is one of the noblest characteristics of the commercial profession, that they are so ready to succour a brother in adversity. If he is really a competent and deserving man, who has kept his integrity untarnished, they are certain to come to his relief. And even if he has fallen into serious errors, there is no class of men in society who will treat his frailties with so much lenity, or be so ready to give him their confidence again, as his fellow-traffickers. But the shameless insolvent whose "misfortunes" are real crimes, whose money is the wages of fraud, whose frequent bankruptcies are the signals of his subtlety and avarice, and whose very offers of kindness, often, are but piratical lights to decoy his neighbours upon the rocks — this man can not expect to be admitted to the fellowship of true merchants. They may use his money in pressing emergencies when they can get no other, but they will be likely to say of it, as has been said of treason, "While we like the loan, we despise the lender."

The great importance of this subject, will justify me in fortifying the views which have been expressed, by an eminent authority, quoted in a former Lecture: —

"In the protracted agony, it has been said, the greatest errors are committed. Can they be avoided? Integrity demands that they should, and it never demands what is impossible. The first thing a man has to do in such circumstances, is to take honest counsel with himself; to state the case firmly, to examine it deliberately, and decide it justly; to go through with it as a work he is bound in conscience to perform; not slightingly, not carelessly, not deceitfully, but thoroughly, as if he were upon his oath to make a true inventory and appraisement. He is to look at his books, not to see the figures there set down, but whether the value is what they represent. Such a work is hard, very hard. Many a man closes his eyes, because he knows what he would see if they were opened. He perceives, but he voluntarily makes his perception indistinct, and persuades himself, or tries to persuade himself, that the truth is obscure, when he knows it is clear. He cannot plead ignorance. He is therefore laying up for himself a store of self-reproach, for finally he will be compelled to confess that he sinned against knowledge. The next thing to be done, is to take counsel with judicious friends. If it be hard for a man to look steadfastly at a painful and humiliating truth, still harder for him is it frankly to make it known to others. Yet it must be done, if we would profit by the advice of friends. And lastly, it is the duty of a man in these circumstances, to counsel with his creditors, for it is their interest that is to be dealt with. Safe counsellors they will be found, and generous ones too, if they are honestly treated. This measure, however, is seldom resorted to, and in these few cases is too long postponed. In the mean time, that is, between the first warning of coming calamity and its final consummation, the ill-directed struggles of the failing man plunge him deeper and deeper into embarrassments and injustice. But we need not attempt to follow him. Let us only add, that the duty of integrity in such circumstances, may be comprehended in a few words — a fair disclosure, a full surrender, and an equal distribution."*

All this, we will now suppose, has been effected, and the debtor, after paying his creditors the stipulated dividend, has received a legal discharge, and is once more a free man. Is he still morally bound for the residue of their claims? I answer without hesitation, he is. The argument on this point is very short. Why is a man bound to pay his debts? Not simply because the law of the land requires it. We might suppose a company of emigrants to land on a desert island, and commence trafficking among themselves, prior to the adoption of any civil constitution. Every one must feel that they would be bound to fulfil their contracts. There is, then, a ground of obligation underlying all human legislation, and which that legislation, in fact, tacitly recognizes. Men are bound to pay their debts because it is *right*. The law of God requires us to fulfil our engagements: to do what we have promised to do. Legislation may, within certain limits, prescribe the

* The Hon. John Sergeant.

methods in which this principle shall be carried into effect, but the principle itself is beyond its jurisdiction.

Nor is it any sufficient answer to say, that in the case contemplated, the creditors have *voluntarily* absolved the debtor from their demands against him. In one sense, it is true, their act was voluntary. They compounded with him, and gave him a release because it was, under the circumstances, as they thought, the best thing they could do for themselves, and an act of kindness towards him. But it was not "voluntary," if by this term it be intended to denote that they would have preferred this course to the full liquidation of their demands, or that they would have acceded to it had there been any prospect, through other means, of collecting their dues. They did it, as it were, under constraint, certainly under the constraint of benevolent feeling, and not with any admission that they regarded their debtor as having complied with his engagements.* It was no part of their design to discharge his *conscience*, to cancel the moral obligation of his dues. They have simply given him a legal acquittance. Is it in his power to change the essential nature of this transaction, from a legal into a moral absolution? Can he

* See Dymond on this point.

take advantage of his own wrong, and make this act of settlement to mean what they never intended it should mean? Has *he* the authority to take the awards of a human jurisprudence, and enrol them among those moral judgments which constitute the unalterable decrees of "heaven's chancery" — to confound the *dicta* of an earthly magistracy, or the concessions extorted by his own errors or misfortunes from his fellow-men, with the decisions of that august tribunal, which reflects, in all its acts, the inviolable rectitude of Jehovah? Because his creditors have absolved him, has GOD absolved him? Because the statute-book obliterates his debts and annuls his promises, does the BIBLE discharge him? No one will maintain this, who has not adopted that sordid theory of virtue, which makes it a commodity to be bought and sold at the shambles. The moral obligation of a debt continues until the debt is paid in full, that is, until payment is tendered to the creditor. If he sees fit to decline it, he may do so. The debtor has discharged his duty by making the offer. Henceforth he is free in morals and in law.

It is easy to account for the misgivings we may feel on finding ourselves impelled towards this conclusion. We picture to ourselves a deserving man, overtaken by reverses, surrendering his property, and discharged by his creditors; and it seems at first sight *a hard case* that he should still be bound for his old debts, and obliged to appropriate his future gains to their liquidation. And the picture appeals to our sympathies with an irresistible pathos, when we reflect that there are, perhaps, thirty thousand* of our countrymen in this situation. Not one syllable shall be uttered here in disparagement of the hardship and suffering involved in very many of these cases. There are few earthly trials more difficult to bear than some which come in this shape: to be insensible to them, were to be not more, but less, than human. But *principles* are immutable. Like the magnetic needle, which points steadily to the pole in all latitudes and in all weathers, indifferent alike to the calms which retard and the storms which shatter the ship, they are unaffected by circumstances. And whenever a people begin to let their circumstances mould their principles, they will become speedily debauched. It is in this way, precisely, that the commercial character of our own country has at some periods suffered a lamentable deterioration. To guard against this danger, we must beware how we blunt the public sensibility on the subject of bankruptcies, or encourage the feeling that a "failure" is a trivial matter, which involves the parties concerned in a little

* See the statistics already cited.

temporary inconvenience, without producing any further ill effects. The prevalence of this sentiment would be far more disastrous to a people, than all the personal and social distress which marks a commercial "crisis." It ought to be felt — wherever there is a healthy mercantile constitution, it *is* felt — that it is a very serious thing for a house to fail. Such an event, instead of being reported as part of the gossip of the day, ought to send a thrill through the whole community. It should be viewed as a common calamity. It should be treated as an occurrence affecting more or less the interests and reputation of the entire mercantile body, and demanding their calm and considerate attention. I do not say that they should visit the suspending house with their displeasure. But they *have* an interest in knowing how and why it has stopped; whether through uncontrollable misfortune or through fraud; whether by some "act of Providence" or by gross imprudence. And according as they find the facts to be, should they frame their judgment on the case and shape their conduct.

It is easy to perceive how potent the moral influence of a state of feeling like this would be in preventing failures. Merchants would be more wary of those habits and risks which define the highway to insolvency. There would be less over-trading and speculating, less borrowing and endorsing, less of regal state in the style of living, and less extravagance among the wives and daughters. Fewer fortunes would be made in a day, but the fortunes that were made, would have some solidity. Fewer men would retire "at thirty," but when they did retire, they would be apt to sleep with a quiet conscience. Fewer families might revel in luxury, but those who had been raised to affluence, would be less likely to wake up of a morning and find the sheriff taking an inventory of their gorgeous drawing-rooms.—All these and many kindred results, would be promoted by the prevalence of correct views on the subject of bankruptcy. Wherever they have prevailed, other prudent maxims have been combined with them, and failures have been extremely rare. Our older merchants can recall such periods in our own history. The annals of Holland will supply other examples. No nation can point to a commercial career so untarnished as that of the Dutch. Their system of small profits and short credits would not suit the mercurial energy of our countrymen; but, combined as it was with the most sterling practical virtues, it conducted them to the very apex of commercial opulence and renown. "Failures among them were rare even in so distressing an era as the occupation of their country by the French, which began in 1795, and involved, from the outset, a stoppage of maritime intercourse with all their posessions in India and America. The consequence of this stoppage was a decay of trade, a suspension of various undertakings, a scarcity of work, miserable dulness in the sale of goods; all leading, in the first instance, to diminished income, and eventually to encroachment on capital: but amidst this distress, the failures were surprisingly few, fewer indeed than occur in Britain in any ordinary season."* There is nothing in all the maritime enterprise and prosperity of the Dutch, which reflects so much honour on them as facts like these. And the extraordinary results here recorded, are to be ascribed in no inconsiderable degree, to the just sentiments they cherished on the subject of bankruptcy. If we would emulate them in their commercial glory, it must be by fostering similar sentiments among our mercantile classes. We must do nothing to subvert the great moral principles which are the buttresses of all honourable commerce, and the decay of which is the sure precursor of embarrassment. Among these principles, are, the inviolability of contracts, the permanent obligation of debts, and the imperative duty of restricting one's pecuniary engagements to what would be deemed, on a candid and prudent survey of things,

* Encyc. Brit.

a just relation to the actual capital at command. A general adherence to these principles, would leave room for but few failures. Most of the paths which lead to insolvency would be closed up. The stoppage of a house would produce the same sensation in Philadelphia or New York, which it occasions in Amsterdam. And while the dishonest bankrupt might look for general reprehension, men of real merit, overwhelmed by misfortune, would experience the most generous sympathy, and be promptly aided in recovering their position.

It would be both easy and pleasant to illustrate this last remark, by an appeal to the history of any of our commercial cities. Numerous examples have occurred, and are annually occurring, of mercantile disasters, which have given occasion for the display of some of the noblest qualities which can dignify our nature. It is one of the finest moral spectacles ever presented in the progress of social life, that of a meritorious merchant struck down in his business by some paralyzing blow, which has left him penniless, surrounded by a generous band of creditors, who come, not merely to soothe him with *words* of sympathy, but to employ their capital and influence in retrieving his misfortune and placing him on his feet again. And if there is any scene which surpasses this in true pathos, it is to see this smitten merchant, now restored by the blessing of Providence to thrift and comfort, reassembling his benefactors, and requiting their munificence by a cheerful liquidation of all their claims. Transactions of this kind have a value above all gold and silver. They make us think the better of human nature. They belong to the *regalia* of commerce. They augment the moral power of the community they adorn, and form, every one of them, a glorious cynosure to the tribes of youth who are pressing on amidst the conflicts and perils of a business-life.

This discussion will hardly be deemed unseasonable at a period when the unparalleled prosperity of the country is alluring so many persons into the very practices we have been censuring. A philosophical French writer has observed, that "the whole life of an American is passed like a game of chance, a revolutionary crisis, or a battle." This is no inapt description of the present state of the country. The tendencies to inordinate speculation in real estate, stocks, merchandize, and other commodities, are too palpable to be mistaken. New schemes are broached with a facility and an assurance which would not have discredited the memorable era of '37. Of these, some doubtless have a substantial basis, while others rest upon thin air; and the last are at such junctures quite as likely to *take* as the first. The adventurers who manage them, are never lacking in effrontery or tact. They know under what auspices to propound a project, and how to conciliate in its favour a community already inflamed with the fever of speculation. They put in requisition the whole machinery of private circulars, newspaper laudations, telegraphic despatches, combinations, fictitious sales, and other appliances; and thus

> "With air and empty names beguile the town,
> And raise new credits first, then cry 'em down;
> Divide the empty nothing into shares,
> And set the crowd together by the ears."

The signs of the times forebode an approaching crash. It may not come next week, nor next year. But if the present inflation of prices continues, and wealth bewitches all classes with its sorceries, and speculation runs riot through the land, the catastrophe *must* come. Let it be impressed upon your minds, then, that *this* is the season of danger. It is at such periods that, "by little and little, circumspection gives way to the desire and emulous ambition of *doing business*, till, impatience and incaution on one side, tempting and encouraging headlong adventure, want of principle and confederacies of false credit on the other, the movements of trade become yearly gayer and giddier, and end at length in a vortex of hopes and hazards, of blinding passions and blind practices, which should have been left, where alone they ought ever to have been found, among the wicked lunacies of the gaming-table."*

If you would escape these calamities, you must stand by your principles *now*. And those principles must be drawn from the WORD OF GOD, and written by his own finger upon your hearts. There is no other adequate safeguard for you. Human wisdom cannot cope with the insidious dangers which beset you. Human virtue is too weak to stand before them. If they imperilled your property merely, it were of less moment. If they put in jeopardy your reputation or your lives, even this might be borne. But they threaten, with the blasting of all your earthly prospects, to destroy your souls—to "DROWN YOU IN DESTRUCTION AND PERDITION!" This it is which makes your situation so fearful, and which invests with such transcendent importance, the demands of the BIBLE upon your instant and lasting homage. Open your hearts to the devout and grateful reception of the precious truth, that "Christ Jesus came into the world to save sinners," and a new passion will spring up within you capable of subordinating to itself every adverse sentiment and

* Coleridge.

habit. Clad in the panoply of the Gospel, you will have the best possible protection against the dangers, and the only adequate support under the trials, of a business-life. Difficulties and losses you may still encounter; but you will be sustained by an Almighty arm, and cheered by the prospect of acceding in the end to a crown of glory and a kingdom which shall never be moved.

Lecture Seventh.

PRINCIPALS AND CLERKS.

THERE are two very different aspects in which a great mercantile establishment may be contemplated. You may enter one of these establishments, and as you pass from room to room and loft to loft, and survey the enormous piles of goods, the regiment of clerks, porters, and packers, the throng of customers, the activity and commotion and amicable strife of tongues, which meet you on every side, your whole impression of the scene may concentrate in the feeling — "What a display of enterprise! What a generous capital! What a thriving business!" While the friend who is at your side, with far other eyes penetrating the materialism of the spectacle, may be wholly engrossed with the reflection, "What a school is this for the training of the heart! How rapidly must the tenantry of this busy hive, principals and subordinates of every grade, be ripening for glory or for shame!" These views are not incompatible: one does not necessarily exclude the other. But with very many merchants, unfortunately, the secular quite neutralizes and absorbs the spiritual view. It is the habit of the commercial world to look at the little community which peoples one of these great warehouses in its exclusively business relations. The tie which binds the inmates together, is simply a tie of convenience or of interest. The principal employs the requisite staff of men to do his work: the work is done, and they receive their wages: and this is the whole of it. But if the BIBLE is to have a voice in the matter, there must be elements recognized in the organization which impress upon it a much higher character. You cannot, with "the law and the testimony" in your hands, sink the man in the merchant. There is nothing in your avocation to absolve you from such divine enactments as these: — "Whether, therefore, ye eat or drink, or *whatsoever ye do*, do all to the glory of God." "Thou shalt love thy neighbour as thyself." "As we have, therefore, opportunity, let us do good unto all men." "To him that knoweth to do good and doeth it not, to him it is sin." These precepts are as binding in the Counting-room as in the homestead; in your commercial, as in your domestic, households. And if you will but allow them their just weight, they will impregnate your trafficking with a leaven of righteousness, and make it no less a ministration of *usefulness* than a means of wealth.

It will be no strange thing, if this should prove, to many merchants, an unwelcome topic. The idea of assuming a responsibility over the moral training of their subordinates, has scarcely occurred to them. They have cares and anxieties enough already: how can they find time to look after the morals of their young men?—But let it abate the displeasure awakened by this suggestion, to reflect that you *are* moulding the characters of these young men, whether you will or not. Providence has placed them, for the time being, under your roof, and you are shaping their principles. They will no more leave your establishment as they entered it, than your sons will come home from Yale or Princeton, the same unsophisticated youths they were when their mother, four years ago, imprinted her farewell kiss upon their cheeks, and sent them forth to share the advantages and the dangers of a college-life. The process of education is going on in the one case with as little interruption as in the other; and the question for you to ponder, is, not whether you will direct this process in your counting-house, but *how* you will direct it.

And here it is very affecting to consider how many mercantile firms there are, under whose administration the wholesome principles which the young men in their employ brought with them from their homes, undergo a sad deterioration. It is not that these firms have any deliberate purpose of corrupting the morals of their clerks; but the commodious virtue which presides in their warehouses, makes this result unavoidable. "You must assuredly know that a certain quantity of what has been called shuffling, has been introduced into the communications of the trading-world — insomuch that the simplicity of yea, yea, and nay, nay, is in some degree exploded; there is a kind of understood toleration established for certain modes of expression, which could not, we are much afraid, stand the rigid scrutiny of the great day; and there is an abatement of confidence between man and man, implying, we doubt, such a proportionate abatement of truth as goes to extend most fearfully the condemnation that is due to all liars, who shall have their part in the lake that burneth with fire and brimstone. And who can compute the effect of all this on the young and yet unpractised observer? Who does not see, that it must go to reduce the tone of his principles; and to involve him in many a delicate struggle between the morality he has learned from his catechism and the morality he sees in the counting-house; and to obliterate, in his mind, the distinctions between right and wrong; and at length, to reconcile his conscience to a sin which, like every other, deserves the wrath and curse of God; and to make him tamper with a direct commandment in such a way, as that falsehoods and frauds might be nothing more, in his estimation, than the peccadilloes of an innocent compliance with the practices and moralities of the world?" * The first stage in this downward process, is, to familiarize the mind of a youth with the conventional deceptions of trade — with its flexible dialect and its equivocal usages. Then let him begin to practise these lessons himself. And, finally, let him undertake, as he will be prepared to do, to initiate his juniors into the mysteries of this artificial code, under which words are no longer the signs of ideas, and veracity becomes a mere item of the Price-Current. This point attained, and he will be qualified to assume the functions of a principal, and direct the *moral training* of as large a corps of clerks as his own business may require.

I come at once to this topic, because it is no part of my plan to discuss in detail the reciprocal duties appertaining to this relation. I cannot, for example, enlarge on the subject of wages — a very important subject surely, and one which it belongs to the character of a true merchant to consider and adjust, with

* Dr. Chalmers.

the utmost prudence and liberality. "The labourer is worthy of his hire." And if there are firms which requite the services of faithful and diligent clerks with a reluctant and niggard compensation — a compensation below the usual tariff of salaries and quite disproportionate to their business — such firms would do well to ponder that apostolic monition, "Behold, the hire of the labourers who have reaped down your fields, which is of you kept back by fraud, crieth: and the cries of them which have reaped, are entered into the ears of the Lord of Sabaoth." (James 5: 4.) It is in allusion to the context of this passage, that Fuller, the quaint historian, says, "The same word in the Greek (ἰός) signifies *rust* and *poison;* and some strong poison is made of the rust of metals, but none more venomous than the rust of money, in the rich man's purse, unjustly detained from the labourer, which will poison and infect his whole estate." — It is undoubtedly good policy, as well as sound principle, to pay the full stipends prescribed by general custom, augmenting them, from time to time, according to some equitable scale, and rewarding signal merit with appropriate testimonials. To do this wisely, a merchant will require to keep his eye upon the persons in his employ. Indeed, it will be both to his credit and his advantage, to note the peculiar traits of each one of his clerks — their faults, their virtues, their habits, their adaptations, and everything pertaining to them. If he is a good judge of character, he will soon learn what they are from those little things which are apt to be deemed of no account. It is said that the fortune of M. Lafitte, the opulent French banker, was made by his picking up a pin. Arriving in Paris (A. D. 1788), a young provincial, poor, modest, and timid, he called with a letter of introduction upon M. Perregeaux, an influential Swiss banker. "It is impossible for me," said Monsieur P. to him, "to admit you into my establishment, at least for the present; all my offices have their complement. If I require any one at a future time, I will see what can be done." Turning away with a downcast look, as the disappointed youth traversed the court-yard, he stooped to pick up a pin, which he stuck in the lappel of his coat. The banker was watching him from the window of his cabinet, and with a sagacious eye, not unaided, we may suppose, by the previous interview, saw in this trivial occurrence the index of qualities which a financier would know how to appreciate. That evening, young Lafitte received from M. Perregeaux a note to the following effect: —

> "A place is made for you in my office, which you may take possession of to-morrow morning."

The banker was not deceived. From simple clerk,

Lafitte soon rose to be cashier, then partner, then head of the first banking-house in Paris; and afterwards, in rapid succession, a Deputy, and President of the Council of Ministers, the highest point to which a citizen can aspire. And what is still more to his honour, he was a generous friend to the needy and unfortunate, and employed his princely wealth in doing good.*

These are large results to flow from the picking up of a pin. And the narrative, suggestive as it must be to every thoughtful clerk, may illustrate the importance of a merchant's observing closely the characters of the young men he has gathered around him.

Another topic on which it might be pertinent to dwell, is, the proper carriage of a principal towards his clerks. The Counting-House is no less a school of manners and temper, than a school of morals. Vulgarity, imperiousness, peevishness, caprice, on the part of the heads, will produce their corresponding effects upon the household. Some merchants are petty tyrants. Some are too surly to be fit for any charge, unless it be that of taming a shrew. The coarseness of others, in manner and language, must either disgust or contaminate all their subordinates.

---

* Hunt's Merchants' Magazine.

In one establishment you will encounter an unmanly levity, which precludes all discipline. In another, a mock dignity, which supplies the juveniles with a standing theme of ridicule. In a third, a capriciousness of mood and temper, which reminds one of the prophetic hints of the weather in the old almanacs—"*windy*"—"*cool*"—"*very pleasant*"—"*blustering*"—"*look out for storms*"—and the like. And in a fourth, a selfish acerbity, which exacts the most unreasonable services, and never cheers a clerk with a word of encouragement.—These are sad infirmities. Men ought not to have clerks until they know how to treat them. Their own comfort, too, would be greatly enhanced by a different deportment. In turning over a magazine, my eye once fell upon a paragraph headed, "The Daily Value of Sunshine." I was at a loss to conjecture what this could mean. On reading it, I found that the writer had employed his ingenuity in calculating the average pecuniary value of each day in ripening the crops of the United States. Thus, suppose the aggregate worth of these crops to be $500,000,000 annually, as the thorough maturing of them depends essentially on the sunshine of the four warmest months, its daily value must be about four millions of dollars. It instantly occurred to me to ask, if sunshine in the fields is worth four millions, what would its daily value be in all the

Counting-Houses of the United States? It might require an adept in the higher calculus to solve this sum, but I apprehend there are clerks in some establishments who would set about it with some *feeling*. Certain it is, that there is the greatest possible difference in the working of establishments, the heads of which are men of a serene temper, whose cheerful and friendly manner inspirits all their subalterns, and those which are managed with a cold reserve or a petulance which extinguishes all vivacity, and adds fresh clogs to the leaden feet of labour. A wise merchant even from policy, and a Christian merchant from principle, will keep all the sunshine they can in their counting-rooms.

But I am wandering from the higher theme, the morals of this relation. Points of casuistry are sometimes obscured by unessential concomitants. Let us transfer the morality of trade to another theatre.— You return from your store, we will suppose, of an evening, and, sitting down in your Library, hear your son in the adjoining parlour describing to some inquisitive visitor various objects of utility or fancy deposited there. "These lounges, sir," (he might say,) "which are of a novel pattern, were made in Boston. The lustres are from the ancient glass-manufactory on the island of Murano, near Venice. This mosaic table my father ordered on his last visit to Florence:

it cost him a thousand dollars. That beautiful water-scene which you admire so much, was painted for him by Horace Vernet, at an expense of seven hundred dollars. It is the only painting we have in the house; as my father does not choose to have his walls disfigured with mere daubs. This ivory cabinet from China is the only one of the kind ever sent to this country." And so, he might go on until the catalogue was finished. On the departure of his guest, your son comes to you, and you meet him with an outburst of surprise and displeasure. "How was it possible, sir, for you to tell that gentleman so many lies? You know very well that you have given him an incorrect account of these articles. The lounges were made in Chestnut street. The lustres are from New England. The table is from Matlock, and cost a hundred dollars. The painting was by Cole; I paid him three hundred dollars for it: and besides, there are a dozen other paintings up-stairs. And as to the cabinet, the Chinese send them here by scores. How *could* you utter such falsehoods?" "Father," we may suppose this promising son to reply, "why do you speak so harshly to me? I have done nothing but what we are constantly doing at the *store*, and I had no reason to believe that you disapproved of it. I knew that this stranger was not a judge of these objects, and that it would greatly enhance not only his astonishment, but his pleasure, to be told these wonderful tales about them. Wherein does this differ in principle from our customs at the counting-house? For example, we clerks are sometimes directed to put French labels on English goods. We sell American cloths for English—just as good, no doubt, but still they never saw England. We are not reproved for calling old goods the 'newest styles,' nor for telling a man that the piece he is looking at, is the only one we have in the store, or the only sample which has been brought to the city. If an article cost twenty-five dollars a bale, we do not think it wrong, in trafficking, to say it cost thirty—which is only five more. We are in the habit of saying that goods are 'all woollen' or 'all silk,' when there may possibly be a *little* cotton in them. And we take it for granted this sort of dialect is justifiable, because we have observed that the members of the firm do not avoid it in their intercourse with customers. Why, then, should I not talk at home as I do at the ware-rooms? Certainly you will not say that a mode of speaking which is wrong in Walnut street, may be right in Market street; or that there is one system of morality for business, and another for domestic life? Indeed, it strikes me, that of the two, there is less harm in dealing in a little exaggeration at home than at the counting-house; because here we do it simply to increase the pleasure of our friends and make their time pass agreeably; whereas we employ it there to get money out of our customers."

Such might be your son's vindication of himself. And I confess, I do not very well see how it could be refuted. In any event, I should be sorry to have the task of answering him, devolved upon me. For I can imagine nothing more embarrassing to a casuist, than to be called upon to prove that the law delivered in the midst of that majestic scene at Sinai, is, after all, nothing but a mere "dissolving view," which vanishes into a totally different thing as a man passes from his dwelling-house to his counting-room.

The idea of so reforming the vocabulary of trade as to make it harmonize with the only true standard, may appear to some persons very chimerical. But there are many firms whose example goes to dispel the mischievous delusion, that some measure of fraud and falsehood is necessary to the successful prosecution of business. With these houses, it would be a grave offence for a clerk to tell a lie. And as to encouraging them in this practice, they would sooner abandon business altogether than do it. They would regard it as a crime to tamper with the conscience of an ingenuous youth who had been confided for the time to their guardianship. It were no trivial wrong, to deny him the proper facilities for obtaining a knowledge of the business, or to refuse him an equitable compensation for his services. But deliberately to subvert his moral principles, by teaching him to ignore all distinction between truth and falsehood, is an atrocity they would shrink from as they would from putting the drunkard's cup in his hands.* And they are right. Among all the contents of their spacious warehouses, and all the interests committed to their management, there are none of higher value, none for their treatment of which they will be held to a more rigid responsibility, than the consciences of these young men. Let them beware how they neglect or abuse so sacred a deposit.

This caution may be extended further. There is one practice, in particular, very current, as it is alleged, in our commercial cities, which deserves to be noticed in this connection. I have been repeatedly requested to speak of it in these Lectures, and the impressions which prevail about it are of the most decided and painful character. The following communication has been sent to me on the subject:—

---

* I am acquainted with a most estimable gentleman in this city, who was dismissed from a clerkship some years ago, because he positively refused to *tell a lie* on his employer's requiring him to do it. The principal broke, and went to ruin: the clerk is now a successful and honoured merchant.

PHILADELPHIA, *Feb.* 21, 1853.

To the REV. DR. BOARDMAN.

Dear Sir: — Will you allow an auditor to ask your attention to a certain usage of commercial men, with the hope that it will not be passed in silence in your public Lectures. The allusion is to what in professional cant, is called *drumming* or *boring.* A young man, on entering into the service of a commercial house, soon learns that his compensation, encouragement, and aid, from the the firm, will depend, not merely upon his urbanity, activity, and address, as a salesman, but, in an equal or greater degree, upon his success *in drawing custom to the house.* This requires him, when the business of the day is closed, to resort to places of entertainment with strangers and acquaintances who come to the city for trade. To mature a mercenary acquaintance and secure his custom, he calls to his aid the cigar and the social glass, and tarries long, it may be, at the wine; he goes in company with him to places of public amusement, or pilots the unprincipled stranger to more hidden scenes of vice. In this service, a young man soon learns to put away a good conscience from him, and barters his fair fame and his immortal interests for the poor profits of another's unrighteous gain.

This evil may be illustrated by a single example. Some time since, a young man in one of our large cities fell under the censure of his employer, when he returned upon his reprover this terrible retort: — "Sir, I came into your service uncorrupt in principles and in morals. But the rules of your house required me to spend my evenings at places of public entertainment and amusement, in search of customers. To accomplish my work in your service, I was obliged to drink with them, and join with them in their pursuit of pleasure.

It was not my choice, but the rule of the house. I went with them to the theatre and to the billiard table: but it was not my choice. I did not wish to go; I went in your service. It was not my pleasure so to do; but I was the conductor and companion of 'the simple ones,' void alike of understanding and of principle, in their sinful pleasures and deeds of deeper darkness, that I might retain them as your customers. Your interest required it. I have added thousands of dollars to the profits of your trade, but at what expense you now see, and I know too well. You have become wealthy: but I am poor indeed. And now this cruel dismissal from your employ, is the recompense I receive, for a character ruined and prospects blasted, in helping to make you a rich man!"

This may be an extreme case; but of the multitudes who crowd our hotels and hover around the places of public resort as *drummers* for their respective houses in the season of active trade, who can doubt that many are led into temptation, and drawn unto death, encouraged by the principal, who, if he does not directly require the service, smiles approbation, with a masterly unconsciousness respecting the iniquitous means by which his trade is increased.

Very respectfully, yours, —— ——.

This letter may serve both for text and commentary. It is not for me to say how far the usage prevails, of which it speaks, nor to what extent its details are sanctioned by the mercantile body. Among the expedients for increasing custom, generated by the competition and enterprise of the times, it is not, perhaps, surprising that young men, answering to the "commercial travellers" of some of the European countries, should be sent out to traverse our distant States, and that others should be charged with the duty of waiting on merchants from abroad as they arrive in the great cities. In themselves considered, these practices involve no principle of morals, and every merchant must judge for himself as to the expediency of adopting them, or either of them. But the latter of them is clearly liable to great abuse; and if we may credit what we hear, is actually abused, to an extent which demands the serious attention of the entire mercantile profession.

I shall not be deemed to take ground adverse to commercial tact and vigilance, if I maintain, that any system of which the case presented in the letter just quoted may be regarded as a fair exposition, must be radically wrong. If any one chooses to assert the indefeasible right of a city jobber to employ young men in "*boring*" country merchants, it would be quite absurd to argue that question here. So the country merchants are willing to be "bored," it were very officious in a third party to come in and say they should not be gratified. But I venture to take my stand between these young men and their principals, and to say, that you have *no* right to commission them to use *such* arts as the letter sets forth, for the purpose of bringing customers to your stores. Nor (that I may forestall any evasion of this proposition) have you a right to connive at their doing the things which are therein described. It will not avail to say, "I have never instructed my salesmen to 'drink' with strangers, and take them to the theatre and other places of vicious amusement." Salesmen may not be "instructed" on this head at all; but unless the public are at fault, they rarely engage in these practices, that their principals do not know of it, and too commonly they are supplied with extra funds for the very purpose. I see no difference in morals between sanctioning the thing directly, and winking at it.*—Nor is it any justification, to urge, that strangers naturally wish to participate in the amusements of a large city, and it is but common courtesy to supply them with a guide. Of the abstract right of strangers or citizens to sustain *such* amusements as are contemplated in these remarks, I shall not now speak. They have their own responsibility in the premises: let them see to that. But whence comes your obligation, or even your authority, to send, or theirs to employ, your

* A gentleman of New York who heard this Lecture, subsequently stated to the author, that he knew of houses in that city, *claiming* to stand in the first rank as honourable firms, which kept a private money-drawer from which the clerks supplied themselves with funds to be expended in the manner described in the text.

clerks on this business? If you choose to go yourselves, very well. I do not say that you would be innocent, but you would escape the criminality which attaches to the existing usage. "Criminality," I say; and I mean it. Take the example in the letter. Can there be two opinions as to the criminality of that firm? "To accomplish my work in your service, I was obliged to drink with them, and join with them in their pursuit of pleasure. It was not my choice, but the will of the house. I went with them to the theatre and to the billiard-table: but it was not my choice; I did not wish to go: I went in your service."—Why, if you could poll the civilized world, you would have a verdict of guilty pronounced against them by acclamation. The ruin of their clerk lies at their door. They thrust him into a thicket of temptations, which they had every reason to believe would destroy him. They knew what was the common result of the career in which they started him. Tens of thousands of young men in their own city, had gone to destruction in the same way: how was he to escape? This, unhappily, was not the question with them. *They wanted customers;* and if customers can be got by offering up to Mammon, one of their clerks, the son possibly of a widowed mother, they are willing to sacrifice him. And when they have so debauched him that he is no longer fit even to be the minion of their avarice, then they consummate their huge iniquity, by branding him with disgrace, and sending him forth to break the heart of the mother that bare him, and, unless saved as by miracle, to go down to a drunkard's grave and the drunkard's hell! Ye ruthless devotees of Mammon! drive on your eager traffic. Roll up your ample profits. Rejoice in your expanding business. Array your households in purple and fine linen. And revel in the gratulations of a sycophantic world. But there is a curse in your prosperity. Your gains are the price of BLOOD. There is blood upon your merchandize; blood upon your coffers; blood upon all your wretched pageantry; blood upon your souls! The blood of that betrayed and immolated youth, cries to heaven for vengeance; the anguish of that broken-hearted mother, pierces the ear of the Lord God of Sabaoth; and sooner or later, except ye be sprinkled with the blood which turns vengeance into mercy, you must confront your victim before a tribunal where the rust of your cankered gold "shall be a witness against you, and shall eat your flesh as it were fire!"

It cannot be that this colossal iniquity is chargeable upon many of the firms which challenge an honourable standing in the commercial world; but there is a principle here which may require to be enforced upon merchants of every class. Your responsibility as to your clerks is not restricted to the hours they spend in your warehouses. The same obligation which forbids your sending them into scenes of dissipation in quest of custom, makes it incumbent upon you to know *where* they are living, and what are their usual evening avocations. A merchant, certainly, who means to fulfil his duties to his clerks in the spirit of the Bible, will see that they are not boarding at unsuitable places. He will interest them, if practicable, in some library company or other institution, which may offer them attractive and rational relaxation. He will caution them against vicious companions and corrupting amusements. He will counsel them to a due observance of the Sabbath, and a regular attendance at some evangelical church. And whenever his quick eye detects about them symptoms of negligence or wrong-doing, he will interpose his friendly aid in a private and judicious manner, to arrest the evil at the outset, and re-establish their goings. These are offices which every merchant would wish to have his own sons enjoy at the hands of a brother-merchant: why, then, should you not all extend them to the entire corps of your clerks? Inexperienced, as many of them must be, absent from their homes, and beset with snares, they need, not merely an employer, but a friend. Who so fit to be their friends as their employers? You cannot, if you would, avoid moulding, more or less, their plastic characters: is it not an object worthy of a generous ambition, to exert your power over them for their highest good; to train them to integrity and respectability as merchants, and to surround them, as far as you can, with influences which are favourable to their eternal well-being? It will be a pleasant reflection on your death-bed, that your Counting-House has been a school of virtue to your assistants; that no young man ever learned there to be sordid or deceitful; that you bestowed a paternal care upon your clerks, and uniformly endeavoured as well to protect their morals and promote their salvation, as to educate them to an honourable commercial life.

I know not that I can better introduce the few suggestions to which I must limit myself in addressing CLERKS, than by quoting a paper which is interesting in itself and from its history. You will all remember the burning of the steamer *Henry Clay* on the Hudson River last summer — one of those wholesale murders with which we have become familiar in this country, and which show how little removed we are as a nation, in our practical estimate of the value of human life, from a state of downright barbarism. Among the numerous victims of that flagitious crime, was the Hon. Stephen Allen, an aged and opulent merchant of New York, who had filled the Mayoralty of that city and various other public offices, with credit to himself and satisfaction to his constituents. On recovering the body of this venerable man, a day or two after the disaster, a well-worn newspaper-slip was found in his pocket-book, of which the following is a copy: —

Keep good company or none.

Never be idle.

If your hands cannot be usefully employed, attend to the cultivation of your mind.

Always speak the truth.

Make few promises.

Live up to your engagements.

Keep your own secrets, if you have any.

When you speak to a person, look him in the face.

Good company and good conversation are the very sinews of virtue.

Good character is above all things else.

Your character cannot be essentially injured, except by your own acts.

If any one speaks evil of you, let your life be so that none will believe him.

Drink no kind of intoxicating liquors.

Ever live (misfortunes excepted) within your income.

When you retire to bed, think over what you have been doing during the day.

Make no haste to be rich, if you would prosper.

Small and steady gains give competency with tranquillity of mind.

Never play at any kind of game of chance.

Avoid temptation, through fear you may not withstand it.

Earn money before you spend it.

Never run into debt, unless you see a way to get out again.

Never borrow, if you can possibly avoid it.

Do not marry until you are able to support a wife.

Never speak evil of any one.

Be just before you are generous.

Keep yourself innocent, if you would be happy.

Save when you are young, to spend when you are old.

Read over the above maxims at least once a week.

This was Mr. Allen's *Vade Mecum*, his pocket-companion and chart. The maxims were embodied in his life, and, by the favour of Providence, conducted him to wealth and honour. You will readily see that, excellent as they are in the main, they are very defective, some principles and duties of prime importance being omitted altogether. It is pleasant to know that these had engaged, more and more, the attention of this upright and useful citizen during the closing years of his life, and that he expressed to his friends, not only his firm belief in the doctrines of Christianity, but his personal reliance upon its SAVIOUR.

The counsels are not cited here as being exclusively applicable to young men: some of them contemplate rather the merchant than the clerk. But both classes may consult them with advantage. Having set them before you, I go on to observe, in the spirit of these hints, that

Every clerk should identify himself with the house he is engaged in. This is one of the most obvious principles appertaining to this relation. From the moment you enter the service of a firm, their interest must be yours. You sustain a relation to them, which you hold to no other house. While you are not to stoop to any immorality for the purpose of serving them, you are to guard their property and their reputation, as though they were your own; you are to avoid whatever may injure them, and do all in your power to contribute to their prosperity. If it is incumbent upon your principals to take a friendly interest in you, the correlative obligation rests upon you to promote, as you may be able, both their business and their personal comfort. It is not always the fault of the principals, that the tie which binds the tenantry of a commercial establishment together is of a mere mercenary character: the most liberal policy on their part may be thwarted by a set of perverse or selfish clerks.

It is only a modification of the principle just affirmed, to insist upon *the strictest fidelity in discharging all the duties proper to the position you occupy*. It cannot be necessary to repeat here the familiar adage, that "whatever is worth doing at all, should be well done." But let every clerk remember, that there is no department of the work entrusted to him, which is not embraced in the obligation, to serve his employers to the very best of his ability. There are many ways in which he may violate this rule, short of going to the safe and thrusting his hand into the money-drawer. He may fail in punctuality. He may so exhaust his energies with an evening's dissipation, as to be unfitted for the next day's duties. He may perform his work in a listless, drowsy manner, not only unjust to the house, but provoking to his fellow-clerks, since their toil will have to bear the brunt of his laziness. He may see goods suffering from exposure or other causes, without protecting them. He may alienate customers by the gruffness of his manner or his offensive volubility. He may disappoint others by failing to have their goods or their bills ready at the stipulated time. He may arrogate an unauthorized responsibility in the opening of new accounts, and thus involve the firm in vexatious and mortifying negotiations. He may neglect to forward goods as per agreement, without writing to apprize the owner of the reason. He may turn town-crier, and publish far and near those private matters concerning the business of the house, which every sentiment of honour should restrain him from breathing outside the ware-rooms. He may recommend for a clerkship some inefficient or unreliable crony, who wants a place, but does not deserve one. — These, and very many other things like these, which a clerk may do, are incompatible with fidelity, and in derogation of his employers' just claims upon him.

The essential quality for a young man in this position, is that *sound moral principle* which is at once the best monitor to duty and the surest guarantee of confidence. I can picture to myself the daily routine of two clerks, one of whom is swayed by principle, and the other by policy. The latter is of that class the apostle had in view when he said — "not with eye-service, as men-pleasers." His performances are all summed up in the phrase, "eye-service." When his employers are present, he is extremely diligent. Behind their backs, he is a model of sloth and unfaithfulness. So it can be concealed from them, he cares not how late he comes to his work, how little of it he does, nor how much he slights it. Whatever time he bestows upon labour, is so much lost: he finds his *life* in lounging and trifling, in idle gossip and trashy novels. — His fellow is of a widely different type. The power which controls his movements, is not in the eye of his master, but in his own breast.

It matters not with him, who is present, or who absent. His work is to be done, irrespective of all outward circumstances. The interpretation he puts upon his articles of agreement, makes him do for his employers as he would do for himself. Always at his post, he pursues his avocation with an unfaltering step. Impelled to diligence and constancy, not by the fear of a discharge, but by the consciousness of right, he enjoys a serenity of mind to which his companion is a stranger, and is as steadily advancing towards honour and usefulness, as the other is sinking into disgrace and contempt. — It cannot be too often reiterated in the ears of our young men, that *this* is the true path to success. "Wait not for great occasions before you begin to act; wherever your lot may be cast, the sphere of duty lies immediately around you. Fill it up with an example of the kindness that attracts, the sincerity that can be seen through like crystal, the diligence that anticipates duty, the trustworthiness that defies suspicion, the openheartedness that opens other hearts, the manly character that commands esteem, the Christian character that arms its possessor with a power more than earthly. Defer not to a distant time the intention to begin." "One to-day is worth two to-morrows." Only treat duty as a sacred thing, and you will find that "in keeping *His* commandments there is great reward."

Among the minor causes of failure with young men in this relation, the subject of *tempers* and *manners* deserves a prominence which cannot be conceded to it in these brief discussions. That a clerkship is frequently a severe school of discipline for the temper, cannot be denied. But this is a part of the necessary training of a merchant. Let it encourage those who are subjected to the caprices of unreasonable employers, who are found fault with when they are guiltless of all wrong, scolded when they have done the best they could, and denied indulgences which others enjoy, that the self-control they are acquiring under this rough tutelage, may be of more value to them hereafter than all the smiles their masters could lavish upon them. And beware of cherishing tempers which might give just occasion for reproof. It is not enough that you be honest and industrious and intelligent. A clerk may be all this, and yet neutralize the impression of his good qualities by a levity which makes him seem a mere trifler. Or he may repel people by his sulkiness or his irritability. He may be foolishly sensitive to affronts. He may be a slave to envy and jealousy. He may be utterly deficient in that good feeling which would make him willing to lend a helping hand to his fellows in time of need. He may be too proud for his station, and deem it an indignity to perform offices which better and wiser men than himself have often performed without scruple. "A man's pride shall bring him low, but honour shall uphold the humble in spirit." Let me quote on this point, a paragraph from a very pleasant letter of Dr. Franklin's (written in his seventy-ninth year) to Dr. Mather of Boston:—

"It is now more than sixty years since I left Boston; but I remember well both your father and grandfather, having heard them both in the pulpit, and seen them in their houses. The last time I saw your father was in the beginning of 1724. He received me into his Library, and on my taking leave, showed me a shorter way out of the house through a narrow passage, which was crossed by a beam over-head. We were still talking as I withdrew, he accompanying me behind, and I turning partly towards him, when he said hastily, 'Stoop,' 'Stoop.' I did not understand him till I felt my head hit against the beam. He was a man that never missed any occasion of giving instruction; and upon this he said to me, 'You are young, and have the world before you: STOOP *as you go through it, and you will miss many hard thumps.*' The advice thus beat into my head, has frequently been of use to me, and I often think of it when I see pride mortified, and misfortunes brought upon people by their carrying their heads too high."

People of every avocation may profit by this lesson; and the clerk who is disposed to take it voluntarily, will fare better than he who waits to have it "beaten into his head" by some mortifying occurrence or positive loss. Rely upon it, if you do not know how to "stoop," you have a rugged path before you — very much such a path as a platoon of soldiers would find who should undertake to march with military precision, carriage erect, eyes straight forward, and muskets a-shoulder, through a tangled and swampy forest. Sooner or later, you will have to "stoop"; and you will do it with more grace and more comfort if you practise the art now, than if you let your muscles acquire such a rigidity that when the inflexion becomes unavoidable, the performance will be certain to savour of the awkwardness of a rustic on his first introduction at court.

One of the common sources of danger and disaster with clerks, is, *extravagance in their mode of living.* The usual scale of mercantile salaries in our cities, is adjusted to the most economical habits. It is, therefore, a perilous thing for those who depend upon these salaries to become smitten with a passion for display. How is a young man to rent a suite of richly-furnished rooms, keep up an elegant wardrobe, decorate his person with costly jewelry, and indulge in expensive amusements, on a stipend of a few hundred dollars? It is natural that the employers of a young man who is seen to be attempting this, should have their eyes upon him. And if the experiment goes on, they will be curious to learn whence he derives his income. It may come from legitimate quarters: he may have collateral resources of which they are ignorant. Or it may come from their warehouse. The love of dress and company may have mastered his integrity, and put him upon a system of peculation. Possibly, he has become a *speculator*. If he occupies a "confidential" position, and has free access to the finances of the firm, some intriguing operator may have enticed him into a course of stock-gambling. Once committed to this nefarious business, the checks of the house are dealt out freely to his partner in iniquity, and for a while, he has no lack of revenues to sustain his luxurious habits. Ordinarily, however, "the triumphing of the wicked is short:" his dishonesties are brought to light, and he is either driven out of society in shame, or consigned to a penitentiary. If any are disposed to argue that in cases of this sort, unhappily become so common, the burden of guilt lies upon the receiver of the funds abstracted, I shall not quarrel with them. The man who will encourage a clerk in such a career, who will stimulate him to obtain by robbery the moneys requisite to carry on one speculation after another, is a hundred-fold more deserving of the State-prison than the wretch who breaks open your store and carries off your goods. The defects inseparable from human jurisprudence, make it difficult to convict this class of offenders; and so it happens that they are apt to go "unwhipt of justice."

justice." But there can be no difference of opinion among honest men as to their moral turpitude. Still, this does not excuse the allies and instruments of their villany. The clerk who allows himself to be drawn into a plot of this kind, richly deserves the reprehension which his treachery and fraud are sure to bring down upon him: — and he deserves it all the more, because his own extravagances are usually the remote spring of his derelictions.

Closely affiliated with the errors just adverted to, are the habits commonly indicated by the word, *dissipation.* This topic has been mentioned already in connection with the custom known amongst us by the technical appellations of "drumming" and "boring." The observations addressed to principals, imply what is the duty of clerks, in respect to that particular usage. But their dangers extend quite beyond this. How varied and imminent they are, must be apparent to every one who has lived for any length of time in a large city, and who considers that the greater portion of the young men in our mercantile establishments, have been brought up in the comparative quiet and purity of the country. The serried temptations of the metropolis come upon them all at once. They have had no opportunity to become familiarized with them by degrees, and fortified against them. They encounter them *en masse,* and at the very moment when they are deprived of the sheltering influences which are bound up in a cherished *home*. The day which transfers them from the paternal fireside, with its wholesome restraints and elevating associations, to a great metropolitan hotel or boarding-house, sees them exposed for the first time to a host of dangers, each one of which has slain its tens of thousands. The wonder is, not that some should fall, but that so many escape. And in so far as our own city is concerned, no thanks will be due to the public authorities of the Commonwealth, if the proportion of those who escape, shall not be diminished from year to year. You will readily understand this allusion. The vice which destroys more of our young men than any other, is Intemperance. And the course of recent legislation in Pennsylvania has been such as to multiply indefinitely the facilities and inducements to intemperance in this city and county. When the Emperor of China was urged to legalize the opium-trade, and thus derive a revenue from it, the answer he made (and it is worthy to be inscribed upon the throne of that empire in perpetuity), was this: — "*It is true, I cannot prevent the introduction of the flowing-poison: gain-seeking and corrupt men will, for profit and sensuality, defeat my wishes; but nothing will induce me to derive a revenue from the vice and misery of my people.*" A voice like this from a pagan throne, might well make the ears of Christian legislators to tingle. But the State of Pennsylvania stoops to put into its treasury the fee of every man who chooses to pay a paltry fifty dollars for the liberty of retailing liquid poison to its citizens. The consequences are equally notorious and appalling. Since the enactment of this law, dram-shops of every grade have sprung up all over our city. The most fashionable avenues are disfigured with genteel groggeries; and at certain hours of the day and evening, you cannot pass along the streets without meeting groups of young men and boys in a state of partial inebriation, sauntering from one of these establishments to another. It is affecting to see what numbers of our youth are, in this way, hastening to disgrace and ruin, each one, perhaps, drawing a cluster of broken hearts in his train. — On the proper remedy for this frightful evil, opinions are divided. All are agreed — all, certainly, who are not implicated in its pecuniary profits — that it ought to be abated. Some would rely upon moral means only. Others would invoke legislation. There is no reason apparent, why the same legislative power which has opened this flood-gate of vice upon society, should not be exerted to close it. Nor should any distrust of the wisdom, the constitutionality, or the efficacy, of one proposed set of enactments, preclude other statutes which would be open to no valid objection. I shall not be drawn into a discussion here of specific *prohibitory* measures. I will give no adversary an opportunity to declaim about "sumptuary laws," "oppression," "tyranny," "persecution," and the like. I stand upon higher and broader ground — upon the ground occupied, as I suppose, by the great mass of intelligent and respectable citizens in this community, of all trades and professions, of all faiths and forms. With all these, I maintain, that the existing license-system is a disgrace to the statute-book; that it is at war with the best interests of society; that its legitimate tendency is to promote pauperism and crime; that it is debauching the morals of our youth, and hurrying them to premature and dishonoured graves; that while it is killing men's bodies, it is destroying their souls; and that on these and many other grounds, it ought to be thoroughly revised and made tenfold more stringent. Very far am I from supposing that this alone would exterminate intemperance. But a suitable law — such a law as should be satisfactory, not to people of extreme views, if any such there are, but to the most considerate and liberal-minded of our citizens — could not fail to check the progress of this gigantic evil, and relieve us of a part of its intolerable burdens. *This* is the demand we make of our legislators. I make it as a Christian pastor, whose office it is, in however humble a way, to seek the social and moral well-being of the community. And *you* make it, Gentlemen, (for I cannot err in believing that we are *at one* on this point,) not only as individual citizens, but as the guardians of a vast body of young men whose morals are in jeopardy every hour from this legalized system for making drunkards. If we *cannot* stand together upon this ground, if we are not agreed in pronouncing this a fit subject for legislative and judicial action, I know of no platform on which the humane and moral portion of society can meet together to petition for the redress of any social grievance whatever.

I may appear to you to have wandered from my subject. But, certainly, every word of this seeming digression, is adapted to warn the young men in our Counting-Houses of the snares which are spread for them. In all ordinary cases, you may date the ruin of a youth from the period when he begins to frequent one of these tippling-shops. For if he begins here, he will not end here. The vices are gregarious. The "gin-palace," the Sunday-drive, the theatre, and sensual pleasure, though not inseparable, are usually linked together. The passions which any of them gratifies, will be apt to court indulgence in the others. The principles undermined by one, are damaged by all. To surrender to one, is to throw down your ramparts and open your gates to the remainder. The merchant who sends you into these scenes to find business for him, need not be surprised, if after a few years he has to dismiss you because you are unfit to do business. The clerk who frequents them spontaneously, may with still greater certainty lay his account for an early discharge. By far other means than these corrupting amusements, are young men to be trained to the toils and the rewards of honourable commerce.

Nor can I refrain here from addressing a word of remonstrance to those *country merchants* who are in the habit of accompanying our young men into scenes of vice or of drinking wine with them. If any such were within the reach of my voice, I would say to them — Reflect for a moment on the course you are pursuing. These young men are, most of them, absent from their homes. They are sent here to earn a support and to acquire a knowledge of business. Many of them are without pecuniary resources or influential friends. *Character* is everything to them. Even those who have property are dependent, under God, on the reputation they establish for integrity, sobriety, diligence, and capacity. To corrupt their morals, is to ruin them. When their principles give way, their prospects for life are blasted. Their employers will discharge them, and they will be thrown upon the world as adventurers and outcasts. *You* would not willingly be accessory to their destruction. You wish them to become upright and successful merchants, an ornament, not a disgrace, to their families. And yet, what are you doing? You allow them to "treat" you. You accept their invitations to the theatre, to go on a "Sunday Excursion," possibly to visit a gambling-house, or worse places. Is not this to ensnare and deprave them? But, "it is their own proposal," you may say. What then? Are you bound to accede to it? If they are already disposed to go astray — if they have actually entered upon the downward way — that enhances your obligation to refuse their overtures. If you comply, you accelerate their ruin. If you decline not only, but remonstrate and admonish them of their danger, you may "save a soul from death, and hide a multitude of sins." Deal with them as you would have others deal, in similar circumstances, with your own sons or brothers. You purchase pleasure at too dear a rate, when it costs the reputation, the virtue, the prospects, perhaps the eternal well-being, of a fellow-creature. Thousands of clerks have been destroyed in this way: when inquisition is made for their blood at the last day, see that it be not found upon your heads!

These remarks on certain kinds of amusements, are made with the more confidence, because the clerks in our cities can never want for means of innocent relaxation. There are always open Exhibitions of various sorts which combine instruction and entertainment. There are Evening Lectures, and Galleries of Paintings. There is social visiting, with its refining influence upon the mind and manners. There are the public Libraries; especially the Institutions provided for the express benefit of mercantile men, and whose well-stocked shelves and spacious reading-rooms open to them a source of elevated and inexhaustible enjoyment. — Surely there is something wrong with the clerk who, in the midst of scenes like these, can find no way of consuming his few leisure hours, without resorting to demoralizing amusements.

There is another topic of vital importance to clerks, as well as merchants, which I had intended to consider at some length; but this would quite exhaust your patience. I refer to PARTNERSHIPS. I will simply refer to the two mistakes which young men are most apt to commit on this subject. The first, is that of entering into a copartnership prematurely. Impatience and ambition are common characteristics of youth; and they show themselves, in your department of life, in an unwise haste to assume the responsibilities of business. A more thorough training would insure a wiser and safer control. The best captains are those who have seen most service before the mast. It is natural for a clerk to feel flattered by the proposal to exchange his subordinate position for a place in the firm, and his salary for a participation in the profits. "These are generally advantageous offers, designed simply to reward assiduous industry, to attach a valuable assistant, or to lay hold of useful business connections. But they are too often accepted with the impatient eagerness of youth, showing off the spirit of the young horse, feeling his strength, activity, and fire, panting and neighing for the dangers of the field, without the training for its duties or a knowledge of its dangers. Such offers are often embraced because the youth would feel himself beginning business, interested in the profits; because he wishes, in his moments of vanity, to boast among his companions of being a member of such a great house. He may be induced, too, by motives the most generous, involving the bettering of the condition of a dependent mother, sisters, or wife. Thousands of motives — not even suspicious and adapted to his every virtue and every vice — recommend his acceptance of such offers. Let him, however, examine well his steps. Let him judge without illusion. Let him here remember that he becomes a partner so far as that relation can be disastrous, while he may in fact be a mere clerk so far as it might be advantageous. Such offers are not to be lightly declined, nor suspiciously received, but they are to be coolly considered: and here the wisdom of age, the advice of cautious friends, become indispensable guides; and patience, not to be too eager to get rich, a necessary virtue. Such offers are very often openings to wealth, character, and influence; also are they sometimes avenues in early life to irretrievable ruin."*

Let these judicious counsels suffice as to the first point adverted to. The second error common with young men, is that of forming partnerships *with unsuitable persons.* We see this continually in matrimonial alliances. People are joined together whose characters and tastes have so little congruity, that every body around is from the outset predicting trouble: and these are among the few uninspired prophecies which are apt to be fulfilled. Similar mistakes in business would be less frequent, if parties duly considered the very delicate and confidential nature of a copartnership. Except in the case of "special partners," for which the wise legislation of modern times has made provision, the power you confer upon your associate, is "nothing less than a power to ruin you." All your pecuniary interests are entrusted to his hands. He can speedily make an insolvent of

* Daniel Lord, Jun., Esquire.

you, and reduce your family to beggary. He may be a visionary man, who will plunge into one wild project after another. He may be an imperious man, who will treat you, not as an equal, but as a servant. He may be an obstinate man, so set in his way, that neither argument nor entreaty will make any impression upon him. He may be an irritable man, or, what is still worse, a sullen man, who, if disturbed in his temper, will go about with a lowering countenance, like a spoiled child, for a whole day or week. He may be a proud man, who will feel himself above doing things which may be essential to the prosperity of the firm, and which other merchants do without any sense of humiliation. He may be an idle man, who will leave you to do the work while he drives out with a "fast horse" in business hours, or roams over the country in quest of pleasure. He may be an extravagant man, who will impair the means and injure the credit of the house, by his luxurious style of living. He may be an avaricious man, who will mortify and vex you beyond measure, with his attempts at a sordid economy, and his penurious higgling with clerks, porters, and every body who has any transactions with him. He may be an ignorant man, who will purchase cotton to ship to Mobile, or oil to send to New Bedford.* He may be a dissi-

* It is not every venture of this class which turns out as

pated man, who will secretly gamble at cards and billiards; or a grasping man, who will still more secretly gamble in stocks. He may be a dishonest man, who will filch away your property, break down the concern, and retire on a fortune. — These are but samples. The catalogue might be largely extended: but this list may suffice to convince you that there is *some* reason for care and caution in choosing as well a business-mate as a mate for life. A partnership lightly formed may move on pleasantly for a time. But commerce has its honey-moon no less than matrimony; and it is well in both relations to consider beforehand, how the mechanism will work when days of darkness and peril come. Sagacious observers have conjectured, nay some satirists (disappointed celibates no doubt) have ventured to assert, that the more intimate of these alliances is sometimes marred by very unconjugal disputations. Without pausing to refute this ungenerous calumny, it is safe to assume, that the ill-assorted unions of mercantile life, must occasionally convert the counting-room or the commercial parlour, into an arena of painful controversy. Perhaps no precaution can guard against

---

well as that famous one of a late opulent Boston merchant, whose cargo of *warming-pans* shipped to the *West Indies*, supplied the planters with capital ladles for their sugar-houses.

contingencies of this sort. But they would seldom occur if parties should take pains to *know each other well* before yoking together:—and if (it may be added) the articles of agreement should prescribe with an unambiguous explicitness, how they were to become *unyoked*, and what should be done with the assets in case of misfortune or embarrassment. Proper attention to these points has made many copartnerships a source of great social enjoyment and a bond of lasting friendship. It is, indeed, refreshing to find, in this region so little adapted to the sentiment and poetry of life, instances of a noble and ardent attachment decorating the rigours of an expanded traffic, and maturing in strength and beauty amidst the cares of a great commercial establishment. Such examples take one's thoughts into those lofty Alpine regions, where the traveller sees, here and there, majestic forest-trees whose spreading branches and exuberant foliage contrast strangely with the savage rocks and glaciers all around. They impart a certain dignity to trade, and keep alive in liberal minds that respect for it which there is so much in the current usages and developments of business to impair. Let *your* copartnerships be formed upon this liberal basis, and fostered in this spirit, and they will yield you peace and honour, where they might otherwise put a cup of gall and wormwood to your lips.

A single suggestion more, and I have done. You may adopt all the measures commended to you in this Lecture, in respect to your training, your habits, your social arrangements, your mercantile plans, and yet lie open to the friendly reproach once addressed to a young man as blameless and as lovely as the best among you — "One thing thou lackest!" What can all these precautions and efforts do for you without the blessing of God? Guard you, perhaps, from premature ruin; secure you the esteem and confidence of your fellow-men; possibly load you with wealth. But you will have lived to little purpose, if you have lived "*without God* in the world." Your earliest, greatest, most constant, most lasting, necessity, is, the favour of God. It is to be obtained only through the atonement and mediation of Jesus Christ. If you are already immersed in the cares of business, his friendship will do more than anything else to shield you from its snares. If you are standing at the threshold of a business-life, every consideration of duty, of gratitude, and of interest, bids you supplicate his mercy, and invoke his aid in the framing of your plans. Whatever your age, position, or employment, the exhortation comes to you with equal authority and wisdom — "Seek *first* the kingdom of God and His righteousness, and all other things shall be added unto you."

Lecture Eighth.

DOMESTIC LIFE, AND LITERARY CULTURE, OF THE MAN OF BUSINESS.

IN an old number of the Merchants' Magazine, there is a communication headed, "COMPLAINT OF A MERCHANT'S WIFE," the writer of which, after protesting against the "unnatural, slavish devotion to business," which characterizes the merchants of the present day, discourses in the following strain: —

"It seems to me, at times, as if there were no more *men* left in the world: they have all become *citizens*. Their humanity seems merged in some presidency or secretaryship. They are good trustees, directors, cashiers, bankers; but they are very indifferent husbands and fathers. They are utterly without social chat; they read no pleasant books; they hate the sound of music; they visit nobody; they scarcely deign to look at the face of nature; and for their unhappy wives, they must put up with cold looks and cold words. This is all wrong, Gentlemen. It is a sad perversion of life; it is cruelly unjust to us and our daughters; and it is the too certain source of deep and lasting misery to those who indulge in it. Home is no longer the garden of the heart, watched over by love, its roses kept in perennial bloom; but thorns and briers cumber its beauty. But I feel this matter too deeply to speak in metaphors. My own domestic circle is fast losing its charms, and becoming more dismal and formal than a hotel. I am beginning to lose all pride in my household. I am growing daily more unsociable. My health and temper are both giving way. In a word, I bitterly feel and lament the want of that sympathy and communion of heart, which are so liberally promised us in the marriage-vow. Come, then, Messrs. Editors, to our relief. Here is a cause worthy of your pens. Exhort, frighten, ridicule, if you can, our erring husbands into a return to their allegiance, and to a more rational and happy life."

I can well imagine with what a zest the merchants' wives and daughters who may be present, will listen to this earnest and intrepid appeal. Whatever else in these discussions may have been dry and distasteful to them, this will have their commendation: they will be ready to exclaim with a common impulse, "A word fitly spoken, is like apples of gold in pictures of silver." I could wish it were in my power to defend the tribes of commerce from these grave imputations. They have assaults enough to bear from other quarters, without encountering volleys of arrows (tipped with anything but *poison*, however) from their own castles. But historic verity demands a qualified admission of the truth of these allegations. It must be conceded that the "men" have, to a great extent, been *transubstantiated* into "citizens," the husbands and fathers into merchants, the wives, though wives still, into widows, and the children, though not fatherless, into orphans. — But let us hear before we condemn.

You will urge, in arrest of judgment, that "the modern methods of business render this abandonment of your homes unavoidable: that the very processes detailed in this course of Lectures, show how imperative and exclusive are the claims of commerce upon the men engaged in it: that the least intermission of vigilance and activity on your part, must involve you in losses: that a mode of life which severs you from your domicils, is not your choice, but your rigorous necessity: and that when the inconveniences experienced by your families, are compared with the hardships they would ultimately suffer should you neglect your business to attend to them, you will be deemed more worthy of praise than of censure for the self-denial you are practising."—Even the wives and daughters must allow that this is an ingenious plea; and parties more disinterested, will feel that it has real force. Within certain limitations, it is impregnable: but, then, it is those unheeded limitations, which impart weight and pungency to such "Complaints" as that we have quoted.

It may turn out, for example, that the alleged absorbing demands of merchandize are restricted to certain portions of the year, and that at other periods there is no invincible necessity laid upon you to be such strangers at your own firesides. With the greater part of the merchants in our large cities, business, instead of being diffused over the year, comes in two mighty torrents or avalanches, of a few weeks or months each. While these last, they have no resource but to surrender themselves, body and soul, to traffic. They have no time for domestic enjoyments. Books, friends, visiting, correspondence, everything must give way. Even the essential functions of eating and sleeping are dwarfed into the most fragmentary performances. Like one of Dr. Johnson's over-busy characters in the Idler, whom he compares to the dogs of Egypt, which, when driven to the Nile by thirst, *run* as they drink for fear of the crocodiles, they "dine at full speed." And long after midnight, the watchmen find themselves jostled by troops of wearied clerks and packers making their way homeward to catch a little repose before the rising sun recalls them to their toil. If it were not for the beneficent provision of a DAY OF REST, they would, many of them, finish in a Lunatic Asylum or an early grave. — For all this, there seems no help. The causes which are at work, no merchant, nor body of merchants, can control. And it were a most unreasonable thing in a wife to complain of her husband for not neglecting his plantation in the harvest-season, in order to wait upon her. Let her, rather, do what she can to relieve him of all domestic burdens, and to soothe and cheer him, as many a wife knows how to do, under his exhausting labours.

But these periodical excitements are followed by protracted calms. Not such calms as would justify remissness in superintending your counting-houses, but periods which, if managed economically, might leave *some* intervals for the domestic circle. It may fairly be required that these opportunities shall be improved; that when no paramount engagements supervene, your time and thoughts, no less than your affections, shall be given to your homes; and that you shall omit no practicable means for forwarding the education and contributing to the happiness of your households. It will not do to forget that the responsibilities which attach to the head of the family, are intransferable; and that while you occupy that position, you must be held accountable for the proper discharge of its duties. This consideration must at times press with great solemnity upon the minds of thoughtful men who are much separated from their children. The training of those children is going forward alike in your presence and in your absence.

Day by day, their faculties are maturing, their principles becoming established, their habits forming, and their whole characters assuming the essential type they are to bear through life — possibly, through eternity. This is your trust — the most sacred, the most momentous, trust, God has confided to you. To fulfil it wisely and well, is of more importance to you than the acquisition of a fortune or the attainment of any other secular end. Nor is it within the compass of any human abilities to do this, unless aided by the Spirit of God. That source of help is, happily, open to you. "If any of you lack wisdom, let him ask of God, and it shall be given him." Every parent who appreciates the relation, will gratefully avail himself of the assistance so freely tendered him in this delicate and difficult duty. But he will not rest here. The temper of mind which sends you to the throne of grace for succour, will put you upon using all the appliances within your reach, to multiply the attractions of home to your families, and to keep their affections in a fresh and healthful state. To do this, you will need, not only to give them as much of your society as you can, but to make your intercourse with them pleasant and improving. For example, it cannot fail to injure them if the whole burden of your conversation at home, is about business, and stocks, and money, and the like; or if they see that you have no relish for any pursuits except those which derive their value from dollars and cents. If *this* is to be the sum and substance of your companionship with them, it is of little moment that you hurry home from your counting-rooms to see them: your absence will do them no harm. Or if, again, you habitually carry into domestic life a fretful or an imperious temper, if you are lavish of harsh words or cross looks, it would be as well to remit the training of your families to other hands. Neither these, nor any other, practical errors on your part, will be harmless. Such is the authority impressed upon the headship of the house, that your every act and word and look and gesture — and what you leave unsaid and undone, no less than what you say and do — will go to fashion the moral lineaments of those deathless beings around you. This would be a serious matter, if it was for this life only they were to be trained. But we cannot limit our parental responsibilities thus. Our obligations extend alike to the bodies and the *souls* of our children. And they who consider the difficulty of extricating one soul from the bondage of sin and the snares of the world, will understand something of the charge involved in preparing a household for heaven. Surely, your children have a claim upon you for all the help you can afford them in combating the temptations of life: and it is neither generous nor just to withhold from the *mothers* that co-operation they are entitled to in the education of your offspring.

It is another weighty consideration bearing upon this point, that unless you avail yourselves of present opportunities, you may miss altogether that endearing and salutary intercourse with your families which I am inculcating. The period you are anticipating, when a discharge from business is to leave you full scope for the culture of domestic pleasures, may never arrive. How many of your contemporaries and neighbours have been arrested by death in the midst of their cares and their traffickings! While you are preparing to enjoy the society of your families, the relentless reaper, who spares no age nor condition, may cut you down. At the very moment, possibly, when your plans have been brought to a successful consummation, and you are ready to *begin to live*, a vacant seat at your table may mark the transitoriness of all human expectations.

Nor is this the only contingency. Should your life be spared, your release from business may come too late both as to your families and yourselves. Too late for them: because their training may be completed. In the education of your children, it is "now, or never." You may bend the sapling, but you cannot bend the oak. You may mould the clay, but you cannot mould the pottery. Your seed will germinate if cast into the genial lap of Spring, but it will get no sustenance from the rugged bosom of Winter. If you mean to have any useful agency in fashioning the characters of those children, this is the time to exert it. — Your prospective season of leisure may come too late for yourselves. When the time arrives for domestic enjoyment, your domestic sympathies and attachments may have become so blunted, that you will be insusceptible of this kind of happiness. There are other things besides iron, which will *rust* from want of use: other attributes of humanity besides bone and muscle, which depend upon exercise for healthful vigour. A neglected home is apt to become an undervalued home. The bird that is long away from its nest, may not care to return to it. And it is somewhat hazardous for a man to discover that, after all, he can "get on" and really enjoy life, without being dependent upon the pure and simple pleasures of his own fireside. The way to shun such untoward discoveries, is to keep the flame burning brightly upon your domestic altars, from the time it is first kindled, until death; to let nothing but the damp of the grave extinguish or enfeeble it. To neglect this, is to forego the purest felicity which the fall has left us. Those who have practised it, have found that life was too short to exhaust the stores of elevated enjoyment bound up in the domestic constitution; too fleeting for that sacred fellowship of home,

> "So friendly to the best pursuits of man,
> Friendly to thought, to virtue, and to peace!"

This is not, unhappily, as well understood as it ought to be. There are no adequate pains taken to perpetuate the freshness of early affection, and to cherish, as time wears on, the sentiments and habits which consecrate the earlier experiences of married life. "A person may be highly estimable on the whole, nay, amiable as neighbour, friend, housemate, in short, in all the concentric circles of attachment, save only the last and inmost; and yet from how many causes be estranged from the highest perfection in this! Pride, coldness, or fastidiousness of nature, worldly cares, an anxious or ambitious disposition, a passion for display, a sullen temper, one or the other, too often proves 'the dead fly in the compost of spices,' and any one is enough to unfit it for the precious balm of unction. For some mighty good sort of people too, there is not seldom a sort of saturnine, or, if you will, *ursine* vanity, that keeps itself alive by sucking the paws of its own self-importance. And as this high sense, or rather sensation, of their own value, is for the most part grounded on negative qualities, so they have no better means of preserving the same but by negatives, that is, by *not* doing or saying any thing that might be put down for fond, silly, or nonsensical, or (to use their own phrase), by *never forgetting themselves*, which some of their acquaintances are uncharitable enough to think the most worthless object they could be employed in remembering. The same effect is produced in thousands, by the too general insensibility to a very important truth; this, namely, that the MISERY of human life is made up of large masses, each separated from the other by certain intervals. One year, the death of a child; years after, a failure in trade; after another longer or shorter interval, a daughter may have married unhappily; — in all but the singularly unfortunate, the integral parts that compose the sum total of the unhappiness of man's life, are easily counted, and distinctly remembered. The HAPPINESS of life, on the contrary, is made up of minute fractions, the little soon-forgotten charities of a kiss, a smile, a kind look, a heartfelt compliment in the disguise of playful raillery, and the countless other infinitesimals of pleasurable thought and genial feeling."*

These suggestions will commend themselves to every truly cultivated mind; but it would be unsuitable for me to enlarge on a topic so engrossing, and

* Coleridge.

which I have had occasion to discuss at some length in a previous course of Lectures.*

There is a second point pertaining to the domestic life of the merchant, which may claim a passing notice here. It is a question often agitated and variously decided, "*Should a merchant consult his wife about his business?*" We cannot answer it categorically. It may be the misfortune of a man to have a wife of so giddy and trifling a character, that the very mention of business would be an offence to her. Or a wife might happen to have so many "confidential friends," that every intimation her husband conveyed to her of the state of his affairs, would be gazetted far and near in the course of a day or two. Again, the answer must be modified by the import of the question. If the inquiry be, "Shall a merchant confer with his wife, as with his copartners, about all the details of his commercial transactions?" the question answers itself. A woman might just as well annoy her husband with all the minutiæ of her household concerns. But in the sense which the question usually bears, it must be answered with a qualified affirmative. Involving, as the matrimonial union does, an identity of interest and fortune, it seems reasonable that a wife should be kept apprized

* "The Bible in the Family."

of any events in her husband's business, having an important bearing upon their mutual well-being. If a benign Providence is bearing him on towards wealth and honour, why should she not share with him the pleasure and the gratitude it inspires? And if he is threatened with reverses, why should he withhold the knowledge of it from her who, of all human beings, will enter into his anxieties with the deepest sympathy? The wife who has no sympathy in her nature, mistook her vocation when she assumed the bonds of wedlock: the husband who will deny a wife the luxury of sympathizing in his trials, has forgotten that memorable day when she stood up with him, a lovely and blushing bride, and he promised before God and man, to "love, honour, and cherish" her till death. It is a poor commentary on this vow, to deprive her of a privilege which, if she have true conjugal affection, she would prize more than all his wealth, or all the conventional attentions he may lavish upon her "to be *seen* of men." The country is just now ringing with a coarse, unseemly clamour about "*Woman's Rights*"—a mere quarrel of certain Amazons with Providence, for making them women instead of men. Here, however, we have an incontestable woman's right, the right of a wife to sympathize with her husband in his joys and in his sorrows. A wife refused this right, may well exclaim,

"Within the bond of marriage, tell me,
Is it excepted I should know no secrets
That appertain to you? Am I yourself,
But, as it were, in sort, or limitation;
To keep with you at meals, comfort your bed,
And talk to you sometimes? Dwell I but in the suburbs
Of your good pleasure? If it be no more,
Then am I not your wife!"

Nor is this the only ground on which the duty may be urged. He knows but little of the weaker sex, who will venture to deny that, as a general characteristic, they are sagacious counsellors on practical matters. I may quote again* on this point, an admirable observation once made to me by an eminent divine of our church:—"We will say nothing of the manner in which that sex usually conduct an *argument*, but the *intuitive judgments of women* are often more to be relied upon than the conclusions which *we* reach by an elaborate process of reasoning." It may not suit our pride to expatiate too often in domestic life on this fact, but there can be no use in denying it, and it is only standing in our own light to refuse to take advantage of it. I can conceive of a merchant's returning home at evening, after a day of profound and anxious consultation with his partners about a projected speculation in lands, merchandize,

* See "BIBLE IN THE FAMILY," Lecture II.

or stocks. You have ransacked your newspaper-files, pored over your commercial dictionaries, reviewed your former operations, examined into your resources, looked abroad upon the state of the world, and canvassed all the agencies, political and financial, which are likely to influence the markets for some time to come, and, after hours of discussing and ciphering, have been obliged to postpone a decision till to-morrow. In this state of mind you meet your wife, and submit the vexed problem to her: and although she hears but the merest outline of it, her mind is instantly made up as to what you ought to do, and she gives you her opinion with the explicitness of a judge upon the bench. Or, your firm is in trouble. Fresh claims are pressing upon fresh embarrassments. You have no conception to-day how the notes of to-morrow are to be paid. Loans and discounts are becoming more difficult to negotiate. You have made sacrifices until you are startled at the chasm created in your late assets. Haunted with apprehensions you scarcely dare breathe to yourself, and oppressed with a burden which is drinking up your spirits, you, at length, in broken accents, lay the case before your wife. What is veiled in impenetrable darkness to your eye, is all luminous to hers. She sees, as by intuition, what you ought to do; and has the mingled courage and kindness to tell you. Unimpeded by the endless array of "Whys" and "Wherefores," of "Ifs" and "Hows," which have confused your calculations, and unsustained, it may be, by any tangible series of Baconian inductions, a single spring has brought her to a conclusion, which she enunciates with as much confidence as though she had received it by revelation.—And in both these cases, the probability is, the wives will be right. If you do not get the counsel you would prefer, you will get that which will be best for you, and which it will be unsafe not to follow. How many firms would this course have restrained from hurtful speculations! How many bankruptcies would it have relieved of their most painful features! Why, then, is it not more frequently adopted? I will tell you.

With one class of men, the reason has already been hinted at: they feel that it is a sort of indignity to consult a wife on matters of business. This is their department, and they are presumed to know how to manage it: to ask counsel of a wife, is to confess their insufficiency. If their pride could stoop to seek advice in any quarter, it would not be from a woman. — This feeling is not only wrong, but ridiculous. It proceeds on the assumption, that they are competent to deal with questions which, by their own admission, have baffled them. And it further assumes, what is notoriously false, that in married life all the wisdom and sagacity are necessarily on the side of the husband. A man of large and comprehensive views will be above these littlenesses. Such a man will have no fear of compromising his own dignity by conferring with an intelligent wife. Inferior to himself, she may be, in strength of mind and in information; and yet she may have qualities which will make her a safe Mentor. The most learned and acute jurists often derive the greatest assistance, in resolving complex cases, from the suggestions of their associates on the bench, although they may be men of only second or third rate talent. And the man who is above asking counsel of any body whom he believes to be a shade below himself in intellectual vigour or various knowledge, merits the penalty which his superciliousness will be sure to bring upon him. In the conjugal relation this is the more censurable, because the preponderance of character may be really with the "weaker vessel"; while the Solon to whom she is wedded, only exposes his own imbecility in denying her any share in his deliberations.

This course may be adopted from a very different motive — an unwillingness on the part of a merchant to harass the mind of his wife with his troubles. This is an amiable and honourable sentiment, and, to a certain extent, it may properly influence the conduct. But it should not be carried too far in those emergencies so often mentioned, when a house is tottering to its foundations. When such an exigency occurs, it is due to a wife that she should be apprized of it. This would preclude the revolting incongruity of which any of our cities could supply examples, of a commercial firm struggling on for months together with impending bankruptcy, while their domestic establishments, the while, were the centres of the most prodigal luxury and extravagance. It is further due to a wife because she *is* a wife, and as such must share her husband's allotments. They took each other "for better, for worse, for richer, for poorer"; and if either is in trouble, the other is entitled to know it and participate in it. Nor is any other policy, in the cases we are considering, compatible with true kindness. When the blow falls, you can no longer conceal the state of things. Your wife will have to know it and to *feel* it. Through your mistaken tenderness, it comes upon her suddenly, "like a thief in the night": whereas, had you dealt frankly by her, she would have been in a measure prepared for the stroke. If you were to submit the question to ten thousand wives in succession, "whether of these two courses would be the more acceptable to them," you would probably hear but one response — "By all means let me know when there is danger threatening, without waiting for the calamity to fall!" — Nor must it be lost sight of, that the course here recommended, might either avert or mitigate the disaster. The timely advice of a discreet wife, might, by the blessing of Providence, save you from insolvency; or, failing of this, it might keep you from those acts which impart to insolvency its keenest sting. The observations formerly made on this subject,* show how important *faithful* counsel is to embarrassed merchants. This you would get from your wives. The thought of your poverty might be distressing to them, but it would be nothing to the idea of your dishonour. They would see and appreciate the danger to which your principles were exposed, and caution you, with all firmness and affection, against bringing the least stain upon your integrity. They would remind you that an untarnished name would be a better legacy to them and their children, than millions of money. They would remonstrate against your postponing the crisis until all your resources were consumed, and encourage you to meet at once the blow which had become inevitable. They would, possibly, soothe your chafed and agitated spirits, not only by the assiduities of affection, but by the higher ministrations of a genuine piety — bringing oil and wine from the Gospel to cheer you, and directing your hopes to Him who is the Refuge of the afflicted

---

* Lecture VI.

and the Healer of the broken-hearted.—These, surely, are objects of some moment to a man harassed with commercial difficulties: a faithful adherence to a simple rule of three syllables, would ordinarily secure them to you — TELL YOUR WIFE.

Will it be out of place to add here, that there are certain correlative obligations answering to these domestic duties of the merchant? If he is bound to bestow all the time he can upon his family, they are bound to make his home as agreeable as possible. If it behooves him to cultivate the household affections, they must not neglect it. If he is to confer with his wife on matters of merchandize, especially in seasons of embarrassment, it will not answer for the wife to manifest an indifference to his affairs, still less to do anything which may increase his difficulties. Examples have no doubt occurred of conjugal officiousness, in which either party has been disposed to intermeddle with the functions proper to the other — the husband with the "house-keeping," the wife with the counting-room. A woman may easily shun this extreme, and yet take that sort of interest in her husband's business, which has been indirectly inculcated in the observations just addressed to merchants. And whatever her tastes may be on this point, she cannot, if she would, avoid having a great deal to do with his business. What he is in his warehouse, in his principles and plans, in his temper and manners, will depend very much upon *what his home is.* And his home, again, will be very much what his wife sees fit to make it. There are homes such as Milton had in his eye (his own, unhappily, was not one of them,) when he wrote the lines —

> "For nothing lovelier can be found
> In woman, than to study household good,
> And good works in her husband to promote."

A greater than Milton had, upwards of two thousand years before his time, drawn the portraiture of one of these very wives with the skill of a master-limner. It is a well-known picture, better known even than the most celebrated "Madonnas" of any of the old painters; but as there is some disposition now-a-days to deposit it in the antique Galleries, as a mere historical gem, I feel inclined to hang it up before your eyes: —

Who can find a virtuous woman? for her price is far above rubies.

The heart of her husband doth safely trust in her, so that he shall have no need of spoil.

She will do him good and not evil all the days of her life.

She seeketh wool, and flax, and worketh willingly with her hands.

She is like the merchants' ships; she bringeth her food from afar.

She riseth also while it is yet night, and giveth meat to her household, and a portion to her maidens.

She considereth a field, and buyeth it: with the fruit of her hands she planteth a vineyard.

She girdeth her loins with strength, and strengtheneth her arms.

She perceiveth that her merchandize is good: her candle goeth not out by night.

She layeth her hands to the spindle, and her hands hold the distaff.

She stretcheth out her hand to the poor; yea, she reacheth forth her hands to the needy.

She is not afraid of the snow for her household: for all her household are clothed with scarlet.

She maketh herself coverings of tapestry; her clothing is silk and purple.

Her husband is known in the gates, when he sitteth among the elders of the land.

She maketh fine linen, and selleth it; and delivereth girdles unto the merchant.

Strength and honour are her clothing; and she shall rejoice in time to come.

She openeth her mouth with wisdom; and in her tongue is the law of kindness.

She looketh well to the ways of her household, and eateth not the bread of idleness.

Her children arise up and call her blessed: her husband also, and he praiseth her.

Many daughters have done virtuously, but thou excellest them all.

Favour is deceitful, and beauty is vain: but a woman that feareth the Lord, she shall be praised.

Give her of the fruit of her hands; and let her own works praise her in the gates.

There is a *merchant's wife* worth having! An Oriental woman, it is true, but there is nothing in her essential attributes and habits which would not grace the Occident as well — the wives of Philadelphia and Boston, as those of Jerusalem and Bagdad. It is the picture, for example, of a *domestic* woman. And is not this meet in a merchant's wife? I do not mean that she should make her house a cloister, and never stir abroad. But let her know what the word HOME means. Let her cherish it until every letter in it becomes precious to her. Let her understand that her empire is there. And let her find her happiness, next to religion, in administering its affairs and augmenting the felicity of its subjects. This need not preclude her from the interchange of social courtesies and the fellowship of friends. But it will certainly present a life in striking contrast with that of some wives, whose houses are to them, from Christmas to Lent, very much what they are to their husbands in the "business-season" — mere hotels.

This is the portrait, again, of an *industrious* woman — always occupied with her maidens or her vineyard, her distaff or her merchandize, her in-door or her out-door cares. Is *this* unseemly in a merchant's wife? The same occupations may not demand her care, but useful occupation of some sort will have a claim upon her. That must be a strange household which supplies the head of it with no employment: and that a curious scheme of life, which permits a woman to surrender herself to her slothful propensities, and while away her years in doing nothing. In a very characteristic letter, poor Burns says of the Muses, "the Nine have given me a great deal of pleasure, but, bewitching jades! they have beggared me: for, like Solomon's lilies, the idle creatures 'toil not, neither do they spin.'" It might be ungenerous to hint that there may have been merchants who were in circumstances to use this identical language respecting their wives. Certainly, a wife who will "neither toil nor spin," nor do anything, except dress and visit and lounge and read novels, *might* "beggar" her husband, even though she "gave him a great deal of pleasure"—and this last would not always happen, for it is only men that have received "one talent," or a fraction of a talent, who take "pleasure" in a wife's spending the same sort of life as a portrait or a doll. Employment is a homely but important element in the cup of domestic happiness: where either party lacks or neglects it, trouble is apt to follow. "The field of the slothful," find it where you will, is more likely to be covered with "thorns and nettles" than with flowers. Even the flowers of affection, the hardiest of all plants, will die out there, or attain only a stunted growth, which will make the spectator exclaim, as one does involuntarily in looking at a cluster of tiny Alpine roses peering through the frost, "Poor things!"

Another obvious feature in the picture we are studying, is, *taste and neatness.* "All her household are clothed with scarlet.* She maketh herself coverings of tapestry; her clothing is silk and purple. Her husband is known in the gates when he sitteth among the elders of the land" — known, not simply by his worth, but by the costly robes her fingers prepare for him. And the whole sketch suggests the image of a domestic establishment impressed throughout with cleanliness, order, and beauty. Our merchant's wife will of course understand this. If she should not, it will be doing her a kindness to say, that these "trivial matters" are of moment with the other sex. *Men* think a great deal of neatness and taste in a wife. It will not satisfy them that you look very imposing when arrayed in your laces and jewelry for a party. This is well enough; but it may be more than neutralized by a careless attire and an untidy house in your ordinary arrangements. Time will gradually blanch your personal charms; and there is, therefore, the greater reason why you should give heed to those

* "Scarlet" — or, rather, as the margin has it, "double garments." So Coverdale — "For all hir householde folkes are duble clothed."

"little things" in dress, and manner, and household dispositions, which have a wonderful, though imperceptible, effect in fostering mutual affection, and the neglect of which will be certain to eat like a subtle cancer at the core of your domestic peace. — This is not to encourage extravagance. You may be ready to appeal to the "tapestry" and the "silk and the purple," of this model housewife, in vindication of your own expensive habits. But have you considered where she procured these elegancies? I do not find that she went to her husband, and got him to draw some thousands of dollars from his business to purchase them for her. As I read the passage, they were her own handiwork. And I venture to express the opinion, that no merchant's wife will be, or ought to be, impeded, in decorating her rooms with all the "tapestry," or her person with all the "silk and purple" — *which she shall weave herself.* You may think it unreasonable to suggest this restriction; and perhaps it is. But it is not more so than the luxury and extravagance which have reduced so many merchants to poverty. The key to no inconsiderable portion of the bankruptcies which occur, is to be found, not in the counting-room, but in the drawing-room, and *there* as often in the wife's hand, as the husband's. If truth could give way to courtesy, this might be spared. But truth will give way to nothing;

and it is too important in this connexion to be suppressed. An old writer, who has given us a revelation of domestic life not peculiar to his own age, brings forward one of his characters as reproaching his wasteful wife with her "change of gaudy furniture," her

—— "mighty looking-glasses, like artillery,
Brought home on engines; the superfluous plate,
Antique and novel; vanities of tires;"

and other articles. He proceeds: —

"I could accuse the gayety of your wardrobe
And prodigal embroideries, under which
Rich satins, plushes, cloth of silver, dare
Not show their own complexions. Your jewels,
Able to burn out the spectator's eyes,
And show like bon-fires on you by the tapers.
Something might here be spared, with safety of
Your birth and honour, since the truest wealth
Shines from the soul, and draws up just admirers."

Whether there were any merchants at the disastrous era of '37, who had occasion to use language of this kind, I shall not inquire; nor would it become one who is no seer, to predict whether there will be any at the next financial crisis which may overtake the country. But there are opinions abroad on both these points, which it might be useful to some people to ponder.

The ready replication to this will be, that "it is ungenerous to impute all the sin of extravagant living to the wives, since they are in many instances but passive instruments in carrying out plans to which they are bound to conform." This would do if "all" the blame were laid at their door. But it is not: where no censure is deserved, none is intended. It is not enough, however, to exonerate a wife, that she has simply acquiesced in a system of luxurious expenditure far beyond her husband's income. It is for her gratification in a good measure, that he has gone into these excesses. In any event, she might have prevented or abridged it. Her influence, always potential at first, could have been exerted to induce a more rational and becoming style of living; and she would not have pressed this point in vain. But the woman who would do this, especially the *bride* who would do it, is one of a thousand. The prevailing passion with people just setting out in married life, is for a pomp and display wholly unsuited to their means. Young merchants have no conception of the drain such an establishment will be upon their profits. They are apt to suppose that if the original outfit is provided (as it may be by a marriage settlement), all subsequent inconvenience is precluded; that the ship once launched will take care of itself. But this conceit is soon dispelled. What with rents and wages and wardrobe, amusements and equipage and entertainments, the charges to private account on the books of the firm, swell with an ominous progression, until the business itself reels under the rapid depletion, and betrays symptoms of an approaching syncope. If they have the moral courage to curtail their expenses and adjust themselves at once to their actual position, they may escape the catastrophe. But when a ship is on her beam-ends, the least delay may be fatal. And the imprudence which brings about a crisis of this sort, is too often combined with a pride and an effeminacy of principle, which will hold back from a manly, straight-forward discharge of duty, until the opportunity is lost and the blow falls. How much better to have studied all these contingencies at the commencement! How much better to begin with moderation, and end with honour and affluence; than to begin with splendour, and end with premature insolvency! If the husbands will not consider this, let the wives think of it. They may miss the hollow flatteries which circulate among the gay and the frivolous, but they will secure the respect of that portion of society whose friendship will be of real advantage to them. And what is of greater moment, they may experience the protection of that benign Being, who alone can crown their plans with success, and make their prosperity a blessing to them.

It is another characteristic of the "virtuous woman" set before us, that "she opens her mouth with wisdom, and in her tongue is the law of kindness;" and she makes it her business to "*do her husband good*, and not evil, all the days of her life." "She shows her love to him, not by a foolish fondness, but by prudent endearments, accommodating herself to his temper, and not crossing him, giving him good words, and not bad ones, no, not when he is out of humour; studying to make him easy, to provide what is fit for him both in health and sickness, and attending him with diligence and tenderness when any thing ails him; nor would she, no, not for the world, wilfully do anything that might be a damage to his person, family, estate, or reputation. And this is her care 'all the days of her life;' not at first only, or now and then, when she is in a good humour, but perpetually; and she is not weary of the good offices she does him. She does him good, not only all the days of his life, but of her own too: if she survive him, still she is doing him good in her care of his children, his estate, and good name, and all the concerns he left behind him."*

And herein also is she a fit pattern for our merchant's wife. For the cares and perplexities of business are very great; and when men come home from

* Matthew Henry.

their counting-rooms, jaded and oppressed with toil and anxiety, they need some one to speak to them in words of kindness and to "do them good." And it is a sad and pernicious thing if, instead of this, they are met with harsh tones and chilling looks, or have the load upon their aching backs increased by a huge accession of petty domestic grievances. This is "in no sense meet or amiable."

"Thy husband is thy lord, thy life, thy keeper
Thy head, thy sovereign; one that cares for thee,
And for thy maintenance: commits his body
To painful labour, both by sea and land;
To watch the night in storms, the day in cold,
While thou liest warm at home, secure and safe;
And craves no other tribute at thy hands,
But love, fair looks, and true obedience: —
Too little labour for so great a debt."

And to refuse even this requital, is to come short, not merely of conjugal duty, but of the magnanimity proper to your sex in general.

It is mentioned as the crowning excellence of the character we are contemplating, that she "*fears the Lord.*" "Favour is deceitful, and beauty is vain: but a woman that feareth the Lord, she shall be praised." In man or woman, there is no adequate foundation for true and lasting esteem but this. Personal beauty, which has so much to do with making marriages, is no infallible index of real worth, and no sure pledge of domestic happiness. It is exposed to the inroads of time, sickness, sorrow, and decay; and may wither at the very meridian of life. The "beauty of holiness," on the other hand, is as indestructible as the soul itself. Earthly vicissitudes produce no impression upon it. It flourishes alike in the shade and in the sunshine. Disease and suffering, trials and losses, only clothe it with fresh lustre. The more it is crushed, the sweeter is the fragrance it emits. The character it embellishes, enshrines the elements of the very highest style of excellence known to created beings. And if there is any attribute which is to be prized above all others, whether in single or in married life, it is undoubtedly genuine religion. I say not that this alone will make a wife what she ought to be: but this is the most essential quality for a wife; and no assemblage of virtues and accomplishments can compensate for the absence of it. Those merchants may well esteem themselves happy, whose homes are lighted up with the beams of a perennial and cheerful piety.

It will be no very violent transition, to pass from the domestic life of the merchant, to his LITERARY OPPORTUNITIES. The subject is one of large extent; but it did not fall within the scope of these Lectures, to discuss it in detail. Some reference to it, however, especially as it may be connected with the morals of trade, will be deemed indispensable.

In the glimpses we have just had of a merchant's household, *as it should be*, one of the scenes which must have passed before the eye of every auditor, is that of the man of commerce enjoying an occasional hour with the great authors in his Library, or seated, book-in-hand, with his family around the centre-table. This is a refreshing sight. It is worthy to be pondered by the restless throng of traffickers who have gradually repudiated all books except Journals and Ledgers, and by the crowds of young men who are just embarking in a mercantile career. There are those, it may be, in whose breasts the scene would only excite emotions of contempt. "Practical men," as they are termed, are apt to despise "book-learning." It was one of these sages, who, having advertised for a clerk, asked each applicant, as he appeared, "whether he understood Latin," and on receiving an affirmative answer, dismissed him without further inquiry. The feeling is, that "learning" tends to disqualify a person for business, that it makes him speculative and "notional," and blunts his wits for scenting out customers and driving bargains. Examples are readily cited, of illiterate individuals who were celebrated for their shrewdness, and made great fortunes. And "if *they* got rich without books, books would be more of a hindrance than a help, to others who are aiming at the same end."—This is merchandize with a witness. The loftiest conception of human life these people are capable of forming, is that of a machine for making money. The nobler part of their nature is not recognized in their theory. They seem not to know that they have souls. They scarcely know that they are endowed with reason. Certainly they ignore all the higher functions and uses of reason, and degrade it, as far as possible, to the level of the better sort of brutes. I disparage not a business-life. I look with no disfavour upon legitimate accumulation. I greatly honour the man who secures, by honest means, a competent or opulent estate, and employs it in doing good. But look at MAN, the crown and glory of this lower creation, the wondrous mechanism of his frame, the more wondrous mechanism of his mind, his capacious intellect, his imagination, his conscience, his immortality, and say whether the end, the paramount end, for which he was sent into this world, was, "to buy and sell and get gain!" Nature, if she were allowed to speak, would rebuke this sordid theory. She would tell you that you were enslaving the understanding to the senses, the man to the animal. She would remonstrate against your setting earth above heaven, and time before eternity. She would remind you that your trafficking must in any event be abandoned, and your gold and silver relinquished after a few days or years, and that if all your training and your happiness were summed up in hoarding, you would be miserably unprovided for a world where trade and its implements are unknown. And she would admonish you, that these faculties, the culture of which you now hold in such contempt, would constitute an essential part of your being for ever, and be a perpetual means of the purest enjoyment or of the keenest suffering, according to your treatment of them here.

It is, in fact, the tendency of trade to cramp the intellect and inspire these mercenary views, which makes it proper even for the pulpit to protest against your neglect of liberal studies. The learned professions are not exempt from this bias. An exclusive devotion to any one of them, will make a narrow, stereotype character, vigorous, perhaps, in certain faculties, but deficient in that amplitude and symmetry which belong to truly great minds. And in your avocation, the danger from this source, is, for obvious reasons, much more imminent. If this consideration were without force, the prejudice against literary studies, more or less prevalent in your ranks, might be refuted on strictly commercial grounds. For there is no kind of knowledge which may not be useful to a merchant in a pecuniary way. The man who is conducting an extensive business, should be at home in the history, geography, and politics, of the leading nations of the globe. He should be familiar with the staple products of every clime, with the principles of political economy and finance, with revenue and quarantine laws, with the commercial usages of different countries and their modes of intercommunication, with the manufacturing processes pertaining to his own branch of traffic, with the adaptation of various articles to land and marine transportation, and with the moral traits of every people whose ports his ships may visit. I know an earnest and accomplished scholar who has said in one of his books, that if he could learn how the topmost stone on Chimborazo lay, he would deem it an item of information worth possessing. A merchant should, in the same spirit, pick up knowledge in every direction and on all subjects. He must "sow beside all waters:" for he cannot tell what he may want. There is a story told of a young man who, when at a university, refused to attend lectures on Euclid, because he was a man of fortune, and never likely to become a *carpenter!* And nothing is more common than for college-students to proceed upon the same vicious principle, picking and culling among the studies, so as to confine themselves to such as will be *of service* to them in after-life — an error for which "after-life" often makes them pay very dearly. — Superior knowledge would give you an advantage over competitors; and save you from those disastrous mistakes into which firms are so often led by a blind confidence. It would help to guard you against disasters: and if disasters came, it would assist you in retrieving your losses, or in turning your attention to some new avocation. It would enhance your personal influence in the community. "Knowledge is power." The very capitalists who affect to despise it, are made to feel this, when they contrast the respect which is paid, in commercial circles, to a really intelligent merchant, with the mere ceremonious homage rendered (not to themselves, but) to their wealth. — On strictly professional grounds, then — on the scale of dollars and cents — it becomes merchants to "give attention to reading."

In our day this has become more important than ever, by reason of the general diffusion of knowledge. Education is no longer the prerogative of the great. It has put off its purple robes and silver slippers, and come down to tabernacle with the masses. The world is waking up to the pregnant fact, that *man* is composed of something besides bone and muscle. The universal clamour is for "Education." The labouring classes are still willing to work, but they are not willing to be mere spinning-jennies and dredging-machines. And science, with a noble philanthropy which outshines all the jewels in its radiant coronet, is stooping to their necessities, and popularizing itself to satisfy these passionate cravings of humanity. This movement is too broad and too powerful for any class or profession not to be affected by it. It has told upon the forum and upon the pulpit, as well upon the politics and the jurisprudence of the world, as upon its literature and its "socialism." The commercial body cannot, if they would, escape its influence. If merchants will not fall in with it, it will leave them high and dry upon the shoals of ignorance, a warning and a by-word to the crowds who sweep past them in the eager strife for knowledge. Nor will it suffice that you *set out* with an education. It is as indispensable to feed the mind as the body. You might as well expect the meals of to-day to keep up your physical strength and elasticity for a fortnight to come, as to rely upon your original stock of ideas to nourish your intellectual faculties through the rest of your life. Men often try this — merchants, perhaps, oftener than any others — and you know how they succeed. You must have seen specimens of the sort — individuals who have trafficked for a score or two of years on their primitive stock of ideas; reading no useful books, shunning all public discussions and lectures, making no efficient use of their powers of observation, adding nothing to their modicum of information except, as a sponge gathers moisture from the atmosphere, by unavoidable absorption, and for ever harping upon one string, and pestering all companies on all occasions with the same petrified topics: — why, what is this better than heading pins for a life-time, or harnessing one's self to the horse who is doomed to the endless gyrations of a bark-mill? *This* is no life for a human being, certainly not for one who aspires to a respectable place in society and expects to be the companion of cultivated men. And the only way to elude it, is, to keep pouring truth into the mind, and recruiting its stock of ideas from every available source. Truth is the soul's aliment, and it is a worse crime against nature to starve the soul, than to famish the body. "It is not the mere cry of moralists and the flourish of rhetoricians; but it is *noble* to seek truth, and it is *beautiful* to find it. It is the ancient feeling of the human heart, — that knowledge is better than riches; and it is deeply and *sacredly true!* To mark the course of human passions as they have flowed on in the ages that are past; to see why nations have risen and why they have fallen; to speak of heat and light and winds; to know what man has discovered in the heavens above, and in the earth beneath; to hear the chemist unfold the marvellous properties that the Creator has locked up in a speck of earth; to be told that there are worlds so distant from our sun, that the quickness of light travelling from the world's creation, has never yet reached us; to wander in the creations of poetry, and grow warm again with that eloquence which swayed the democracies of the old world; to go up with great reasoners to the FIRST CAUSE of all, and to perceive in the midst of all this dissolution, and decay, and cruel separation, that there *is* one thing unchangeable, indestructible, and everlasting; — it is worth while in the days of our youth to strive hard for this great discipline; to pass sleepless nights for it, to give up to it laborious days; to spurn for it present pleasures; to endure for it afflicting poverty; to wade for it through darkness and sorrow and contempt, as the great spirits of the world have done in all ages and all times."

"All this," I can fancy I hear some of my auditors saying to themselves, "is very true and very fine: but why tantalize us in this way? We are overtasked now: how is it possible for us to find time for reading?" This question is fairly put, and shall be as fairly answered.

I should be extremely sorry to have the merchants or clerks before me suppose, that I am insensible to the disadvantages they labour under in repect to literary culture. At certain seasons of the year, particularly, to exhort them to reading, would be about as rational as to ask them to fly. It would be worth while, for example, to see the *look* with which a corps of clerks in one of our jobbing-houses, would receive a philanthropic citizen who, on any day of *this coming week*, should make his way into their establishment through draymen and porters and coopers and packers and messengers, and the throng of impatient customers from the "far West" and the far South and all the sub-cardinal points between, and blandly request them "to peruse the very interesting and valuable" octavo he might tender to them. I am sure they would say nothing rude in reply to him. The ludicrousness of the thing would banish every harsh feeling, and light up their shrewd and care-worn faces with a smile of blended astonishment and incredulity which would at least do *them* good, even if it failed to enlighten their benevolent visitor. But *March* does not take up the whole Calendar. You are no more buried amongst bales and boxes during the entire year, than is the husbandman employed from January to December in harvesting his crops. During most of the months, a just sense of the value of time, combined with a well-arranged *system*, would secure you frequent opportunities for study. You may not think so if you consult simply your present habits, or inquire of your associates and neighbours. But go, when you have a breathing-spell, to that noble monument of Christian philanthropy, the "INSTITUTION FOR THE BLIND," in the north-western part of our city, and learn whether your path up the hill of science, is a rougher one, than that which these children, who dwell in perpetual darkness, are treading with so elastic a step. Or, take up the volumes entitled, "THE PURSUIT OF KNOWLEDGE UNDER DIFFICULTIES," and see what was accomplished by Arkwright and Ferguson, Saunderson and Heyne, Franklin and Fulton, and hosts of others whose names shine in the glorious galaxy of self-made men. If *they* did, why may not you? There can be few among the young men in our Counting-Houses, whose situation in respect to intellectual improvement, is not superior to that of any one of the six individuals just mentioned in their early days. One great secret of their success lay in the profound art of economizing time. You have stood, doubtless, by one of the ingenious machines in our Mint, and seen the brilliant and beautiful coin dropping into the receiver at the rate of a hundred to the minute, and your feeling has been, "How happy should I be if I could coin money for myself at this rate!" But you are all coiners — and that, of something which might be worth more to you than all the deposits at the Mint. Every fleeting second receives from you a brand more indelible than any which the die imparts to the metal; and if you are careful to have every impression what it should be, you will, in the end, be richer in intellectual and moral wealth than Crœsus ever was in the gold that perisheth. It was by taking care of these seconds, "the gold dust of time," that the men we have named and their fellows, rose to eminence and honour. I have styled this "a profound art," and so it is. Not one in a thousand understands it. Franklin himself declares that in carrying out his curious scheme for "arriving at moral perfection," his rule of *Order*, which ran thus, "Let all your things have their places: let each part of your business have its time," gave him more trouble than any other part of it. By perseverance, however, he mastered it in some good degree; and we may all do the same.

Many of those who imagine that they cannot possibly find leisure for useful books, actually devote a great deal of time to certain kinds of reading. It is one of the incidental results of the science and enterprise of the day, that our country is flooded with a "cheap literature," native and exotic, no small portion of which is very trashy or very pernicious. Young men are apt to resort to publications of this sort for pastime. The latest French or German novel (pamphlet edition, double column, and miserable paper), or the last volume of "Capital Trials" or "Awful Murders," might be found lying upon the small table in their dormitory, or tucked away on one of the shelves of the warehouse, to be devoured by snatches when the principals "are not about." As a natural consequence, they have no relish for substantial reading. The palate pampered on highly-seasoned dishes, revolts at simple and nutritious food. The more the imagination is indulged with these stimulating doses, the stronger will be its cravings. It is a well-authenticated fact, that "the inveterate thieves of London make it a practice to attend all the executions, not so much for an opportunity of picking pockets, as for the pleasure of excitement, which, through the very exciting nature of their lawless pursuits, they become incapable of deriving from any ordinary source." And on the same principle, a mind accustomed to such reading as has been referred to, will collapse unless supplied with overwrought narratives and extravagant fictions.

But light literature has an accomplice, which must also be arraigned here. Dr. Franklin, in writing from Philadelphia to the Bishop of St. Asaph, in 1786, complains that "the reading-time of most people was so taken up with *Newspapers* and periodical pamphlets, that few now-a-days ventured to attempt any solid reading." So far as I have been able to ascertain, there were at that period printed in Philadelphia, two small weekly newspapers, and one daily, commenced two years before. I think it must have been this last paper, the "Pennsylvania Packet," (which finally ripened into that sedate, time-honoured journal, "Poulson's American Daily Advertiser,") that did the mischief the venerable sage so feelingly deplores. However that may have been, if the newspaper press of that day laid itself open to this grave censure, what must be said of it now? — This is delicate ground. Who stands upon so proud an eminence that he can rebuke his neighbours for their devotion to the newspaper, without exposing himself to the retort — "Physician, heal thyself!" I frankly confess, not I. My house is of glass, I fear very *thin* glass, and it is not safe for the tenant to be too forward in throwing stones. There are few bills I pay more cheerfully, than those for my newspapers.

> "This folio of four pages, happy work!
> Which not ev'n critics criticise; that holds
> Inquisitive attention, while I read,
> Fast bound in chains of silence, which the fair,
> Though eloquent themselves, yet fear to break;
> What is it but a map of busy life,
> Its fluctuations and its vast concerns?"

And yet I cannot in my heart approve of the prevailing passion for newspapers: nor endorse at all the common plea of mercantile men that they have "no time for books." In particular cases, this is no doubt true. But look at one of these gentlemen as he goes home to his tea: what is that huge roll in his hand or projecting from his surtout pocket? Newspapers. And if it happen to be a Friday or Saturday evening, when the "Weeklies" are superadded to the "Dailies," he will have typography enough in his parcel to make a large octavo volume or a pair of them. And what is more, he will go through with it. This "very busy" merchant, who is so oppressed with care that he has not "a moment's time for reading," will travel through one folio page after another until he has mastered the contents of his entire pacquet. Not satisfied with the articles pertaining to commerce, and a general survey of the affairs of the world, he has acquired a sort of morbid taste for the endless miscellany that makes up an ordinary journal, even down to the "Police Reports," the broken arms, the collisions of omnibuses, the "accidents" in distant cities, the state of the "weather" on the other side of the globe, and, when these items are exhausted, the "Lost and Found" and other weighty matters in the advertising columns. Now, I will not retract the sentiment, that "knowledge of every kind may be useful," but, really, one cannot see this process going on, day by day, with thousands of merchants, without having two reflections forced upon his mind. The first is, that these gentlemen are under a strange delusion when they imagine tha' they have "no time for reading." And the other is that newspapers are great moths. One of the familia headings they present to city readers, is, "Bewar of Thieves!" What is this but the cry of the pilfere who runs away from the scene of his depredation shouting, "*Stop thief!*" Certainly, if a man make inquisition for his lost time, he will be very apt t find that his favourite newspapers have robbed him of a good share of it. *They* are the culprits: and it is only half their criminality, that they have stolen his time. They have broken up his early habits of reading, perverted his taste, impaired his mental discipline. and indisposed him to all vigorous thought and patient research. He can scarcely summon energy enough to sit down to one of the Quarterly Reviews, or to listen while his son or daughter reads to the family circle from any standard History or Biography. His literature and his resolution have disappeared like Pharaoh's fat kine, and there is nothing but the *newspaper* to show for them!

Thus much for the supposed "want of time," which reconciles so many merchants and clerks to the neglect of all instructive literature. The common effect, as just intimated, is, to generate a distaste for solid reading. It becomes a formidable thing to grapple with a book: to overcome the *vis inertiæ* which oppresses the mind on the very suggestion of such a task. If the habit has been matured by time, it may be invincible. No one expects to see the merchant betaking himself to Bacon and Milton and Irving and Prescott, who has had the ominous interdict inscribed over the gates of his mind for forty years, "No admittance, except on business."* Authors (in print, at least) are proverbially benevolent and courteous. You may have hundreds of them together in your house without being disturbed by them. They neither quarrel with each other, nor break the peace of the family. They are tolerant of dust and neglect and all kinds of harsh treatment. They stay where they are put, and never come except when they are called. The only case in which they show any spirit, is the one just hinted at, where an individual undertakes to dally with them who has passed by them every day for a score or two of years, without deigning to speak to them. This they *do* resent. And the offender is apt to find them so punctilious about a reconciliation, that after a few advances he gives it up in despair. But this is an extreme case. A simple indifference to books, may usually be conquered, if you but *will*

* See the Hon. George S. Hillard's admirable Address before the Boston Mercantile Library Association, 1850.

to do it. For example (I quote from Sydney Smith), "sound travels so many feet in a second. Nothing more probable: but you do not care *how* light and sound travel. Very likely; but *make* yourself care; get up, shake yourself well, *pretend* to care, make believe to care, and very soon you *will* care, and care so much, that you will sit for hours thinking about light and sound, and be extremely angry with any one who interrupts you in your pursuits, and tolerate no other conversation but about light and sound, and catch yourself plaguing every body to death who approaches you, with the discussion of these subjects. I am sure that a man ought to read as he would grasp a nettle: — do it lightly, and you get molested; grasp it with all your strength, and you feel none of its asperities. There is nothing so horrible as languid study; when you sit looking at the clock, wishing the time was over, or that somebody would call on you and put you out of your misery. The only way to read with any efficacy, is to read so heartily that dinner-time [or bed-time] comes two hours before you expect it." And many a young man, at first very shy of books, has learned the art of reading in this way so well, that he now counts the hours of business which keep him from his favourite nook at the Mercantile Library or from the few chosen authors that grace the shelves in his chamber.

Others might rouse themselves to a similar course, but they "know not how or what to read." The very magnitude of the public libraries to which they have access, bewilders them. "What can they do in such a wilderness of books? With what subjects shall they begin? Which are the best authors? What is the most profitable method of reading?" Questions like these crowd upon them, and extinguish the half-formed purpose to set about the culture of their minds and aspire to something more worthy of their rational nature than the character of mere money-makers. The difficulty is real, but it is not serious. The topics to which it points, it is not my province to discuss; but I may say, in a single sentence, that satisfactory information on these topics, is within the reach of every person who desires it. There are gentlemen connected with these libraries, and others in your own profession, who would cheerfully aid you in arranging a course of reading. Or better still, perhaps, there are books on this very subject, containing ample information respecting every department of letters, and designed to meet in a judicious and competent manner, the very wants which have been described.* No

* See, especially, "A Course of English Reading, adapted to every taste and capacity, with Anecdotes of Men of Genius. By the Rev. James Pycroft, B. A., Trinity College, Oxford." (A. Hart, Philad.) A most instructive and entertaining book.

young man, with such helps at hand, need be at a loss what to read, nor how to read to good purpose.

The importance of this habit in a simply professional view, and as going to counteract the influence of a too exclusive devotion to merchandize, has already been adverted to. It is no less useful to young men in our cities, as a shield against temptation. "The ruin of most men," says Mr. Hillard, "dates from some vacant hour. Occupation is the armour of the soul, and the train of Idleness is borne up by all the vices. I remember a satirical poem, in which the Devil is represented as fishing for men, and adapting his baits to the taste and temperament of his prey; but the idler, he said, pleased him most, because he bit the naked hook. To a young man away from home, friendless and forlorn in a great city, the hours of peril are those between sunset and bed-time, for the moon and stars see more of evil in a single hour than the sun in his whole day's circuit. The poet's visions of evening are all compact of tender and soothing images. It brings the wanderer to his home, the child to his mother's arms, the ox to his stall, and the weary labourer to his rest. But to the gentle-hearted youth who is thrown upon the rocks of a pitiless city, and stands 'homeless amid a thousand homes,' the approach of evening brings with it an aching sense of loneliness and desolation, which comes down upon the spirit like darkness upon the earth. In this mood, his best impulses become a snare to him, and he is led astray because he is social, affectionate, sympathetic, and warm-hearted. If there be a young man thus circumstanced within the sound of my voice, let me say to him that books are the friends of the friendless, and that a Library is the home of the homeless. A taste for reading will always carry you into the best possible company, and enable you to converse with men who will instruct you by their wisdom and charm you by their wit, who will soothe you when fretted, refresh you when weary, counsel you when perplexed, and sympathize with you at all times. Evil spirits, in the Middle Ages, were driven away by 'bell, book, and candle'; — you want but two of these, the book and the candle."

It is another consideration of great moment, that merchants, in this country, are often called to high public stations. They may be found among our Legislators. They have graced the Cabinet, and represented us at European Courts. A profession thus identified with our national affairs, should be no less distinguished for its general intelligence than its integrity and enterprise.

The importance of literary culture as a preparation for retiring from business, has been adverted to on former occasions, and the length of this Lecture forbids me to enlarge upon it here. But the argument may be seen in its best form, if those who are curious on the subject, will take the trouble to estimate for themselves, the intellectual and moral resources, and the honour and comfort, of a merchant who carries into his retirement a well-disciplined mind and established habits of reading, as compared with the closing years of another who, on bidding adieu to his Counting-House, is ready to say, with Micah, "Ye have taken away my gods which I made, and what have I more?"

The paramount reason, however, why mercantile men should bestow this care upon mental culture, grows out of its connexion with their spiritual interests; — and that, not simply in those indirect methods which have already been mentioned. The argument drawn from the conservative and elevating influence of literary occupation generally, is sound and forcible. But the higher bearings of this habit will be understood at once, when I mention the BIBLE as the book which must of right claim a precedence in every scheme of reading. Regarded simply as a means of intellectual discipline, no other work can be studied to equal advantage. Its themes are the sublimest and the most ennobling which can be contemplated; and the mind which is brought into reverential and habitual contact with them, will grow rapidly in strength and comprehension. But not only does the Bible speak to us of God: it is God who speaks *to* us in its sacred pages. And, therefore, while other books may be read, this book *must* be read. Not to read it, is to contemn its Author. Not to read it, is to miss the manifold blessings, and to incur the fearful retributions, it reveals. There alone is the WAY OF SALVATION laid open, and that question, the most momentous which can engage the attention of a rational being, authoritatively answered, "What must I do to be saved?" Whatever may be neglected then, neglect not the faithful, systematic, devout study of the Sacred Scriptures. Ignorance of the Bible were not merely disreputable to you as men of intelligence: it would jeopard, and might destroy, your souls. And "what shall it profit a man if he shall gain the whole world, and lose his own soul!"

Lecture Ninth.

THE CLAIMS OF THE SABBATH UPON MERCHANTS.

A FEW days since, stepping into one of our great commercial houses, the floor of which was covered with boxes of merchandize awaiting transportation, I said to one of the clerks, calling him by name, "What would you young men do without a Sunday?" "What would we do?" he replied, "we could not do at all. It would be impossible for us to get on without Sunday in the other portions of the year; and not to have it at this season, would *break us right up* at once. It is indispensable to us," he added, "for physical rest, and a great deal more so that our minds may get repose from this care and anxiety which are so crushing to us." His appearance gave emphasis to every word he uttered. I had seen him at the commencement of "the season," and marked his fine, bright countenance and his elastic step. Again, in the interval I had seen him, and heard him say, on a Saturday afternoon — "I have not been in my bed until one or two o'clock, a single night this week." And now his cheek was blanched, he had become very thin, and his whole aspect and gait were stamped with lassitude and exhaustion.—I have cited him as a witness on this subject, because while he is a very estimable young man and a most faithful and efficient clerk, he is not, I believe, a professor of religion: and with a certain class of persons, this circumstance may impart additional weight to his testimony. But in truth, it would not be requisite to *select* witnesses in order to establish the necessity of a weekly rest. You would be safe in going at random into any of our Counting-Houses, or in polling the entire mercantile community on this question: — there could be but one response to the question, "Is Sunday essential to the proper prosecution of commercial business?" This, however, is but a partial statement of the truth. The Sabbath is not essential to the merchant only, but to men of every occupation, and of all climes and kindreds. This is the teaching alike of the Bible, of science, and of experience.

Our Saviour has affirmed it in that much-perverted saying, "The Sabbath was made for man, and not man for the Sabbath." (Mark 2: 27.) As the word Sabbath means a *rest*, this language implies that man *requires* a day of rest. He who "knew what was in man," foresaw that he would need a weekly respite from labour. Had he been differently constituted, or differently situated, this might possibly have been dispensed with; or instead of one-seventh, some other portion of his time might have been demanded for repose. But as he is, he must have a "rest-day"; and so his bountiful Creator has given him one. To quarrel with the Sabbath, therefore, is for a man to quarrel with his own constitution. And the people who declaim so much about this institution as an invention of "priestcraft," would be more rationally employed in inquiring how and why they came to be created with a physical and moral frame-work which would soon shiver to pieces without a Sabbath. If "priestcraft" *has* invented the Sabbath, it deserves for once their thanks rather than their maledictions. Let us hear an eminent scientific authority on the subject: —

"As a day of rest," says Dr. Farre, in his testimony before a Committee of the House of Commons, "I view it as a day of compensation for the inadequate restorative power of the body under continued labour and excitement. A physician always has respect to the preservation of the restorative power, because, if once this be lost, his healing office is at an end. If I show you from the physiological view of the question, that there are provisions in the laws of nature which correspond with the divine commandment, you will see from the analogy that 'the Sabbath was made for man' as a necessary appointment. A physician is anxious to preserve the balance of circulation, as necessary to the restorative power of the body. The ordinary exertions of man run down the circulation every day of his life; and the first general law of nature by which God (who is not only the giver, but also the preserver and sustainer, of life,) prevents man from destroying himself, is the alternating of day with night, that repose may succeed action. But although the night apparently equalizes the circulation well, yet it does not sufficiently restore its balance for the attainment of a long life. Hence one day in seven, by the bounty of Providence, is thrown in as a day of compensation, to perfect by its repose the animal system. Take that fine animal, the horse, and work him to the full extent of his powers every day in the week, or give him rest one day in seven, and you will soon perceive, by the superior vigour with which he performs his functions on the other six days, that this is necessary to his well-being. Man, possessing a superior nature, is borne along by the very vigour of his mind, so that the injury of continued diurnal exertion and excitement on his animal system, is not so immediately apparent as it is in the brute; but in the long run he breaks down more suddenly; it abridges the length of his life and that vigour of his old age which (as to mere animal power) ought to be the object of his preservation. I consider, therefore, that in the bountiful provision of Providence for the preservation of human life, the Sabbatical appointment is not, as it has been sometimes theologically viewed, simply a precept partaking of the nature of a political institution; but that it is to be numbered amongst the natural duties, if the preservation of life be admitted to be a duty, and the premature destruction of it a suicidal act. This is said simply as a Physician, and without reference at all to the theological question: but if you consider further the proper effect of real Christianity—namely, peace of mind, confiding trust in God, and good-will to man—you will perceive in this source of renewed vigour to the mind, and through the mind to the body, an additional spring of life imparted from this higher use of the Sabbath as a holy rest."

The principle elucidated in these philosophical observations, has been recognized by the worst enemies of the Sabbath. So thoroughly satisfied were the French Theophilanthropists, of the necessity of a day of rest, that when they abolished the Sabbath they replaced it with a *decade*, making every tenth day a holiday.

It follows from the argument just presented, that the Sabbath could have been no mere local or transitory enactment. The nature of man remaining unchanged, a restorative "rest-day" would be equally essential under all dispensations and among all nations. Accordingly, there are distinct traces of such an institute from the creation to the *exodus*: under the theocracy it was formally incorporated in the decalogue: the Saviour confirmed its authority: and from his ascension until now, Christendom has recognized it as an ordinance of God. The change from the seventh to the first day of the week (a point which the limits of this service forbid my entering into here), does not affect the essence of the institution. The vital thing—that which was originally appointed — that which was republished with fresh sanctions at Sinai — is, the "Sabbath," the "*rest-day.*" That which the human constitution demands, and has always demanded, is, a weekly rest extending, in the aggregate, over *one-seventh part* of man's allotted period upon earth. To use a familiar illustration, we might suppose a company of Christian tourists to start from Pittsburg and travel westward, until they had compassed the globe and returned to some isolated spot on the mountains within a few miles of their former home. If they had kept each Sabbath as it came, avoiding all intercourse with other Christians, and should now settle in their new abode without communicating at all with their neighbours, they would have lost a day by their journey, and we should have the anomaly of two adjacent communities, of the same faith, keeping the Christian Sabbath *on different days.* Can any one deny that the observance of these travellers would be a substantial accordance with the Sabbath-law, or doubt that it would be acceptable to God? It is not, then, incompatible with the original enactment, that the day should be changed — especially by the Lord of the Sabbath himself.

All this may be conceded by individuals who will, nevertheless, argue, that "as the Sabbath 'was made for man,' man must have a right to do what he chooses with it. If he sees fit to open his store and sell goods on that day, to send his mowers into the field with their scythes, to run his stages, to keep his journeymen at tanning, marble-dressing, building, weaving, or whatever his trade may be, no one may resist it as an infraction of the Sabbath. And if governments and corporations choose to keep canals and railways in operation, as well on the first day of the week as on the other six, they are not contravening the Sabbath-law."

This, however, will depend on the *design* of the law. No sweeping conclusions like these can be deduced from the proposition that "the Sabbath was made for man." You may say to your son: "Here is a watch which I have had made for you." Would that authorize him to throw the watch into the sea, or to take it to pieces and use the machinery in patching together his broken toys? You may erect a costly mansion, and say to your bridal daughter: "I have built and furnished this house for you, as a wedding-present." Would this justify her in setting fire to it, or in renting it for a grocery-store? You may say to one of your clerks: "I have had this additional ware-room constructed expressly for you, and I wish you to take charge of it." Would this warrant him in storing other people's goods there, or in trafficking in articles which you disapproved of and which might damage you in business and reputation? — Neither does it follow, because God has made the Sabbath for you, that you may do what you please with it; — especially as he has in fact made it over to you *in trust* only, and without divesting himself of his own right in it. In the deed by which He has conveyed it to you, the general uses to which it is to be applied, are carefully specified. It is to be a *holy rest* — a day of religious worship — a day specifically dedicated to God and the soul. Yet not so rigidly spiritual as to preclude any and all non-spiritual offices in all conceivable circumstances. There are secular matters which may be attended to on the Sabbath. But what they are, it is *His* prerogative, not ours, to decide. And He has decided. He has settled the principle, by his teaching and his example, that *works of necessity and mercy* are not in derogation of the sacredness of the day. Beyond this, no man can go without usurping a control over the whole institution, and impugning the right of the "Lord of the Sabbath," to say how it shall be kept. There is no intermediate ground. If the Bible is not to be recognized as the paramount authority, as well in respect to the *exceptions* as to the rule itself, then the rule is a nullity and the Sabbath a figment. For what does the command, "Remember the Sabbath-day, to keep it holy," amount to, if each man may bend the day to his own caprices? The principle which would sanction your trafficking on that day, would no less legitimate the military reviews and public amusements to which Sunday is appropriated in most of the European capitals. Any one who has spent a week in Paris, must know what we might expect if this mode of interpreting the declaration, "the Sabbath was made for man," should become prevalent in this country. But the Bible has not thus stultified itself by ordaining a law, and then allowing every individual to put what construction upon it he chooses. The Lawgiver has expounded his own statute. And under this authority, our secularities on that day are restricted to the two classes of offices just specified. Whether any proposed service be a work of "necessity" or of "mercy," we must decide for ourselves, under our responsibility to God. To abuse this liberty by turning the Sabbath into a day of pastime or of needless toil, is to practise a paltry deception upon our own consciences, and to insult the Deity. The spirit of the divine legislation on this subject, any candid inquirer will readily comprehend; and the more such an one investigates it, the clearer will become his conviction of the unbounded wisdom and goodness involved in this whole economy of a perpetual weekly Sabbath.

There is another serious error in the reasoning of

the plea I have quoted. Because "the Sabbath was made for man," if your interest as individuals or as corporators in a joint-stock company appears to require it, you may exact of your clerks and journeymen, your steamboat crews and railroad servitors, any amount of Sabbath labour which you see fit. So you argue: but with bad logic and worse humanity. If "the Sabbath (the *rest-day*) was made for *man*," who gave you the right to monopolize it? These book-keepers and salesmen and packers and porters — are they not *men?* These engineers and conductors and stokers and switch-tenders and baggage-masters and machinists and depôt-keepers — are they not *men?* And if they are, was not the day of rest made for them as well as for you? It is nothing to the purpose that you are rich and they are poor; or that you are principals and they subordinates. With God, there is no respect of persons. And if He *made* the Sabbath for "man" — for every man, and for one man as much as for another — it is to be presumed He will not regard with indifference any attempt on the part of the opulent or the powerful to intercept from the poor, the boon He has intended for them. Their right to it is as indisputable as your own. They do not receive it from you. It is not yours to give; and if you cannot confer it, you cannot take it away. God has bestowed it upon them and upon you alike, as he has the atmosphere and the light; and it is an invasion of His prerogative, to deprive them of their chartered rest. The title under which they hold it, is paramount to all human compacts: older than any patent of nobility, above all crowns and constitutions. The image and superscription upon it, are those of the KING OF KINGS AND LORD OF LORDS; and, as if to impress upon it a sacredness still more awful, it is sealed with "BLOOD DIVINE." By such an instrument is a weekly rest guaranteed to all your helpers and subordinates, from your confidential cashier down to your errand-boy. By such an instrument is it secured to all the tribes of labour — to the men who wheel upon the wharves, to the operatives in every mill, the mechanics and apprentices in every shop, the clerks in every Post-office, the working staff of every canal and railroad. The Sabbath is no gratuity bestowed upon them by their employers. Their employers have it for themselves by virtue of their being *men*, but it is not theirs to give away. GOD has given it to every *man;* and they would do well not to interfere with His gift.

The pretension against which I am arguing, is, indeed, monstrous. It is the deliberate assumption of a right to invalidate a Divine grant! to wrest from a large portion of the human race, a priceless possession which they hold directly from God himself! I say, "from a large portion of the race," and it is even so. For if the principle contended for be admitted, that the affluent and the great may constrain (and *moral* means may be so used as to amount to coercion) the dependent classes to work for them on the Sabbath, where no office of "necessity or mercy" is involved, then the weekly rest which was "made for man," may come to be the exclusive appendage of those who are blessed with wealth or station; and these are a mere fraction of any community. Nor is this all. The motive which prompts to this oppression of the poor — the entire basis upon which this usurpation of the Divine prerogative rests — is, a sordid self-interest. It is to inflame still more the feverish excitement of commerce and increase its gains, to make the rich richer and the poor poorer, that large bodies of deserving men are to be robbed of the rest-day which God *made* for them. Avarice is never satisfied. It might have been supposed, that when science and art had brought the remote portions of a country like this into juxta-position, and, in the matter of travelling and transportation, well-nigh condensed days into hours, the trade-spirit would be content to pause for one day out of seven, and let all its servants enjoy the repose the Creator had provided for them. But so far from this, the disposition is to make every new railroad a fresh instrument of Sabbath-desecration. The faster goods travel, the faster they *must* travel. The traffickers from the country, who would certainly reach the city or their homes on Monday, are not satisfied with this: they must "save a day" by travelling on Sunday. With a similar economy of time, the metropolitan merchant takes Sunday for his transit to or from a contiguous city. "Business requires it." Excuse me for telling you, that you are mistaken. As a general rule, business does *not* require it. Legitimate business never can require that you should habitually desecrate the Sabbath, and deprive some scores or hundreds of your fellow-men of their chartered rest. It is cupidity that requires it. It would make more money, or make it faster: and in this greediness after gain, it does not scruple to tyrannise over those whose circumstances place them at its mercy, and to wrest from them the only day of the seven which they can call their own.

I would press home upon you, your own favourite text, "the Sabbath was made for man." It *was* made for man; and if you consider how invaluable it is to those who are consigned to a life of toil, you will feel that it must be a flagrant wrong to despoil them of it. The human constitution, as has been shown, demands this periodic rest. Men who have to labour without it, are sure to break down and die.

I do not ask, will Christian principle, but, will common humanity, justify us in prosecuting business on any plan which must be fatal to the health and the lives of our fellow-creatures? And if you take away the Sabbath, what time has the labourer for his family? It may be a light thing for *you* to go off on a Sunday from your homes. But look out of your window of a morning, and see these men, after a hurried breakfast, before their children are up, hastening to their work, each one carrying a basket or kettle with his noon-day lunch; and see them again returning, after sun-down, fagged and weary, and much fitter for bed than for the companionship of their families: — and say, whether such men ought to be denied the only day they can devote to domestic affection and household joys. The Sabbath is, under God, one of the main ramparts which guard the poor-man's habitation from the exactions of power and the rapacity of avarice. And to subvert this, is to rob him of his HOME.

"Hail, Sabbath! thee I hail, the poor man's day.
On other days the man of toil is doom'd
To eat his joyless bread, lonely, the ground
Both seat and board, screen'd from the winter's cold
And summer's heat by neighbouring hedge or tree;
But on this day, embosomed in his home,
He shares the frugal meal with those he loves;
With those he loves he shares the heartfelt joy
Of giving thanks to God."

This scene has been described by a "Labourer's Daughter" as no one could depict it except from experience. I will quote from her sketch but a single paragraph, as the volume is within the reach of all, and eminently worthy to be read of all.*

"What a delightful scene of tranquil enjoyment is to be met with in the family of the labourer where the Sabbath is properly appreciated and actively improved! Has the reader ever spent a Lord's day in such a family? Has he seen the children, awaking from the light slumbers of the morning, glance round on the more than usual order, cleanliness, and quiet of the humble apartment, and then ask, 'Mother, what day is this?' and heard the reply, 'This is the Sabbath, the best of all days, the day which God has blessed!' Has he seen their father dandling the baby, till their mother should finish dressing the elder children, and then, when all were ready, heard the little circle join in the sweet morning hymn, and seen them kneel together, while their father offered up a simple but heartfelt thanksgiving for life, health, and reason preserved, through the toils of another week; and for the privilege of being again all permitted to enjoy, in each other's society, the blessed light of the first day of the week; that morning light which brings to mind an empty grave and a risen Saviour; those peaceful hours, which, undisturbed by the labour, hurry, and anxieties of the week, they can devote to the advancement of that spiritual life in their souls, which

---

* See "*Prize-Essays on the Temporal Advantages of the Sabbath,*" by *Working Men:* which also includes the "*Pearl of Days*, by a *Labourer's Daughter.*" Presb. Board of Pub lication.

shall outlive the destruction of death itself? Has he heard the words of prayer, the questions of the father, and the replies of the children; and has he not felt assured that the mind-awakening influences of such subjects of thought, and such exercises, would be seen in the after-years of these children?"

This last thought would bear to be expanded — "the mind-awakening influences" of the Sabbath, not only in its domestic, but in its public, religious services. For it is no less the chief means of mental improvement to the labourer, than his indispensable season of physical repose. But above all these, it supplies him with his only adequate opportunities for spiritual culture and preparation for eternity. This is so apparent, that it would be a waste of words to *prove*, that to subject the labouring classes, or *any* class, to habitual toil on the Lord's day, is, to cut them off from the sanctuary, to deprive them of the requisite leisure for the study of the Bible, to subvert their religious principles, and, under ordinary circumstances, to corrupt their morals and destroy their souls.

But some one may be ready to exclaim — "What is all this to us? Why address *Merchants* on the importance of the Sabbath to the poor?" I answer, because most of the usages which go to deprive the poor of their Sabbath, have the sanction of the commercial body. To advert to a topic repeatedly mentioned — *the railroads of the United States are, for the most part, controlled by its merchants.* It is at your bidding that the Post-office is made an exception to the rule which regulates every other department of the government, and its incumbents deprived of the rest enjoyed by all other public servants. It is your merchandize (I address the profession as a whole) which sends these long trains of freight-cars along the rails on the Sabbath. It is your patronage, beyond that of any other class of citizens, that sustains the "passenger-trains" on Sundays. Whenever an effort is made to suspend the Sunday-traffic on any particular road, it is commerce that remonstrates against it. It has even claimed in some instances, that a road should be kept in operation on that day, although, on its own concession, the passenger-trains would have to be run at a positive pecuniary loss — the pretext being, that the suspension of the trains might divert travel to other lines. The only medium through which this great moral question is contemplated, is that of business and profits. The improvement and comfort of the working people and their families, go for nothing. The authority of God goes for nothing. Commerce, uninstructed by religion, has but one standard of value, and casts all commodities, from iron and cotton up to ethics and devotion, into the same scales, —

"Nor is it well, nor can it come to good,
That through profane and infidel contempt
Of Holy Writ, she has presumed t' annul
And abrogate, as roundly as she may,
The total ordinance and will of God,"

and to degrade the Sabbath, in so far as "business" may seem to demand it, to a mere secular day. This "cannot come to good" even as regards her own affairs. It is demonstrable that the general and permanent prosperity of any country, in a simply commercial view, will be promoted by a due observance of the Sabbath. This is implied in the argument already presented on the Sabbath-law as being founded in the very structure of the human constitution. It is no less evident from the intimate connexion between the business of a people and the state of the public morals, and the dependence of this, again, upon the respect paid to the Sabbath. It is of the last importance to the mercantile body, that the country should be pervaded with a healthful morality. Whatever lowers the tone of integrity, multiplies the discomforts of trade and augments its losses. If you do anything to impair the general reverence for the Supreme Being and for his law, you are counterworking your own pecuniary interests: and, sooner or later, unlooked-for delinquencies and frauds among your customers or clerks, may remind you of your error. But the desecration of the Sabbath is a measure of this sort — and one of the most decisive you could put your hands to. For the preservation of religion and virtue among a people, depends essentially, under Providence, upon the Sabbath. Christianity has her Bible, her sanctuaries, her systems of religious education, her munificent array of benevolent institutions: but what are all these without a day of rest? The Sabbath is *the* PLATFORM *on which this whole machinery stands;* and to strike that down, would be well-nigh to paralyze the agencies by which the Gospel is carrying forward its sublime mission of regenerating the world. If men loved Christianity, the case were different. But they do not love her. They will not of themselves seek her out and supplicate her blessings. She must come *to them*, as her Divine Founder came from heaven to "to seek and to save that which was lost"; and to do this, she must have a season appropriated to the purpose, a day set apart by authority, when business shall intermit its traffickings and pleasure its frivolities, and politics its debates, and housewifery its toil, and all the tribes and conditions of humanity be allowed to pause and listen to the *voice of God* as He speaks to them in His Word. The Sabbath supplies this opportunity. It is in itself a most wholesome and impressive memorial of a superintending Providence. The tranquil wharves of a Sabbath-keeping city, the long rows of closed warehouses, the peaceful streets, the silent Banks and Exchange, all proclaim that THERE IS A GOD. This weekly rest is a *Witness* for Him in a world which is perpetually prone to forget Him. It is a Witness to his power, in the work of creation and in the resurrection of Christ; to his wisdom, in ordaining this season of repose; to his goodness and grace, in providing its manifold benefits; and to his sovereignty, in the right he herein challenges to control our time and all our affairs. — If just conceptions of the Deity are essential to sound morality, then must it be admitted that the Sabbath is one of the main buttresses of the public morals.

Again, experience has shown, that Sabbath-keeping is friendly to all the virtues, while Sabbath-desecration readily affiliates with all the vices. Dealing with men in masses, those who observe this day in the spirit of the institution, will usually be found on the side of industry, frugality, honesty, intelligence, and good citizenship; while those who habitually profane it, will generally be more or less addicted to idleness, fraud, prodigality, swearing, intemperance, or other vices. The true way to secure trust-worthy clerks and faithful warehouse-men, to gather around your great establishments a body of subordinates and helpers who can be relied upon in all exigencies, and who will do your work thoroughly and cheerfully, is, to encourage all in your employ to honour the Sabbath. Loyalty to God is the best guarantee of fidelity to man. And he who can trample upon a Divine command, has weakened, if not subverted, the principle which binds him to be upright in his dealings with his neighbours.

On a still broader view, this "rest-day" has an imperative claim upon the citizens of this country. It is scarcely a figure to characterize it as the palladium of our liberties. The historical fact is of pregnant import, that despots, whether political or sacerdotal, have always been hostile to the evangelical Sabbath. It was in logical harmony with the whole genius of the Stuart dynasty, that James I., and, after him, Charles I., should attempt to break down the Sabbath by imposing the "Book of Sports" upon the British people. It is in keeping with the spirit which controls, and has always controlled, the European despotisms, that they should encourage their subjects to turn the Sabbath into a day of amusement. A nation that moils for six days and frolicks the seventh, is about as fit material for a tyrant as could be desired. But a tyrant could do nothing with a people who had free access to the Bible, and assembled every Sunday in their sanctuaries to listen to the faithful preaching of the Gospel. Such a people would have too much intelligence to wear the yoke of an oppressor. They would understand their rights and have the courage to assert them. Neither crown nor mitre could terrify them into a servile submission to wrong, nor put off their demand for their proper franchises with a sop of beggarly amusements. This is but too well understood in the countries referred to. In Spain, in Austria, in France, in Italy, the grand policy of the reigning authorities, civil and ecclesiastical, is to keep the people in ignorance of the Bible; to deny them all instructive preaching, prevent even the private study of the Scriptures, and make the Sabbath (after the morning service!) a scene of mirth and dissipation. If we are to preserve and transmit to other times, a government the reverse of all these — a government, free, just, enlightened, beneficent in all its tendencies, and supported, not by the bayonets of a standing army, native or *foreign*,* but by the generous affections of its citizens, we must reverse the means and implements of their policy, and secure to our entire population an OPEN BIBLE and a SCRIPTURAL SABBATH. This will be no precarious defence against domestic usurpation and foreign aggression, against the turbulence of faction and the violence of anarchy, against the

* Look at the Papal throne.

subtleties of priestcraft and the ravings of atheism. That all these evil agencies should be hostile to the Christian Sabbath in its true import, is a fact which deserves to be pondered by candid and patriotic men of whatever sect or party: it might help to open the eyes of some who have inconsiderately discountenanced measures designed to rescue "the Lord's day" from desecration. In every aspect in which the question can be viewed, they will find that this invaluable institution is identified no less with all our material interests as a nation, than with the improvement and happiness of individuals and families.

I know not how these general views may impress the minds of the Merchants whom it is my privilege to address, but it will be proper to show that the Sabbath has other and more direct claims upon your homage: — I mean, a Sabbath kept in the true spirit of this divine ordinance. You might yield a vague assent to the reasonings which have been urged, and reckon yourselves among the friends of the Sabbath, while, nevertheless, you would deem it no infraction of the fourth commandment, to appropriate the day, or a considerable portion of it, to the posting of books, to your commercial correspondence, to the revision of your plans or the projecting of new ones, or to a journey to some neighbouring city. But this is not keeping the Sabbath. The command is, "Remember the Sabbath-day to *keep it holy.*" This surely imports something more than that you are not to open your Counting-Houses and require the attendance of your clerks and porters, and make that day in all respects like the other six. No merchant can do this in our cities without losing *caste* among his brethren. It is not deemed *respectable* to do it; and it were, therefore, a very equivocal sort of compliment to applaud a man for abstaining from it. The commercial sentiment still sanctions the transaction of Post-office business on the Sabbath, although without any adequate reason. In particular cases this is, of course, proper: "necessity or mercy" may demand it, and to proscribe it in such instances, were to be "righteous over-much." But there is no sufficient reason for converting the exception into the rule. If there is any city in the world which requires a general delivery on Sunday, it must be the financial centre of the world, London. It is preposterous to claim in behalf of any community, an extent of Post-office accommodation beyond that which satisfies the two millions of that great capital. And they are satisfied with having their Post-office closed on the Sabbath. This was demonstrated three years ago in the most conclusive manner, by the memorials sent up to Parliament from the metropolis, in favour of closing all the Post-offices throughout the United Kingdom on that day. These petitions, which were very emphatic in their language, were signed by many thousands of citizens, including nearly all the principal bankers and merchants. If the commerce of London thrives under an arrangement of this kind, that of Philadelphia or New York would not suffer from a similar one.*

---

* As a specimen of the papers alluded to, I subjoin one which was circulated among the London BANKERS. Similar "Declarations" were signed by the leading Mercantile firms, the principal Surgeons and Solicitors, and the Aldermen, of the Metropolis. This honourable example of a great commercial community coming forward to secure to the public servants in the numerous Post-offices of the realm an *unbroken Sabbath*, is in striking contrast with the spirit displayed on the same question in some of our own cities. May it not be hoped that something of this magnanimity will yet be exhibited on this side of the water?

DECLARATION.

LONDON, *January*, 1850.

We, the undersigned, being strongly impressed with a belief that there exists no greater necessity to justify the transaction of the ordinary business of receiving and delivering letters on the Sabbath-day, in any of the Post-offices of the United Kiugdom, than in those of the Metropolis, do hereby earnestly request her Majesty's Government to take into immediate consideration, the expediency and propriety of causing the same to be discontinued, by ordering the Post-offices in the country to be altogether closed on that day.

This belief is grounded on the following facts: —

1. That the Metropolis, containing a population of 2,200,000 souls, has never experienced any necessity for the opening of the Metropolitan Post-offices on Sundays.

But I have no intention to discuss this topic. I am simply insisting upon a faithful dedication of the Sabbath to its legitimate uses, as an object of the greatest moment to the commercial body. My young

2. That the great acceleration which has recently taken place in the postal communications throughout the empire, must necessarily diminish, to a very great extent, any inconvenience which it might otherwise be supposed would arise from closing the Provincial Post-offices on Sunday.

And believing that the effectual preservation of a seventh day of rest from their ordinary labour, is a principle of vital importance to the physical and social well-being of the poorer classes of society, whilst the due observance of the Lord's day is a duty of solemn obligation upon all classes of the community, we agree to take such measures as may appear best calculated to press the foregoing considerations on the attention of the Government and the Legislature.

Baring Brothers,
Williams, Deacon & Co.
Hankeys & Co.
Barclay, Bevan, Tritton & Co.
Jones, Lloyd & Co.
Masterman, Peters & Co.
Robarts, Curtis & Co.
Smith, Payne & Smiths,
Denison & Co.
Price, Marryatt & Co.
Barnett, Hoares & Co.
Hanbury, Taylor & Lloyd,
Rogers, Olding & Co.
Bosanquet, Franks & Co.
Spooner, Attwood & Co.
Brown, Janson & Co.
Sapte, Muspratt, Bunbury & Co.
Fullers & Co.
Barnard, Barnard & Dimsdale,
Drewett & Fowler,
Cunliffes & Co.
H. E. Gurney,
Samuel Gurney, Jun.
A. & G. W. Alexander & Co.
Charles Hoare & Co.
Goslings & Sharpe,
Child & Co.
Praeds and Co.
Dixon, Brooks & Dixon.
Strahan & Co.
R. Twining & Co.
Herries, Farquhar & Co.
Ransom & Co.
Bouverie & Co.
Charles Hopkinson & Co.

friend whom I quoted in the opening of this Lecture, spoke of its absolute necessity to the merchant and his coadjutors as a season of physical rest. But it is (as he, indeed, intimated) far more than this. It is an institution demanded by our *intellectual* nature. Repose is as essential to the mind as to the body. A British writer has observed, "We never knew a man work seven days in a week, who did not kill himself or kill his mind." The records of our Insane Asylums will supply painful confirmation of this remark. Scores of merchants have paid, in these Institutions, the penalty of a devotion to business which robbed them of their weekly rest. The brain will not bear the continued tension of the Counting-room — the feverish excitement of an insatiate craving after wealth. It gets dizzy with looking for ever at figures and calculations, flitting from one speculation to another, counting its losses, anticipating its gains, contriving new schemes, plotting and counter-plotting against competitors, all its energies on the stretch, all its time swallowed up, its whole being concentrated in the one inexorable passion of accumulation; — how is it possible that the brain *should* stand all this? "I should have been a dead man," said a distinguished financier and capitalist, referring to the memorable epoch of '37, "had it not been for the Sabbath. Obliged to work from morning till night through the whole week, I felt on Saturday, especially on Saturday afternoon, as if I *must* have rest. It was like going into a dense fog. Everything looked dark and gloomy, as if nothing could be saved. I dismissed all, and kept the Sabbath in the good old way. On Monday it was all sunshine. But had it not been for the Sabbath, I have no doubt I should have been in my grave." There was sound philosophy as well as piety in his course. Some men would have said he "lost a day" every week by it. He knew that *a clear head* for six days, would be of more value to him than an additional twenty-four hours with an overtasked and distracted brain; and he took the only way to secure it. The common mistake lies in overlooking this. Amidst the whirl of business, confounded with the magnitude and variety of the cares which are pressing upon you, the only want you are conscious of, is "more time." And so, when you have used up all your own days, you seize upon that day which your beneficent Creator has reserved to Himself, (or, which is the same thing, given to you *in trust*,) and appropriate this also to your purposes. The Sunday you have taken to mature an "operation," to write some important financial letters, to hold a conference with certain friendly brokers, to make a trip to New York or Harrisburg — is jotted down in your memoranda as so much "clear gain."

But no good ever comes, in the long run, of taking what does not belong to us. What you have "gained" in time, you have more than lost in the violence done to your mental frame-work, and your consequent incapacity (comparatively speaking) to administer wisely the interests you have in hand. The point does not admit of proof, but if a guess may be allowed, the failure of many a firm is to be charged to the Sunday-lines on our railroads. I do not allude to those "Excursion-trains" so needful, as certain philanthropists contend, to the "relaxation" of the working-classes, which often bring back their passengers at evening, draggled and worn out, and all the worse in health, purse, and morals, for their day's "pleasuring." I speak of the strictly business-jaunts of mercantile men, who, to "save time," turn the Sabbath into a day of travel. It must frequently happen with others, as with the financier just quoted, that Saturday afternoon finds their affairs all in a "fog," or, in any event, finds *them* so weary or so excited, as to be quite disqualified for the calm solution of any commercial problem. If they were content to use their "rest-day" *as* a rest, its hallowed influences would recruit their strength, allay their perturbation, restore their powers to their proper balance, and prepare them to grapple with difficulties on Monday in a very different condition from that in which they retired to their homes on Saturday evening. But suppose they carry their perplexities (or their brilliant projects of self-aggrandizement, as the case may be,) to their pillows, pore over them all their Sabbath morning, with the same servile and absorbing devotion they lavished upon them through the week, and, in the afternoon, throw themselves into the cars and hurry off to New York to consummate on the morrow, the measures they have digested:—will it be a strange thing if, in the sequel, a policy thus begotten shall prove an opprobrium and a vexation to its authors? And can it be doubted, that this precise form of Sabbath-breaking has had a potential agency in the ruin of very many of the firms which have become bankrupt in our cities? A candid investigation of our commercial disasters, could not fail to set in its true light this too popular expedient for "saving a day." It would show our merchants, that in the long run, all the days thus "saved," were pretty certain to gravitate to the debit side of the Profit and Loss Account. And it might satisfy them of what they are so "slow of heart to believe" on the authority of the Bible, that success and failure even in temporal matters, are closely interwoven with the manner in which the Sabbath is observed. (See Isa. 56: 2. 58: 13, 14. Neh. 13: 15—22, and various parallel passages.)

This, however, is but a part of the truth. A well-spent Sabbath does much more for the mind than secure to it needful rest and refreshment. It helps to counteract that cramping and mercenary tendency so often alluded to, as incident to a life of trafficking. It supplies in a measure those opportunities for intellectual culture, the want of which merchants so frequently deplore — and *that*, without their resorting to any pursuits which are incompatible with the sacredness of the day. A simple change of scene or occupation is useful to all the powers. Our perceptive and reasoning faculties, if kept to a monotonous routine of subjects, lose either their vigour or their symmetry. You can well understand what sort of a mind a boy would have, who should study nothing but arithmetic, or nothing but orthography, from one year's end to another. And the case must be still worse with an individual whose whole time and thoughts are absorbed from New Year's to Christmas in buying and selling. Every merchant knows the relief derived from a summer's excursion into the country or to the sea-shore. You return from these rambles not simply with improved health, but with a sensible increase of mental activity and energy. Fresh air and exercise have done their share of this; but they have not done it all. Instead of looking for ever at Ledgers, and counters, and shelves of ginghams and calicoes, and packing-boxes, and drays, you have been looking upon the green fields, and the ocean, and the starry firmament. You have been sauntering through the woods, climbing mountains, displaying your awkward equestrianism on country horses, riding in waggons without springs over country roads, making hay with the farmers for amusement, shooting, angling, sailing, bathing, sleeping — watching the endless phases of human life at a watering-place— the grave, the gay, the consequential, the profound, the taciturn, the flippant, the choice few whose sterling worth and attractive manners make a ready place for them in every group and coterie — and you have come back from your rustication, all the better for the very trifles which have served to amuse you. The secret of this, is, that you have thrown off for a while the drag-chain of business, and given mind and body a holiday. Your established trains of thought have been broken in upon. Goods and customers and discounts and bills payable, and the other common-places which constitute your daily intellectual rations during so large a portion of the year, have been replaced, for the time, with condiments of a very different character. New objects have called dormant powers into exercise. The indomitable trade-spirit has been mitigated by a larger development of the social sympathies. Taste and imagination have begun to flutter their pinions. And you have returned to your Counting-Houses, with broader views of life and a juster consciousness of your powers, than you had before you took this vacation.

Let this illustrate what the SABBATH will do for you — what it actually is doing for all who keep it properly. One of its most obvious and uniform effects, is to enlarge one's horizon. As you sit from day to day in your counting-rooms, or make your diurnal visit to the Exchange, or lose yourselves in abstruse calculations, or hurry through one transaction after another with your customers and agents, you are very apt to suppose that what you see and hear and feel around you, is *the world;* that this great domain of commerce, ("great," as you view it,) comprises the centre and circumference of your being; and that, so matters prosper here, you need not concern yourselves about objects and interests which "lie beyond." The day of rest dispels this illusion. It takes you to an eminence which shows you how insignificant a portion of "the world" the realm of merchandize is, and how fatally you wrong your own intellectual nature, by shutting it up among the ships and spindles of commerce. Not only does it suspend the current of secular thought and feeling which is wearing such deep and jagged channels into your moral being through the week, but the themes it offers to your contemplation, are the noblest to which the human mind can be directed. "The instruction dispensed on this day" (I use the eloquent language of a Working-man) "is of a character calculated to expand, refine, and sublimate the mind. It embraces a boundless range of topics, from the simplest elements of knowledge appreciable by the dullest intellect, to the most recondite mysteries that baffle the highest reason. It unseals the fountain-head of truth in the nature of God. It unlocks the treasures of divine philosophy in creation, in providence, and in redemption. It impresses into its sacred service whatever is beautiful in nature, grand in science, and instructive in art; whatever is pure in ethics, lovely in virtue, and sublime in revelation; whatever is monitory in the past, perilous in the present, and inspiriting in the future. It leads the mind backward to the ages before the flood, to the paradisaical state of man, to the origin of the universe, and thence to the vast solitudes of a past eternity; or it urges the shrinking spirit forwards through the valley of the shadow of death — through the dark and populous empire of the grave — into the august presence of the Judge of all the earth — to the home of the beatified — to the pandemonium of the wicked — and outwards into the immensities of the everlasting future! It addresses itself to all the faculties and passions of the soul; it illumines the understanding, sobers the judgment, thrills the heart, softens the feelings, energises the conscience, and sanctifies the deepest affections of our mysterious nature." *

It is impossible for any person of the least candour to contemplate this process, without feeling that a well-spent Sabbath is of the highest value in promoting the intellectual culture of individuals and the general diffusion of knowledge among a community.

Its importance to the mercantile classes in another view, as restoring them for one day in seven *to their families*, and giving them, even at the busiest seasons, opportunities for those domestic duties and enjoyments of which they are much of the time deprived, must be too apparent to escape notice. This is, in fact, one of the most interesting and grateful aspects in which the *Merchant's Sabbath* can be viewed. No man need be a stranger in his own house, nor a cipher in respect to the training of his children, who has his periodical day of rest at his control. Nor are there any families bound together by such tender and enduring ties, as those which appreciate these weekly "re-unions," and keep the day in a spirit of cheerful piety and true household fellowship.

But I must waive this theme for another still more important. The danger which waits upon you in all

---

* "*Heaven's Antidote to the Curse of Labour*": the First of the "Prize-Essays on the Sabbath."

the walks of trade — the sin which spreads its toils around your feet, and beguiles you onward in the road to ruin — is that of *neglecting your salvation.* The tempter plies you with the insidious plea, that you have "no time" for religion, until you come at length to believe this with a confidence which repels alike the solicitations of the Gospel and the warnings of Providence. It would be very easy to expose the fallacy of this notion even as regards the six working days: for it were wiser and better to neglect business, property, family, *everything* earthly, than to neglect the soul. But it is not necessary to do this. Christianity does not demand it: its tendency is, rather, to make men better merchants, better husbands and fathers, better citizens, and more thoroughly qualified for the duties proper to these relations. And, then, as if to meet this very difficulty of a "want of time" for your spiritual concerns, it has given you the weekly rest to be appropriated primarily to these interests. Foreseeing that business, if permitted, would monopolize your whole time, and cheat you out of all opportunity to prepare for heaven, God was pleased to put the seal of a peculiar sacredness upon every seventh day, and to convey it to you in trust for this specific purpose. He "made the Sabbath" for you, that you might not have it to say, "I have *no time* to repent and make my peace with God."

He shut it in from the encroachments of avarice, from the usurpations of ambition, from the seductions of sensual pleasure, from the exactions of authority, from the turbulence and impiety of a selfish, grasping, atheistic world, from all the multitudinous influences which are combined to keep man in an interminable subjection to sin and Satan — he shut it in by his own omnipotence, that you, and all his creatures, might be able constantly to recruit your strength for the duties and temptations of life, and to prepare for death, judgment, and eternity. So munificent a gift should be faithfully applied to its prescribed objects. To pervert or neglect it, is to superadd the guilt of a base ingratitude, to the criminality of a most perilous neglect of your own souls. The Sabbath comes to you as a messenger of mercy, as the harbinger of peace and hope and heaven. It spreads before you those sacred pages written all over with words of truth and grace, and supplying the only chart which can conduct you to the skies. It brings you to the Sanctuary that you may hear of God and redemption, of heaven and hell, of the "great white throne" and the awards of eternity. It leads you into your chambers, that you may "commune with your own hearts," and invoke the Divine Spirit to cleanse you from sin with the blood of the cross and make you sincere and humble followers of Christ. It places you in the midst of your households, and, while it enkindles your mutual affection, revives the impression of your responsibility as well for their spiritual as their secular training. It admonishes you of your stewardship, and shows you whose hand it is that has prospered you, and to what uses it behooves you to appropriate your wealth. It deadens your grovelling attachments, refines and elevates your feelings, brings you into fellowship with the wisest and best of the race, and makes you "co-workers with God" himself in saving and blessing a lost world.—All this the Sabbath does for every one who remembers it, "to keep it holy." Many among you have found it so in your own experience. Let those who have hitherto neglected it, make the trial, and they will learn, as they never learned before, the import of that saying, "THE SABBATH WAS MADE FOR MAN!"

Lecture Tenth.

THE TRUE RICHES.—LIVING TO DO GOOD.

In the progress of these Lectures, I have had frequent occasion to refer to the subject of *retiring from business*. This phrase has a definitive signification, which is well understood. As a practical question, it is frequently involved in great embarrassment; but there are few Merchants who would willingly give up the hope of being one day released from the cares and responsibilities of the Counting-House. To prepare for this change is, with many of you, the grand employment of life; and you are impatiently reckoning the years which must elapse, before you can have amassed a fortune which will justify you in renouncing the bustling domain of commerce, for the repose and comfort of a genial Home. I censure not these longings. I see but one thing to condemn in your calculations. It is, that you are apt to restrict your views of "retiring from business," to so narrow a compass, and to make your arrangements for the thing itself on so meagre and insufficient a scale. You think of it only as a matter of choice — as the privilege of the favoured few who may rise to affluence — and as comprising merely the evening of an active life. But the words may fairly be taken to mean a great deal more than this. You are *all* to "retire from business" — whether you desire it or not — and your season of respite will have no measurement short of the cycles of ETERNITY! When it is added, that this discharge from the pursuits which now engross you, may come at any moment — long before you may be "ready" to give up business — the question will be set before you in something of the grandeur and solemnity which really belong to it.

If this be sober verity, and not fiction, it is the most obvious and urgent duty of every individual, to inquire into his state of preparation for the scenes before him. You have known men give up merchandize prematurely, leaving their affairs involved, or with resources quite inadequate to their support: and you have had your own opinions as to their prudence and sagacity. But what would be your condition, if an unseen power should now interpose and withdraw you from life itself? Are you equipped for that realm to which life is the mere vestibule? Have you laid by a competence of those

"TRUE RICHES" which will avail for your support and comfort there? Or, are you guilty of the neglect you rebuke in others, the only difference being that their improvidence has respect to this transitory state, yours, to the endless future of the soul?

You will not, in reply to questions like these, point to your capacious warehouses, your well-filled coffers, your elegant mansions, and your honourable position in the community. This might answer, if the inquiry were, "Shall we now 'retire' for the few remaining years or days that may remain to us of life?" But what have these matters to do with retiring for ETERNITY? Who is so visionary as to think of transferring the implements and avocations of commerce to that world? or of resuming there the strife for the gold which perisheth? Our great Epic Poet, in his sketch of that sublime spectacle, the Council in Pandemonium, has, indeed, made Mammon say,

"This desert soil
Wants not her hidden lustre, gems and gold;
Nor want we skill or art from whence to raise
Magnificence; and what can Heaven show more?"

But the only Teacher empowered to speak of that world, has presented us with another portraiture eminently affecting and suggestive — that of a man once "clothed in purple and fine linen," lifting up his eyes in torment, and pleading in vain for a drop of water! This spectacle may stand in place of a thousand homilies, to illustrate the madness of living merely to acquire wealth and revel in luxury. There can be no greater folly than for a man to place his happiness in objects and interests from which he must soon be for ever ravished. The loss of his idols, painful as that may be, is but a small part of the inevitable penalty of his error. The blow which strips him of his possessions, leaves his whole moral being under the sway of those evil passions which have long tyrannised over him. He goes into eternity, the wretched minion of avarice, or at least the bond-slave of a sordid secularity — all his principles, all his habits, all his aims, susceptibilities, and desires, adjusted to this world, and utterly alien from the constitution of things in the spiritual empire of which he is henceforth to be a denizen. Could he destroy his identity, or annihilate his memory, existence might be tolerable. But this cannot be. The passions he has nurtured into such gigantic strength, are a part of his being; and now, deprived of their proper external objects, and energized by an avenging conscience, they will turn upon the soul with unmitigable fury, and "their torment will be as the torment of a scorpion." For it is no arbitrary decree, but a law of humanity, that "whatsoever a man soweth, that shall he also reap." Nor does it furnish any ground to impeach the justice, or even the goodness of the Deity, that He should abandon men hereafter to the retributive mastery of those appetites, which were permitted to usurp His authority over them while here.

In an enlightened community like our own, the grossness of the conception, that mere wealth can prepare a man for that final abdication of business of which we have been speaking, may go far to prevent its obtaining currency. But there is another sentiment fraught with equal peril to the soul, which comes clad in the garb of an angel of light, and is certain of a cordial greeting among the mercantile classes. The opinion to which I allude, may, not improbably, have fortified itself, in some minds, from the very discussions that have occupied us in these Lectures; for it can readily pervert to its own purposes, arguments designed to expose its fallacy.

My object has been, to get the BIBLE installed in the COUNTING-HOUSE, as the only arbiter of duty, and the regulator of all the diversified concerns of Commerce. The domain we have been traversing together, is that rather of morality than of theology. The whole burden of these discourses has been in the direction of practical godliness — the actual exemplification of veracity, integrity, diligence, moderation, and kindness, in the daily routine of traffic. And the ready conclusion which some auditors may deduce from these premises — the speculation too rife in the walks of commerce wherever her masts or her warerooms are to be found — is, that a compliance with these precepts, *is all that is required in order to* SALVATION: "this do, and thou shalt live." We derogate nothing from the intrinsic excellence nor the indispensable importance of these virtues, when we admonish you that this is a most serious and fatal error. The Bible challenges a control over all your relations and occupations, and exacts a rigid conformity to its pure ethics in every transaction, and even in every word and thought, of your lives; but it is careful to apprize you of two things which are fundamental to the Gospel system. One is, that all obedience, to be acceptable, must be animated by faith in the Redeemer and love to God: and the other is, that by no possibility can our own works avail to our pardon and salvation. "By the deeds of the law shall no flesh be justified." Our integrity may be unimpeachable, our lives may be radiant with acts of unostentatious charity, a whole community may unite in applauding our virtues; but if our hope of heaven have no better foundation than this, it is built upon the sand. For we must be saved either by works or by grace: the two cannot coalesce. "If by grace, then is it no more of works; otherwise grace is no more grace. But if it be of works, then it is no more grace: otherwise work is no more work." If we elect to try works instead of grace — to get to heaven through the merit of our own obedience — then, clearly, we must obey the Divine law *perfectly:* for an imperfect obedience can entitle no one to its rewards. But who can meet the full requisitions of a law which extends to the thoughts and intents of the heart, forbids the slightest improper feeling or emotion, and enjoins a holiness as immaculate as that of the seraphim before the throne? The thing is impossible. We can make no remote approximation to it. Human nature is radically diseased, and demands as radical a cure. The very examples which seem to approach nearest to the Scripture standard of morality, are not infrequently vitiated by a latent element of self-righteousness which must make them "an abomination in the sight of God." His eye is upon the heart; and *that* it is His own prerogative to renew.

> "The transformation of apostate man
> From fool to wise, from earthly to divine,
> Is work for him that made him."

This work the SPIRIT OF GOD accomplishes. It is an essential step in that free salvation which is the only alternative to the delusive and hopeless scheme of salvation by works. Simultaneously with this change, the Spirit convinces the sinner of sin, shows him the corruption of his heart, the imperfection of his obedience, the criminality of his unbelief; wakes up in his bosom an ingenuous sorrow for his sins; and constrains him, as an humble penitent, to cast himself upon the mercy of God in JESUS CHRIST. Trusting in the atoning blood and the finished righteousness of Christ for salvation, he obtains as a free gift, that plenary pardon which he never could have earned by his obedience, and that peace of mind which can be found no where in the universe but at the Cross. Henceforward he "loves much" because he has "much forgiven." He carries the spirit of true religion into his life, and faithfully, though still imperfectly, endeavours to keep the law of God. His integrity, truthfulness, and benevolence, now rest upon an impregnable basis. And the sentiment which animates his conduct, is no longer the mercenary temper of a servant, but the loving gratitude and loyalty of a child. He serves God, not that he may be saved, but *because* he is saved. And his obedience, consequently, is impressed with a breadth and a comprehension, a generosity and a cheerfulness, as remote as possible from the penurious homage he formerly rendered, while trying to *merit* salvation by his own works — a fellow-labourer therein, though of a more dignified character, with the ascetic iterating his parrot-like devotions in a damp cell, with the Mohammedan on his burning pilgrimage to Mecca, and with the Hindoo swinging through the air by a hook inserted in the sinews of his body. *This* is the true place of practical morality in the Christian scheme—not the foundation, but the superstructure; not the roots and the trunk, but the foliage and the fruit—the effect and evidence of salvation, not its procuring cause. A due apprehension of this truth would dispel the precarious hopes to which very many are now trusting, and turn off their thoughts from their own imaginary or superficial goodness, to Him who is equally able and willing to "save to the uttermost all who come unto God by him." Just in proportion as the mercantile classes are brought under the influence of a genuine faith in Christ, will the Bible exert its sacred prerogative in their Counting-Houses, and their current secularities effloresce with the graces which cement and embellish the social state. Herein too consists the panoply they require for an exchange of worlds—that preparation for "retiring" ultimately and for ever from business, and all that pertains to it, which every man should make, who shrinks from going portionless into eternity. There is nothing in eternity—nothing in the dark and chill passage which leads to it—to intimidate the soul that is united to Christ. It is all one empire;

its several provinces acknowledge the same Sovereign; that Sovereign is "THE LORD OUR RIGHTEOUSNESS," who has all power in heaven and on earth; and the pillars of his throne must fall, before he will suffer a soul that has trusted in Him to perish. How well His people are fortified against all possible want or suffering for the future, can be known only to those who have considered the resources of Omnipotence. In receiving them into a vital union with himself, Christ endowed them with his own inexhaustible wealth: they became "HEIRS OF GOD AND JOINT-HEIRS WITH JESUS CHRIST"—language which overpasses our comprehension, and makes one exclaim, in thinking of the believer's heritage,

> "My soul, with all the powers I boast,
> Is in the boundless prospect lost!"

These treasures, comprising, as they do, the hopes and consolations of the Gospel here, and its ineffable and eternal rewards hereafter, may well be styled the "TRUE RICHES." Unlike earthly riches, they have a substantial and indestructible character. They never deceive. No one is ensnared by them. No one is disappointed. No one who has trusted in them, is liable to have his property wrested from him. They satisfy the soul. They fill its utmost capacities. No moth nor rust can corrupt them. No thief can break through and steal them. They resist the corrosion of time. They survive all changes — even death itself. The departing spirit, compelled by an inexorable law to relinquish everything else, even to the very tabernacle in which it has dwelt, soars aloft, bearing its treasures in triumph to the skies — not merely retaining all it has previously owned, but invested, at that moment, with fresh honours and estates as much transcending in extent and splendour the proudest demesnes of earthborn royalty, as these excel the veriest hovels of barbarism. And as it hastens to join the white-robed company of the ransomed, and to cast its crown at the Redeemer's feet, those pregnant words in its charter, just begin to disclose their profound and wonderful significance — "ALL THINGS ARE YOURS!"

I may possibly seem to you, in this glance at the only inalienable portion of the soul, to have wandered quite away from the range of topics which immediately concern you as *Merchants*. I might answer, that although Merchants, you are men, and, as such, heirs of eternity, and vitally concerned in the acquisition of a heritage beyond the grave. But I choose rather to avail myself of the state of feeling just hinted at, as an indication of the repugnance, or at least the want of congeniality, there is, between the prevailing tone of the commercial world, and the spirit of true Christianity. That religion of which I have been speaking, as indispensable to prepare you for "retiring" from all sublunary affairs, is not a loose garment, to be caught up and gathered hurriedly around you in the moment of your dissolution. If we would be sustained by the consolations of the Bible in death, we must live by its precepts. And, in particular, as regards yourselves, its paramount authority must be recognized in all the departments of commerce, and the settled feeling of the trading classes must be — "I am not ashamed of the Gospel of Christ." Business is not to be prosecuted for its own sake. Commerce is one of GOD'S agencies for governing and blessing the world. Its silver and gold, its mills and factories, its canals and railways, its fleets and cities, are all His. The multitudinous tribes of human beings occupied in its various callings, "live and move and have their being *in Him.*" The allegiance they owe Him, comprehends all their powers, property, plans, time, influence. The just requisition He lays upon them, is, that they make His glory the ultimate end of their lives; that they regulate their conduct by His Word; and that they carry the spirit of genuine piety into all their transactions. What less could He require? What other code would comport with our relations to Him and to our fellow-creatures? What other principles would consist with our own happiness? These elements are the only proper corrective to the debasing effects of commerce. Dignified and controlled by religious principle, it is one of the most beneficent institutions which adorn the globe. But divorced from this alliance, it is surcharged with mischief. The majestic tides which sweep through its crowded thoroughfares, bear men away from God. The constant tendency is to nourish their inferior appetites, to make them set an inordinate value upon money and the objects money will procure, to impair their reverence for the Deity, to weaken their sense of moral responsibility, to blunt their consciences against the reproofs of Scripture, and, in a word, to shut out eternity from their thoughts and degrade them into practical Atheists. No human power or skill can cope with this evil. The current will overwhelm your dykes, as the ocean does the puny structures of children on the strand.

> "The STILL SMALL VOICE is wanted. He must speak,
> Whose word leaps forth at once to its effect;
> Who calls for things that are not, and they come."

He has spoken. And his word, lodged in the heart, raises the only successful barrier against the encroachments of the monopolising trade-spirit. Let it, then, have free course. In theory at least, we have a principle in religion, the principle of *faith*, which can master the strongest passions of the human breast. It has mastered them all — fear, love, revenge, lust, pride, avarice, have yielded to it in instances without number. Its benign influence is felt in all the great centres of commerce. And there are firms in every city which might be cited as most honourably exemplifying its benign results, when admitted to its legitimate place in a business-life. But these are the exceptions. The Bible is only beginning to make its way into the Counting-House. Many who imagine themselves to be quite ready for it, who even suppose they have long ago received it, have a very crude conception of what this involves. They think simply of conducting their establishments with integrity, avoiding every approach to deception and falsehood, requiring all their subordinates to be truthful and courteous, fulfilling their engagements with scrupulous fidelity, and shunning all collateral speculations. This is well, very well, as far as it goes. But if they pause here, the Bible is not yet "enthroned" in their counting-rooms. Nothing will satisfy it but an earnest, aggressive Christianity, which shall be ever intent upon doing good, to the utmost measure of its capacity. It is as much the law of the "true riches" to diffuse themselves, as it is of cupidity to hoard. And the more a merchant possesses of this incorruptible wealth, the more he will be inclined to share it with others. The opportunities for this, in an extensive business, are equally varied and important.

To revert, for example, to a topic formerly discussed — you have, in each of your great establishments, a numerous tenantry, sustaining to you a relation analogous to that of your own families; constituting, in fact, a second household. Your Bible will remind you that this is the ordering of Providence. In the successive steps which have conducted you to your present position, you may have been chiefly influenced by selfish motives. But an invisible hand has led you on, until you find yourself the centre of a little community, who are your daily and intimate companions, who go and come at your bidding, and whose exertions are contributing to your wealth. As a Christian man, you will not fail to ask, "Why is this? For what end has Providence committed this large and growing business to my hands, and gathered around me this group of Young Men? How is it that one youth from Tennessee, another from Kentucky, a third from Ohio, a fourth from Missouri, a salesman from Virginia, a book-keeper from Maryland, have all been guided to my counting-house and confided to my tutelage?" These are grave and interesting questions. The longer you ponder them, the more you will be disposed to say, "This is the finger of God!" And the less will you be disposed to decline the mission to which the dispensation so obviously calls you. A base cupidity might thrust it

31

upon you as the one predominant and daily inquest, "How can I turn the services of these clerks to the best advantage, and make the most money out of them?" But your inquiry will rather be, "How can I do the most good to these young men?" It is, certainly, a noble field of usefulness which God has opened to you; and if you cultivate it as you ought, you will not regret your fidelity, when you come to see the sheaves gathered into the garner. *How* you are to do this, must be left to your own enlightened discretion. With a clear impression of your obligations and an abiding sense of the love of Christ, you will not be at a loss for means and occasions to commend religion to them. Whatever agency you may employ, a consistent example must be combined with it; for young men are shrewd observers, and disposed, beyond any other class in society, to insist upon a rigid congruity between profession and practice. But a really consistent example will rarely be alone. The spirit which insures *that*, will prompt you to kind and judicious efforts, as occasion may offer, to bring the claims of religion before their minds; and efforts of this sort rarely fail of a blessing in the end.

If the inmates of a commercial house have a peculiar claim upon the Christian sympathies of its principals, it is not an exclusive claim. Your profession introduces you to a great variety of persons, many of whom it might be possible to reach with a wholesome moral influence. We are apt to disparage and neglect familiar and incidental opportunities of doing good. Great occasions we can improve: they have a palpable shape and magnitude: we know how to lay hold of them: and they seem *worthy* of our care. But the opportunities which occur in the ordinary routine of life, in buying and selling, and in the trivialties of social intercourse, are allowed to glide away while we are considering whether it is worth our while to improve them. — There has always been a class of *reformers* in the world, whose philanthropy confines itself to grand achievements. They are happily hit off by Mrs. More in her "*History of Mr. Fantom*," a London tradesman, who turned philosopher, and set about rectifying the world at large, with a zeal that left him no heart for cases of individual suffering. He would "alter all the laws, and do away all the religions, and put an end to all the wars in the world." He would "abolish all punishments, and not leave a single prisoner on the face of the globe." But when applied to by a benevolent neighbour to contribute a trifle towards liberating an unfortunate debtor from prison, he "had no attention to spare to that business, though he would pledge himself to produce a plan by which the national debt might be paid off in six months." When asked to co-operate in bringing a tyrannical workhouse-keeper to punishment, he excused himself on the ground, that "the wrongs of the Poles and the South Americans so filled his mind, as to leave him no time to attend to such petty grievances." A poor man's house in his vicinity having taken fire and burnt down, he justified his neglect in not going to the help of the sufferers, by alleging that he was just then "engaged in a far nobler project than putting out a fire in a little thatched cottage" — he was "contriving a scheme to extinguish the fires of the Inquisition!" Mr. Fantom has his proper archetype only amongst the infidel socialists of the day; but in the feature of his character presented in these extracts, he may stand for the representative of many wiser and better men. Perhaps we are all too much disposed to make our Christianity a matter, if not of Sundays and sacraments, at least of times and seasons, and still more of systems and societies. The imperative demand of the age, is, for *organized* benevolence, for "Institutions"; and it is a demand which must be met, unless the Church would see a large part even of the territory she has wrested from heresy and barbarism revert to its former masters. But we must guard against the subtle feeling, that these combined efforts are to supersede private philanthropy; that our contributions to Societies, can absolve us from the obligation of personal exertion. Better to abolish all Societies, than that they should absorb the benevolence of the Church, and become the sole medium of intercommunication between the people of God and a perishing world. Christianity will not bear to be swathed and *splinted* up in this fashion. You will either crush its life out, and leave it a worthless mummy; or it will rend your compresses asunder, and reassert its inalienable freedom. It is cause for thankfulness that we can do good by proxy in so many ways; but it would soon stifle our religion to do good only by proxy. It will never do to remit to Boards and Associations the exclusive prerogative of deciding how, and when, and to what extent, our Christianity shall go forth on errands of mercy. This were scarcely better than to commit the whole business of our salvation to a priest. Our own souls would famish under this vicarious sort of piety. It is good for us to be brought into contact with the errors and wants, the dangers and sufferings, of humanity. Our SAVIOUR did this; the apostles did it; all the early Christians did it; the whole genius of the New Dispensation presupposes it. The very lowest conception of the Christian system which can be formed, must embrace, as one of its radical elements, the obligation to relieve the necessities and contribute to the well-being of others, in every practicable way. And any wish to be released from this obligation, must discredit the sincerity of the profession with which it is allied.

In *your* case, it is not "suffering" which appeals to you in the ordinary course of your business; but there must be many persons thrown in your way whom you might benefit by an occasional friendly word or kind office — by placing a Bible in their hands, by encouraging them to a due observance of the Sabbath, by a timely caution against profaneness, drinking, or idle habits, by manifesting an interest in their families. Something, too, might be done in the way of reaching your customers. The Counting-House, I am aware, is not a place for "preaching"; nor is there anything more disgusting than that loquacious, pharisaical religion, which is for ever spreading its tawdry plumage, and mixing up the most sacred themes with the common topics of business. But there seems no sufficient reason why a Christian merchant should meet with a set of gentlemen from different parts of the country, year after year, without opening his lips to them on the most important of all subjects; still less, why he should permit them, season by season, to spend one or more Sabbaths in the city without tendering them the hospitalities of his pew in the house of God. And what hinders but that our opulent importers should have an eye to the crews of their ships, and try to do some good among them? This, it is true, is "the Captain's charge." But it is your office to select your Captains, and to decide whether your vessels shall go to sea under the care of debauchees and tyrants, or of men of sound morals and humane tempers. And it were not unworthy of your position to see that their sailors are supplied, each of them, with a Bible; and to take some pains, on their return to port, to have them directed to proper boarding-houses, and told where they might find a mariners' chapel on a Sunday.

All these are, properly speaking, professional duties: they *come in your way* as Merchants, and you cannot well pretermit them, without a positive repression of your religious instincts. But there may be scenes and objects outside of your beaten thoroughfares, which have a claim upon your sympathy. Every great city embraces a vast amount of degradation and wretchedness—heterogeneous hordes that are but a step removed from savage life. In close agglomeration with its wealth, refinement, and intelligence, its splendid mansions and luxurious entertainments, are masses of ignorance, poverty, vice, and suffering, such as can be found no where else within the verge of civilization. Indeed, the very magnitude of the evils to be provided for, and the frequency with which examples of crime and misery pass under one's notice in such a community, have a tendency to check the flow of benevolence. If it were possible to take up a small section of one of the worst courts or lanes of Philadelphia or New York, and transplant it with its miserable tenantry in their rags and filth and vices and sicknesses, into some quiet rural town of two or three thousand inhabitants, it would become at once the paramount object of interest there: every family would feel concerned to do something for their relief, and every bosom would thrill with emotions of pity or of horror. But *we* can pass these very objects on the side-walks by scores, without noticing them. We can traverse whole squares lined with their dwellings, and be conscious only of some transitory feelings of sadness and disgust which we are but too happy to throw off by hurrying away from the neighbourhood as fast as possible. Yet these are our fellow-mortals, with minds as susceptible of cultivation, and souls as precious, as our own. They are more than this: they are our neighbours, constituent parts of the same community with ourselves, living within sight of our schools and sanctuaries, and therefore committed, in some sort, by Providence, to our guardianship. To say that they are *your* charge specifically —that it belongs to the mercantile body to look after all the vagrancy and depravity of the cities — would be very unreasonable. But considering that these cities are essentially commercial in their character, that they owe their growth and opulence and power to trade, it is certainly equitable that the mercantile classes should assume a liberal share of this responsibility. In any event, Christianity requires that you should bestow upon this work whatever personal attention and labour you can command; and that the abstruse social problems forced upon us by these aspects of pauperism, should have the benefit of all the experience and sagacity you can bring to the solution of them. It will not answer to become so engrossed with traffic as to lose sight of the claims of humanity; so absorbed with questions of finance and merchandize, as not to see the throngs of deathless and accountable beings around you, who are hastening to eternity without God and without hope, and preparing, it may be, to confront you at the bar of Christ, for your neglect of their souls. What is all your merchandize, all your riches, all your social influence, compared with the meanest and unworthiest of these objects! There is not a vagrant in the vilest haunt of the vilest vicinage of the city, whose salvation would not be worth more than all the ships and warehouses of our metropolis, nor whose perdition, a more terrible catastrophe than the destruction of all the implements and ensigns of your commercial greatness. This will fall upon your ears, doubtless, as a trite sentiment. You "know it already. No sane man would think of proposing money, or diadems, or anything earthly, as an equivalent for the soul." But while every one "knows" this, how few have risen to the point of treating it as a reality — of *living* as though they knew it! How rare are the Counting-Houses in which it is felt with the force of an inwrought, practical conviction! Even those in your ranks who are most fully imbued with the spirit of the Gospel, must be painfully conscious of a tendency to let the things which are seen, blind them to the things which are unseen — of allowing business to blunt their spiritual sensibilities, and chill their zeal in seizing upon opportunities of usefulness. And so it comes to pass, that while Commerce can be charged with neither indifference nor parsimony in this matter, her aggregate efforts in behalf of the mendicancy of our cities, are as incommensurate with her resources, as they are with the evils to be removed. What she lacks, is, THE BIBLE IN HER COUNTING-ROOMS.

The great lesson I have wished to enforce in these discursive remarks, is, that we should live *to do good*. We are not to confine our exertions to one set of objects, nor to periodical occasions, but be always ready, as we can find or make opportunities, to minister to the well-being of our fellow-creatures or to the prosperity of religion. It is one of the most beautiful pictures the inspired writers have given us of the Founder of our holy religion — a biography in a single sentence — "HE WENT ABOUT DOING GOOD." And if we would approve ourselves to be His disciples, we must cherish His spirit and tread in His steps. There is no incompatibility between the two great classes of interests which solicit our benevolence, the physical and the spiritual, the necessities of the poor and the salvation of souls. "Experience demonstrates that the heart which responds to the cries of a world perishing through lack of knowledge, is the heart which most readily thrills at the cry of bodily want; that those who care most for the souls of the heathen, are among the most active agents of patriotic and local charities; that genuine Christian charity, while it leaves no object unattempted on account of its vastness, overlooks none on account of its minuteness. Copying, in this respect, the example of Him who, in his way to the cross to save a world, often stood still to give health to the sick, and to wipe away the tears of the mourner; sowing, at each step, the seeds of those various institutions of mercy, which are still springing up in his church; and who, while suspended on the cross in the crisis of human redemption, still thought of his filial relation, and tenderly provided for a mother's comfort." *

Imbued with this spirit, you will find a genuine satisfaction in performing those philanthropic offices upon which the Saviour has, both by precept and example, impressed so high a value. And the same feeling which sends you forth upon these ministrations among the poor, will lead you to write "Holiness to the Lord," upon your PROPERTY. There is no lesson which the Church is slower to learn, than the true doctrine on this subject; no duties which the mass of Christians are more backward in discharging, than those involved in the scriptural idea of stewardship. I have dwelt too much in these Lectures on the sin and danger of covetousness, to warrant me in expatiating on that topic here. And yet I cannot bring the Course to a close, without again reminding you, that God has committed your property to you in trust for Him, and will hold you to a strict responsibility in the management of it. There are few themes of higher moment to you, than the moral limits of accumulation, and the true use of riches; and you will be brought to one or another conclusion on these points, according as you examine them by the current maxims of commerce, or by the infallible utterances of revelation. If you are willing to rely

* Harris.

upon the teachings of the Bible, it will not prescribe the precise arithmetical proportion of your gains which shall be set apart to religion. Discarding this principle of the old economy, it will reveal to you, rather, the character of the DEITY, in the plenitude of its matchless perfections, as the only rightful and adequate object of your homage. It will unveil to you that munificent Providence which has watched over you through life, defended you in danger, healed you when sick, extricated you from embarrassments, retrieved your losses, crowned your business with success, gathered around you the endearments of your cherished homes, and bestowed upon you the institutions and ordinances of a pure Christianity. Above all, it will take you to the CROSS, and bid you look upon that wonder of wonders, the SON OF GOD bearing our sins in his own body on the tree, and dying an accursed death that we might live. It will show you how, for His sake, your iniquities have been blotted out, and your hearts renewed. It will remind you of the long-suffering and patience of your Heavenly Father in bearing with your provocations; of His faithfulness in reproving your errors, and His tenderness in recovering you from your falls; of the fortitude with which he has nerved you to bear reverses, and the consolations with which he has assuaged your sorrows. It will conduct you to the verge of the fathomless abyss, and to the borders of the land of promise, and afford you some transient glimpses of the unutterable misery you have escaped, and the everlasting glories in reserve for you. And having done all this, it will leave it to your own grateful and adoring hearts, to answer the question, "*How much owest thou unto my Lord?*" This is the spirit of the New Dispensation; and it is under the pressure of motives like these, you are to decide what proportion of your revenues shall be laid at the Saviour's feet. He needs, as He has a claim to, the utmost resources you can bring to his support. The contest He is waging with the powers of darkness, He might terminate by an exertion of his omnipotence; or He might commit the prosecution of it exclusively to His angels. But as our globe is the theatre on which it is waged, and the soul of man its object, He has chosen to employ our unworthy agency in carrying it forward. And the question for you to decide, is, how far your obligations to the Redeemer require *you* to go, in assisting Him in this conflict with His and our enemies. By what form of personal service, by what measure of pecuniary contribution, are you called upon to attest your loyalty to Christ and your sympathy for a perishing world?

There are no ends to which money can be applied, so honourable and so beneficent as these. The universal spread of the Gospel, is an object impressed with true moral sublimity, and fraught with blessings for our race, surpassing all the visions of poetry. It will be a greater distinction at the last day to have borne even the humblest part in promoting it, than it will to have owned a province or wielded a sceptre. And, other considerations aside, it is every way worthy of the dignity and the opulence of Commerce, that she should repay, in a measure, the manifold obligations she owes to Christianity, by dedicating her exuberant resources to this work. It is meet that the merchant-princes of our land and of other lands, should identify themselves with those great Institutions which are engaged in evangelizing the nations. To a certain extent, you have done this. But it would be trifling with your intelligence, to suppose that you regard the prevailing spirit of Christian liberality in business circles, as fully up to the Scripture standard. Allowing for numerous exceptions, the disposition is, to appropriate to religion, simply the crumbs which fall from overloaded tables; to give the pounds to earth, and the farthings to heaven; to lay up imperial fortunes for children, and put off with a pittance the millions who are clamouring for the bread of life. To complain that there are no sacrifices made for the Gospel's sake, would, in this connexion, seem scarcely serious — so far away from the actualities of the case, is anything approximating to a "sacrifice." We need not even, at this point, speak of retrenching superfluities. The reigning type of benevolence may be carried up many degrees without molesting "superfluities." In truth, the very foundations are out of joint. The elementary principles of Christian stewardship are not recognized. Let these be once lodged in the great heart of Commerce, and energized by a baptism of the Spirit, and there would be no occasion to go among the merchants to *solicit* funds: the silver and the gold would flow into the Lord's treasury as did the offerings of the Hebrews for the building of the tabernacle, until His servants might be obliged, with Moses, to bid the people desist.

But the Christian casuist who propagates sentiments like these, is certain to have a text of Scripture thrust at him from some quarter, to admonish him that "if any provide not for his own, and specially for those of his own house, he hath denied the faith, and is worse than an infidel." It is a wholesome sign that there should prevail, in any community, a horror of being classed with "infidels." But it must be deemed a little curious, that nothing in nature or in art should excite this emotion to such a pitch, as a subscription-paper or a collection-box. There are many men to whom skepticism never appears so atrocious, as when they are approached for means to drive skepticism out of the world. Nor will any other incident stir them up to such paroxysms of parental affection, or make them so resolute in the purpose of "providing for their own." Let us not quarrel with this feeling. The Bible is friendly to all the domestic sympathies; and the tighter the bonds of household love are drawn, the better. But there is still something to be said on the subject mentioned in this much-abused admonition of the apostle.

It is a striking illustration of the insidious nature of avarice, that not one rich man in a hundred, perhaps not one in a thousand, is disposed to stop hoarding. The point of acquisition which constitutes "wealth," is pushed along as men approach it; so that the amount of property which, at setting out in business, supplied their definition of "opulence," and at which they meant to forbear further accumulation, comes, in time, to dwindle into a paltry "competence," with which "no one ought to be satisfied." A simple change in the *definition* keeps conscience quiet, and allows the beguiling process to go on. The more they get, the more they want. And even when an estate has swelled to colossal proportions, the idea of arresting its growth, or of giving away a generous part of the revenue it yields, is almost as painful as that of losing a child. Singularly enough, this morbid tenacity of income prevails where there is a distinct purpose of making a posthumous appropriation of large sums to charitable uses. The Will is already drawn up to this effect, and duly signed and sealed; but the Testator, entranced by the mysterious power of gold, cannot summon the resolution to become his own Executor. He has seen many a Will broken, and many an inheritance alienated from its proper destination; and he knows this may happen in his own case also. But, again, "it may *not* happen"; and he will run the hazard. If it were not for the spell which is upon him, the pleasure of applying his bounty and witnessing the benign effects of it, would outweigh the sordid satisfaction he derives from seeing his huge heap of gold dust growing larger and larger. But the hallucination cannot be thrown off: the glittering treasure will assert its mastery against any rival power except the universal Conqueror.— Or, he is, possibly, one who is guiltless even of any prospective benefactions. His sole aim is, to "provide for his own"; to go on turning revenue into capital as long as life lasts, that when his eyes are closed in death, his mammoth estate may descend to his heirs unimpaired.

I shall not be suspected of deprecating the accumulation of property even up to the most generous limits, or of discouraging a becoming foresight and liberality on the part of parents towards their families, if I ask you to consider how irrational all this conduct is, and how incompatible with the precepts of the Bible. Assuredly, it proceeds upon a most mistaken theory of the proper uses of wealth, and a practical denial of the Scripture doctrine of stewardship. To argue these points, would imply that the arbitrators of the cause were themselves under the sway of the same enchantment upon which they were called to pronounce judgment. But the facts may be employed to caution you against the wiles of this imperious passion, and to impress upon your minds the importance of administering your affairs, on the wise and safe principles of Christian duty. Property is as much a trust, as intellect or learning, and is equally to be consecrated to the glory of God and the good of man. One of the prime questions connected with it, is that referred to by the apostle in the verse which has been quoted—providing for one's household: and this must be adjusted, neither under the impulse of blind affection, nor at the bidding of pride and cupidity; but with an earnest and prayerful desire to know the will of God, and a faithful use of all the helps He may proffer us in ascertaining His will. It would be very unwarrantable to say that an overgrown estate ought never to be bequeathed to a child: such a step might be demanded as a simple act of justice, or ratified by an enlightened piety on grounds of expediency. But as a general rule, experience and observation combine to discourage this practice. The course of things perpetually going on in this country, and which nothing but the re-enactment of the laws of primogeniture could arrest, is for one generation to collect a fortune, and the next (one or two) to disperse it. Where are the estates of the leading Philadelphia, New York, and Boston merchants, who died half a century ago? Gather up the fragments, if you can find them, in the hands of their children and grandchildren; and see what there is to show for all the planning, and toiling, and saving, those fortunes cost! You have but to look around our own city, to see even contemporaneous patrimonies melting away like a March snow, almost before the mansions once tenanted by their frugal owners have put off their *crape*. Whether this parental munificence is commonly requited with a corresponding gratitude, and men are held in filial honour in proportion to the ingots they leave, and the time and pains they have taken to fabricate them, each one must decide for himself. But if it entered at all into the aims of these parties to establish a reputation which their fellow-citizens, or even their own descendants, should cherish as a sacred legacy, a very brief return to the scene of their former toils, would probably satisfy some of them, that they had sadly mistaken the means for compassing their end. There are men who have judged more wisely. The grave has lately closed upon one of this class in an Eastern city. A venerable and successful merchant, he had for many years before his death, left off accumulating, and made it his inflexible rule to give away the whole of his large surplus income. Now he was endowing a college Professorship; now founding an Academy; now bestowing a princely benefaction upon some judicious Charity; and now another upon some noble religious enterprise. One of his favourite methods of doing good, was to purchase, and put in circulation, hundreds of copies, or perhaps whole editions, of any useful book which happened to commend itself to his taste and judgment. And after his death, a memorandum among his papers was found to contain the names of a large number of village pastors, whose scanty stipends he had been in the habit of supplementing from year to year. These are but hints and samples of his life: but they may suffice to show that he was not a man to be forgotten. It is something for a private citizen so to live that when he dies, the whole community to which he belonged, and other distant communities vying with them, shall take up his name and breathe a blessing upon it. It is for yourselves, under Providence, to decide (I speak especially to the wealthy among you), whether *your* memories shall be thus embalmed, or handed over to a speedy oblivion. And in making this observation, I am far from commending it to you as a becoming object of your ambition, to purchase a posthumous fame by your charities. I have in view simply the ordinance of heaven, that "the righteous shall be held in everlasting remembrance." "The memory of the just" (and this epithet includes the idea of benevolence) "is blessed." Whether you take the case of a secluded female, who employs her leisure hours, like Dorcas, in making coats and garments for the poor, or the faithful missionary, who wears himself out in distributing the bread of life along the lanes and alleys of a city, or the paternal landlord, who, like the "*Man of Ross*," puts the impress of his kindness upon all the homes of his neighbourhood, and associates his name with every measure which can augment the common comfort, or the generous capitalist whose benefactions are a sure reliance to the great religious charities of his age — it is alike the ordering of Providence, that their memories shall be blessed. You may not aim at this result. Your humility may shrink from the thought of having your names repeated from one to another, even by friendly and grateful lips. But you cannot well avoid this, if you are faithful to your trust, and employ your property, or a reasonable portion of it, in doing good. Sooner or later, many *will* "rise up and call you blessed." It is meet that it should be so. And the marvel is, that you do not all perceive how superior in dignity and worth, in honour and influence, is a scheme of life regulated by these principles, to one which looks only, or mainly, to indefinite accumulation. You *must* perceive it. It is forced upon you in the current intercourse of society. It is impossible not to observe the widely different positions occupied, respectively, by individuals belonging to the two classes of which we are speaking. They may be equal in intelligence, social standing, and wealth; but there is no equality in the general respect and esteem accorded to them. No right-minded community will admit a purely selfish person, one who lives for himself and his own exclusively, to the confidence and gratitude they bestow upon a man who shows himself a lover of his kind, and a ready helper where there is any good to be done. They have, each of them, their reward; and the rewards are, very properly, as unlike as their characters. These are facts as patent as the sun at noon-day. They run all through the annals of every city. They meet us as we pass along the streets. They find quiet but significant utterance at many a funeral. And if tombstones would speak the truth, the cemeteries would fairly bristle with them.

Why, then, are they not more operative in society? How is it, that Commerce is still so much under the sway of selfishness? that there are so few in any walk of life, who have learned the true use of money? Let those who ask these questions, ponder them. They are not to be answered in a breath. To do justice to them, we must go back to the fountain of corruption in the human heart. We must dissect our school-books. We must analyze our systems of domestic training. We must inquire into the maxims and usages which determine the proper place of wealth in the social economy. We must weigh the course of our legislation and our jurisprudence. We must gauge the tone of the popular press. We must revise the teachings of the pulpit. We must ascertain whether the prevalent Christianity of the Church, is in all things coincident with the Christianity of the New Testament. — Let these sources of information be explored, and some light will be thrown upon the problems we have to cope with. This office I cannot enter upon. I have detained you too long already. But whatever may be the secondary causes which have invested the love of money with so fatal an ascendancy in our country, there is but one effective antidote for it. The sorcery of wealth can be dissolved only by the BLOOD OF THE CROSS. And for yourselves — unless you are prepared to barter the

"TRUE RICHES" for the "mammon of unrighteousness," that disastrous error which has consigned so many Merchants to irretrievable and eternal bankruptcy, you must admit the Gospel of Christ to its legitimate supremacy in the realm of Commerce, and ENTHRONE THE BIBLE IN ALL YOUR COUNTING-HOUSES.

Lecture Eleventh.

SUGGESTIONS TO YOUNG MEN

ENGAGED IN

MERCANTILE BUSINESS:

A DISCOURSE OCCASIONED BY THE DEATH OF MR. ARCHIBALD SLOAN, AT THE MERCHANTS' HOTEL, PHILADELPHIA, OCTOBER 9TH, 1851.

CORRESPONDENCE.

PHILADELPHIA, *Nov.* 1, 1851.

Dear Sir: — Having listened, with great interest, to the sermon you delivered on Sunday evening last, addressed to "the Mercantile Classes," and desiring that its usefulness may be extended, by affording an opportunity for its perusal to the community at large, we respectfully request, on our own behalf and on that of many others who heard you, that you will furnish us with a copy for publication.

With much respect, your obedient servants,

T. G. MOSS,
W. R. CASON,
G. M. PROCTER,
H. J. SMITH.

Rev. Dr. BOARDMAN.

PHILADELPHIA, *Nov.* 1*st*, 1851.

To the Rev. H. A. BOARDMAN, D. D.

Dear Sir: — The undersigned listened with great satisfaction to the sermon delivered by you on Sunday evening the 26th ult., occasioned by the death of one of our companions, Mr. ARCHIBALD SLOAN, and are deeply impressed with the belief that its publication and general circulation would be productive of much good in this community, more particularly to that class to which we belong, and to whom it was especially addressed. With that view, we most respectfully ask from you the manuscript for publication.

FRANCIS SQUIRE,
W. M. F. MAGRAW,
ROBERT A. CRAWFORD,
C. C. HAFFELFINGER,
E. W. DAVIDSON,
JACOB ZELLER,
LAMBERT THOMAS,
J. ALLISON EYSTER,
ALEX. T. LANE,
H. T. M'VEIGH,
GEORGE T. HEATHER,
SAML. P. DARLINGTON,

E. C. HUNTINGTON,
C. D. RUSSELL,
HENRY C. LAUGHLIN,
LOWBER BURROWS,
BENJAMIN F. GROVE,
S. H. SMITH,
HARRY A. GLEIM,
GEO. W. WANAMAKER,
JOS. S. BROWN,
JOS. WEBSTER,
W. M. RECKLESS,
JOHN C. RALSTON,
J. W. WHITEMAN,
FRANCIS A. FERRY,
WM. T. DORTCH,
JOHN JORDAN,
A. EMSLIE NEWBOLD,
HUGH P. SCHETKY,
WM. J. BARR,
HENRY LELAR, JR.
J. M. TAYLOR,
H. A. LEAVITT,
GEO. S. TOBES,
W. AUG'S ANDREWS,
WHARTON GRIFFITTS,
HARRY STILES,
WM. H. NICOLS,
ALEX. OMENSETTER,
JAS. W. VEAZEY,
JAMES H. COCHRANE,
W. N. ASHMAN,
FRANK COOKMAN,
ISAAC W. WEBB,
RICHD. PARKER,
JOHN B. PENN,
H. D. LAWRENCE,
GEORGE C. BARBER,
J. M. CARSKADDEN,
E. S. HOWELL,
L. LEAVITT,
HUGH B. M'CAULEY,
J. H. MEEHAN,
DAVID I. HAUN,
JAMES W. WROTH,
EDMUND B. ORBISON,
H. HADDOCK,
JAMES W. LINVILLE,
WILLIAM CHAFFEE,
J. W. STOUT,
SAML. H. STERETT,
CHAS. D. HURLBUTT,
WM. P. ROCKHILL,
M. JNO. MOORE,
A. W. NASH,
GEO. S. SCOTT,
C. B. SLAGLE,
JOHN C. WEBER,
SAML. SPARHAWK,
THOMPSON RITCHIE,
EDWIN A. MERRICK,
J. P. BURROUGHS,
GEO. W. GILL,
JOHN S. WENNER,
F. C. POTTER,
B. A. BUCK,
WM. F. WILKINS,
C. W. YARD,
C. W. SYDNOR,
SAML. MILLIKEN, JR.
WM. H. GREGG,
D. M. SWARR,
C. J. SHOWER,
DAVID E. OAK,
WASHINGTON DANNER,
ALFRED NESMITH.

PHILADELPHIA, *Nov. 3d*, 1851.

Gentlemen: — Having been led by the lamented death of Mr. SLOAN to reflect on the position and relations of the large body of Young Men in our commercial houses, the unwelcome conviction was forced upon me, that our Pastors generally, myself included, had scarcely recognized them as a distinct class in the community, much less put forth any suitable efforts for their welfare. Under the influence of this feeling, the discourse you have in such kind terms requested for publication, was written. You will need no assurance from me that it was prepared without the slightest reference to the press; but I do not feel that this is a sufficient reason for withholding it, if, as you seem to suppose, its suggestions are adapted to be useful to those who listened to it from the pulpit. The manuscript is herewith placed at your disposal.

I am very truly and faithfully yours,

H. A. BOARDMAN.

To Messrs. T. G. MOSS,
W. R. CASON,
FRANCIS SQUIRE,
W. M. F. MAGRAW, and others.

Lecture Eleventh.

SUGGESTIONS TO YOUNG MEN ENGAGED IN MERCANTILE BUSINESS.

But seek ye first the kingdom of God and his righteousness; and all these things shall be added unto you. — Matt. vi. 33.

Funeral pageants are too common in large cities to attract notice, unless they are marked by some peculiar circumstances. About two weeks since, on a mild and serene afternoon, a procession passed along our streets to a cemetery in the southern part of the city, which did for the time bring the eager throng in the thoroughfares to a pause, and excite at least a transient feeling of interest. It was a train of Young Men following the remains of a friend and companion to the grave. He came here from Tennessee three or four years ago, as a clerk in an eminent commercial house. His integrity and capacity, his fidelity and diligence, his modest demeanour and generous disposition, secured him the confidence of his employers, the cordial esteem of his associates, and the respect of all who met with him. No one will be found to gainsay the assertion that he was a general favourite; and that any of his contemporaries may esteem themselves happy, who are as much beloved as he was. He retired to rest of a Saturday night in his usual vigorous health — his athletic form and manly countenance betraying no indication of the insidious foe which had entrenched itself in the very citadel of life. Before the morning he was seized by an impetuous and unconquerable malady, which, after four brief days and nights of dreadful suffering, left him a pallid corpse. All that medical skill and faithful nursing (such nursing, perhaps, as is rarely enjoyed in a great hotel) could do, was done to save him. If sympathy and affection could have averted the blow, the kind ministrations and the tears of the young men who were constantly around his bed, and who supplied, as well as might be, the place of relatives, must have insured a reprieve. But his hour had come. He died — died with the flush of health upon his cheek, before disease had wasted his flesh, and, as it were, in the fulness of his strength — as a noble ship, her timbers all sound, her spars complete, and all her canvass spread, has sometimes disappeared suddenly beneath the sea.

The startling severity of the blow sent a thrill through many hearts. A large concourse of his companions, with many of our merchants, assembled to do honour to his remains; and as the sad *cortege* passed on with a slow and solemn tread to the place of sepulture, it was honourable alike to the living and the dead to see how many hearts were touched by this spectacle — the funeral of a young man!

If God speaks to us in his providence as well as by his Word, an event like this should not be treated with indifference. It is charged with a mission which it deeply behooves us to understand. We shall not, probably, misinterpret one of its lessons if we make it the occasion of considering, for a little, the position and relations of the class of young men to which our deceased friend belonged, and the importance to them of personal religion.

I speak of them as a class by themselves, for such, in fact, they are. The young men in our mercantile establishments — those particularly in our "jobbing houses"—are, most of them, from abroad. They are neither natives of this city, nor are they here for a year or two simply as students. They have come here to reside, and are ultimately to become merchants themselves. This is one circumstance which marks them as a distinct class.

Another is that they usually board at the hotels. Commercial ends are secured by this, which are thought to be of much importance.

They have, again, a common occupation. They are in the same, or similar, kinds of business. The received methods of our inland commerce impart a substantial identity to their duties, their temptations, their pleasures, and their general mode of life, and separate them, in a measure, from the rest of the community.

These attributes of the class, as such, must suffice to show that their position is not altogether favourable to the cultivation of virtue and religion. There is a great deal involved in taking a young man from his home, and setting him down to do for himself in a large city. The mere removal of a youth from a good home to any other situation — to a school or college, to the house of a friend or relative, to a shop or a store — brings with it a serious trial of character. But here the case is a very strong one. Compare a modest, tranquil dwelling in a small town or hamlet of Kentucky or Tennessee, with one of our mammoth HOTELS, and you will begin to understand the ordeal which some thousands of young men in our city have passed through. It is not easy to conceive of any greater social change which they could have experienced, than this. At a single bound they have passed from all the genial influences which sheltered, restrained, and nurtured them in such a home, into a scene which contains scarcely an element of domestic life. Instead of sitting down at a snug family board with the same little group from month to month, they sit at a table with two or three hundred guests, and these changing every day. In place of the sympathy, the tenderness, the mutual confidence and refining fellowship of a mother and sisters, they are surrounded by *men*—respectable and worthy persons, no doubt, but all *men*—and as such, no adequate companions to replace the circle they have left. For an atmosphere of love, where there was some one to share in every joy, and divide every trouble; where their every want was promptly supplied, and every indication of pain or anxiety was made the occasion for fresh offices of affection; they have been transplanted into one which, though not destitute of this element, savours far more of indifference and selfishness. They are in a throng who are thrown together by interest or convenience, business or pleasure; the most of whom are not stationary long enough to form any attachments; and who sever the precarious tie which constitutes their transient bond of union, with as little feeling as they formed it.

This change in their domestic relations is emblematical of that which has taken place in their situation at large. They have relinquished the seclusion and simplicity of the country, for life in a great metropolis. Everything here is widely different. The outward face of things is so unlike the country, that a young man is often bewildered when he is first dropped in the heart of a city, with its multitudinous streets and lanes, its interminable ranges of houses and shops, its imposing public buildings, the rapid succession of vehicles of every pattern which sweep along the avenues, and the endless crowds of human beings that jostle each other on the sidewalks. It is to such a youth a new world — stranger and more exciting even than it would be to an intelligent and travelled American or European, to be put down in the streets of Pekin or Jeddo. Nor is the exchange very advantageous on the score of morals. Natural scenery, it is true, will never renew the heart. Voltaire wrote many of his infamous libels upon Christianity, and some of his most licentious tales and essays, while looking out from his villa at Ferney, upon as glorious a panorama as mortal eyes ever gazed upon. And humanity has few more degraded specimens of its handiwork to present to the sympathy of the philanthropist, than some which can be found among the most picturesque regions of the globe. Still, there is much in nature, as contrasted with a great city, that is adapted to refine and improve the character —

"Scenes formed for contemplation, and to nurse
The growing seeds of wisdom; that suggest,
By every pleasing image they present,
Reflections such as meliorate the heart,
Compose the passions, and exalt the mind."

It is certainly a material advantage that in the country, the objects which meet the senses speak of GOD, while in the city we are reminded only of man. Not only do the mountains and forests, the valleys and rivers, illustrate the wisdom and majesty of the Deity; but "the spectacle of active nature is no less favourable to the cultivation of religious feeling than the contemplation of its passive scenes; every bird and every animal has its habits of life independent of man; it has a sagacity which man never taught; and propensities which man could not inspire. The growth of all the plants and fruits of the earth, depends upon laws over which man has no control: out of great cities there is everywhere around and about us a vast system going on utterly independent of human wisdom and human interference; and man learns there the great lesson of his imbecility and dependence, not by that reflection to which superior minds alone can attain, but by those daily impressions upon his senses which make the lesson more universal and more certain. But here everything is man, and man alone; kings and senates command us;

we talk of their decrees and look up to their pleasure; they seem to move and govern all, and to be the providence of cities; in this seat of government, placed under the shadow of those who make the laws, we do not render unto Cæsar the things which are Cæsar's, and unto God the things which are God's; but God is forgotten, and Cæsar is supreme; all is human policy, human foresight, human power; nothing reminds us of invisible dominion and concealed omnipotence; we do nothing but what man bids; we see nothing but what man creates; we mingle with nothing but what man commands; it is all earth and no heaven." *

In the letter, this pertains to London; in its spirit, it applies to all great cities. Nor does it state the whole truth. Not only have we to do here with man's works, man's laws, man's projects, with everything that is of man and that is fitted to fasten the attention upon man, but we "live and move and have our being" amidst a *crowd* — and it must be a robust integrity which can stand this. We are admonished against the danger from this source on high authority. "Be not ye the servants of men." "Thou shalt not follow a multitude to do evil." The best of us need to have these warnings frequently sounded in our ears. And how essential are they to the class whom I am addressing! No man can be blind to the whole-

* Sydney Smith.

some restraints which are imposed on vice, in a city like this, nor to the powerful agencies which are here originated for the support of real religion. It is in no small measure through metropolitan capital, energy, intelligence, and piety, that the mighty conflict with sin is carried forward, which is, by the blessing of God, to result in the general diffusion of Christianity. But it cannot, on the other hand, be denied, that a perfect torrent of worldliness is perpetually pouring itself through all the streets and marts of such a city. The multitudes have their eyes fixed, not on heaven, but on earth. Their employments, their conversation, the motives which drive them on in the fierce race of competition, the institutions and implements of commerce, the whole network of their daily associations, are secularizing in their tendency. And when you superadd to these influences, the fascinating amusements and gilded vices which impregnate the atmosphere with their grateful but deadly malaria, and infuse a new and most effective element into the reigning levity and hardihood of the crowd, you cannot fail to see what imminent peril waits upon every young man who places himself within the reach of these potent seductions. The strong impulse of those who come here from the interior especially, and are severed from their homes, must be, to fall in with the current and let it bear them where it will. It is natural and easy to do as others do around us — to conform to the popular usages and fashions. Men cease to be nice casuists when they are mixed up in a crowd. The practical verdict of the multitude supersedes their inquiries into the right and wrong of actions, and sweeps away their scruples — or, at least sweeps *them* away, even though their scruples remain. The motives which induce this passive acquiescence in the ways of the majority, may be commendable. It may spring from modesty, or from a dread of singularity. "Who am I, that I should set myself up as wiser and better than those around me? Why am I called upon to condemn practices and habits which have the sanction of so many older and abler men? Can that be wrong which has so general an approval? I am but an humble individual; can any harm result from my living as other people live?" With such specious sophistries as these, young men too often persuade themselves to barter their independence and their rectitude, for a listless and unworthy subserviency to the opinions of their neighbours. On any other subject they might dare to be singular. On questions of politics, of trade, of education, of literature, they venture not only to think for themselves, but to utter their sentiments with manly freedom, and shape their conduct accordingly. But where morals and religion are concerned, they are either seized with a timidity which makes them suppress their convictions, or paralyzed by an apathy which produces a servile assent, where there ought to be a fearless resistance. If we could cull a few leaves from the private journals of mercantile life, such as are filed away, not in the pigeon-holes of an escritoir, but in the recesses of the heart, it might appear that no small portion of the young men of this class have brought themselves to fall in with one practice and another of the commercial world, only through a tedious series of unavowed misgivings and remonstrances; while many others have been content to take things as they were, without inquiry or reflection. It cannot be disguised that, as a body, their morals are exposed to more or less danger from the preternatural excitement which pervades the whole realm of commerce. This excitement may be detected wherever there is trafficking on a large scale; but it has its *foci* in our great cities; and these young men, like the angel in the sun, are just at the burning point. Allowing that the rivalries and conflicts which occupy them are of a generous nature, still they are a crucible to character, and it is well if they come out of them unscathed. In the customary routine of their duties, they are selling goods to men of every type, seeking customers at their hotels for the houses they represent, carrying on a large correspondence, taking long and hazardous journeys, repelling what they regard as calumniatory statements from adverse sources, sometimes brought into immediate collision with the agents of counter-interests, and tempted, not unfrequently, with a view to mere mercantile ends, to accompany strangers to places of vicious amusement; — and it were a marvel if their principles should suffer no damage in a life like this. Let it be recorded to the lasting honour of the profession to which they have devoted themselves, that amidst these hostile influences there are constantly moulding characters of noble strength and symmetry; and that, in the aggregate, they maintain in their proper sphere, the high reputation of the commercial class for candour and probity. Still, there are disasters. This is a coast where too many fine barques have been wrecked, and too many shattered, not to put us on our guard against its dangers. How these can be eluded or surmounted must be a question of absorbing interest with every young man engaged in mercantile pursuits. It is a question quite too comprehensive to be answered in a single sermon. A few suggestions must, in the present service, supply the place of a formal dissertation on this subject.

Nothing effective can be done in the right direction, until a young man awakes to his PERSONAL RESPONSIBILITY. So long as we move in a crowd, swayed to and fro by its eddies—like the twig entangled in a mass of rubbish on the bosom of a running stream—we cannot but miss the proper end of our being. The servitude of *caste* must be broken. We must think and act for ourselves. We must be impressed with the conviction that there is not only a fitness and an unfitness, an expediency and an inexpediency, a beauty and a deformity, in our specific actions and our general plans and aims, but also A RIGHT AND A WRONG; that this is, beyond all comparison, their most important relation; and that the standard by which it is to be adjusted is not usage, but the LAW OF GOD. It may very well happen that your principles and life are in harmony with those of the great commercial brotherhood to which you belong, and that they justly secure to you the respect and confidence commonly awarded to such virtues as adorn your characters. But is there not another tribunal to which you are amenable? "With me," says the apostle Paul, "it is a very small thing that I should be judged of you, or of man's judgment: yea, I judge not mine own self, but he that judgeth me is the LORD." This is as true of each one of us as it was of Paul. We need not disparage the opinions of our fellow-men; we may, within proper limits, court their approbation. But it is a fatal error to confound their commendation with the Divine sanction, to mistake the *vox populi* for the *vox Dei*, the voice of the people for the voice of God. The balances in which motives and actions are weighed, are hung high above the tumults of commerce — beyond the reach of all those influences which beguile our consciences and bias our judgments. And he alone is likely to go on in the path of rectitude, with an unfaltering step, who has his eye steadfastly fixed on them, and labours to poise his motives and conduct by their unerring decisions.

This cannot be done by one who lives only in the crowd. It is indispensable, if we would attain it, that we HAVE OUR SEASONS OF SELF-COMMUNION AND COMMUNION WITH GOD. If our Saviour found it needful to retire frequently for prayer, how essential must secret meditation and devotion be to us! The very circumstance of withdrawing for this purpose — the consciousness of being alone with God — is peculiarly adapted to foster that feeling of personal responsibility of which we have just spoken. There, in that solitary chamber, the noisy world shut out, the tramp and hum of the crowd heard only as a distant murmur, the cares of business and the enticements of sin left behind — there, with your Bible open before you, and your thoughts going up to the throne of the Omniscient, you cannot well help feeling that you have an existence of your own, an individuality which cannot be merged in the activities of the surrounding multitude, but which is as complete and intransferable as though you were the only rational tenant of the globe. The legitimate effect of these seasons of seclusion is to restore those impressions of the invisible and the spiritual, which continual commerce with the world tends to efface. They supply us with a new stand-point from which to survey the world at large, and our own particular relations to it. You must sometimes have noted in travelling, how different are the views you get of a region of country, as you stand upon a lofty ridge, and retrace your route, from those which beguiled you by the way. And the difference will be far greater in the estimates you form of yourself and of the world in your own dormitory, with the Scriptures for your guide, as compared with those which have engrossed you while actually pursuing your daily avocations. It is here you will be likely to get a fresh sight of that immutable standard of *right and wrong*, which is so often obscured or distorted by the mists of passion and prejudice. Here you will measure yourself, not by your fellow-worms, but by the perfect Exemplar proposed to us in the Gospel. Here you will detect the unworthy motives of some of your actions which have elicited the applause of your friends, and be led to see that you have less cause to be exalted before men, than you have to be abased before God.

Here, in a word, you will have those momentous themes presented to you which we are all so apt to lose sight of, and a due appreciation of which is essential both to our present comfort and our eternal well-being. Whatever is neglected, then, let provision be made, in the adjustment of your time, for a daily season of devotion.

From private to public devotion, the transition is easy and natural. Look again at your position. Immortal, accountable, and dying creatures, you are placed in circumstances where you are in imminent danger of being swept away by the torrent of secularity which breaks over you with all its force during six days of every week. Duty, interest, happiness, your everlasting salvation, are all involved in your escaping or repelling it. What are you to do? To breast it in your own strength, would be like attempting to breast the rapids of the Niagara, and must equally lead to a fatal catastrophe. But our heavenly Father has not left us to so hard a fate. He has offered us his own Almighty arm for a support, and taught us how to avail ourselves of it. Pre-eminent among his merciful arrangements for this end, stands the CHRISTIAN SABBATH — an institution so fraught with blessings of every kind, that to contemn it would argue a mind dead to all sense of gratitude, and to all proper consideration for the improvement of the race. In your situation, the Sabbath has a value which no words can express. It comes to you with its sweet repose, to refresh you from your toil and weariness. It comes to turn the current of your associations; to repeat for you the miracle of the Red Sea, and roll back, for a few hours, the swelling tide which threatens to submerge you; to take you out of the beaten track in which you are treading your ceaseless rounds, and open to you the green pastures and still waters of paradise; to change the scene for you, from warehouses and customers, merchandize and trafficking, to the house of God, the reverence and the solemnity of a worshipping assembly, the songs of Zion, and the sublime themes of revelation. An alternation like this is invaluable, in a mere intellectual view. The mind dwarfs and rusts if it is kept to a stereotype routine of functions. To give breadth and comprehension to its powers, the subjects on which they are employed must be diversified. It were better to change sometimes to trifling objects, than not to change at all. And if this principle be sound, the advantage, simply in the way of mental culture, must be incalculable, when the subjects presented for consideration are at once the most majestic and the most urgent which can engage the attention of rational beings. The time forbids me to go into this inquiry now, but the fact must be apparent to every hearer, that you render an individual a most useful service, aside from any moral benefit he may receive, when you replace, even for an hour or two, the mass of earthliness which fills his heart and monopolizes his faculties from day to day, with ideas of God and eternity, the soul and its destiny, redemption and perdition. You startle him from his torpor. You wake up his powers. You open to him a new creation. You send off his thoughts into regions he had scarcely dreamed of. You enlarge the grasp of his faculties, and qualify him to pass with a discrimination and an acuteness previously undeveloped, upon the common pursuits and familiar topics of life. So true is it, that "the fear of the Lord is the beginning of wisdom," even taking "wisdom" in its lowest signification.

But the Sabbath has a much stronger claim upon you than this, and it is insisted upon here because this is precisely the pivot upon which the career of thousands of clerks in our cities hinges. *The Sabbath is the point in their scheme of life at which the road forks;* one track leading on to honour, success, and usefulness; the other to ultimate ruin, and frequently to premature failure and disgrace. If you consider the matter (for I can do little more than state the fact), you will find that the proper observance of the Sabbath is affiliated with every virtue and every good habit, with all the agencies which are favourable to self-improvement and solid happiness, and all those which go to prepare men for heaven; while the habitual desecration or neglect of this day is as closely interlaced with the evil propensities of the heart, with vicious habits, and with those pestiferous influences which subvert men's principles and destroy their souls. The profanation of the Sabbath implies a want of reverence for the Divine authority, and of gratitude for the Divine goodness, which is itself an evil omen. There is a flaw already in the character or the conscience of the man who can permit himself to invade the sanctity of that day which Jehovah claims as his own, and upon which He has impressed his image and superscription. This conduct denotes an absence of that plenary integrity towards God which is the best guarantee of inflexible integrity towards man. Honesty may co-exist with irreligion and with downright infidelity. But its only immutable and adequate basis is faith in Jesus Christ. A merchant who looks only to his own interest, and who is as indifferent to the spiritual welfare of his clerks as he is to the thrift of the dray-horses in the street, would nevertheless pursue a wise policy by encouraging them to a faithful observance of the Sabbath. The more they feel their obligations to God, the more conscientious will they be in serving their employer; for, it is the same principle which puts a man upon fearing God, and upon rendering to all their dues — which makes one loyal to heaven, and upright in all that pertains to earth. The neglect of the Sabbath involves a disreputable neglect of the Bible. It fosters a disrelish for serious things. It blunts the conscience. It promotes indolence and instability. It frequently contributes to nourish a taste for demoralizing books. It leads to bad company — Sunday-drives — drinking — theatres — and other pernicious recreations. It lays men open to the subtle approaches of skeptics and scoffers. While, on the other hand, it removes from them the restraints, and deprives them of the helps, which we all require in our warfare with sin, and which they certainly require, who rush unbidden into all these temptations. A volume would scarcely suffice to discuss this topic. But the occasion precludes my doing more than to exhort you by every motive which can be addressed to your interest, your duty, or your desire of happiness, to guard your Sabbaths from desecration. God has given you this day as your own: "The Sabbath was made for man." The world has no right to it. Business has no lien upon it. Friends may not deprive you of it. He has bestowed it upon you for your own use and benefit; and, if your eyes are not holden, you will see that it is a more munificent gift than if he had made you a grant of all the ships that float on our waters, or all the gold they have brought here for coinage. Dedicate it to its high and holy purposes — to the worship of God, to your preparation for eternity, and to philanthropic labours for your destitute or suffering fellow-creatures. HAVE A PLACE IN SOME EVANGELICAL CHURCH — a place which shall be your own. This will make you feel like occupying it, and take away that illusive and fatal pretext, which keeps so many young men from the sanctuary, that they "have no place to go to." It will do more. By identifying yourselves with a congregation, you become sharers in their sympathies and their prayers. You participate, more or less, in their spiritual blessings. The very relations you sustain towards them will become fresh incentives to virtuous conduct. You will be conscious of occupying a more conspicuous, and, I may add, a more honourable, position in the community; of having friendly eyes turned upon you, and friendly expectations cherished concerning you; all which will be wholesome props and stimulants in the race of life. Above all, this will bring you within the sound of the Gospel. It will set home upon your consciences at stated intervals, those lessons of our mortality and responsibility which we are all so prone to forget, keep you admonished that it is your duty to "seek first the kingdom of God and his righteousness," and supply you with the aids essential to the achievement of this great end. Let nothing, then, prevent you from attaching yourselves, not by the precarious tie of caprice or fashion, but by the firm bond of principle and duty, to some evangelical congregation.

It will not do, however, to rest here. "The kingdom of God" must be sought until it is found. By nature and by practice we are alienated from God, and rebels against him. Our prime duty, our most urgent necessity, is to be restored to his favour, and transformed into his image. We must be pardoned through the blood of Christ, and renewed by the Divine Spirit, or we are lost for ever. We require this, as already intimated, on other grounds. It were a theme well worthy your attention — true religion as an element in the commercial character— a subject of peculiar interest, and happily illustrated in numerous examples around us, of accomplished merchants whose lives are transfused with the spirit of genuine piety. It would be a grateful office to trace the influence of a steadfast and intelligent faith both upon the intellectual and the moral powers — to see how it operates in imparting strength and symmetry to the character — how it fosters integrity, prudence, sagacity, and industry — how it excites to the cultivation of all the faculties — how it represses evil tendencies and wards off temptations — and how it inspires general respect and confidence. These are important bearings of personal religion as regards mercantile character and success. But we have no time to consider them in detail.

To a single one of them I may be allowed to advert briefly; I refer to the temptations incident to your peculiar vocation. What these are, you know a great deal better than I can tell you. That they are neither few nor small, might be inferred from the sketches already given of your general mode of life. You have your homes in those great establishments (conducted, often, let it be said, with admirable skill and efficiency) into which steamboats and railway trains are constantly pouring crowds of travellers. Imbued with a becoming zeal for the success of your respective houses, you adopt all honourable measures to extend their business. Among the eager and shifting multitude with whom you are thus brought in contact, are men who are curious to see the sights of the city, and others who are bent on amusements and indulgences which the small towns and villages they reside in do not supply. Your aid is invoked as guides and companions — possibly, sometimes, tendered where it is not invoked. You will not thank me, perhaps, if I go further. But how can I do you good unless I tell you the truth? Let me remind you, then, that this very process has brought many a promising young man to ruin. It too often conducts them to the theatre, and other places of vicious amusement. It carries them out on Sunday excursions. It leads to drinking and card-playing. It makes them acquainted with gamblers and profligates — the marauders that may be seen at almost all hours of the day, lounging about some of the most conspicuous corners in our city, and who, if tolerated, will entrench themselves in the hotels. A salesman will vindicate this policy to his own conscience, on the ground that it is designed to subserve the interests of his principals. This it may do for a time, and in a limited degree; but it seldom works well in the end. Business may be increased at too large a cost. Gun-cotton was at first hailed as a wonderful achievement in the arts, and one likely to be of high public utility. But it has been found that the process of preparing it is attended with imminent hazard to the operatives, and that when manufactured, it is a very dangerous tenant: the risk of it is greater than its value. Custom that is got by *treating* and frequenting scenes of dissipation, is very like gun-cotton. It jeopards health and character to get it, and when secured, it is very apt to blow up and scatter your property to the winds.* How can it be otherwise? No man

---

* I have heard one of the most accomplished and influential salesmen in this city, say, that in the whole of his

can be an eligible customer, who is not a man of correct principles and habits. If he lacks this requisite, the larger his purchases the more perilous for the house that sells to him. What reliance, then, can be placed upon a man whose morals are already so debauched that he spends his time while in the city, in sensual pleasures? or upon one of so little intelligence and energy, that a bottle of wine or a complimentary visit to some place of amusement, will control him in buying his goods? It is suicidal for a house to countenance *any* measure which may tend to weaken the moral sense of a customer, or foster his inferior appetites. How many have been inoculated in our Atlantic cities with the fatal virus of intemperance or gambling, who have gone back to their distant homes and indulged these propensities for a while in secret, until at length, after a few more visits to the seaboard, they have been mastered by their evil passions, and ruined in health, fortune, and character. "Wealth gotten by vanity shall be diminished." There is a Providence as much in commerce as in religion: and it can excite no surprise in a reflecting mind, that a traffic which it has corrupted the morals of clerks and customers to gain,

---

experience, he never knew a customer secured by the course alluded to, who did not prove, in the end, a scourge to the house he dealt with.

should sooner or later entail losses, if not dishonour, on all concerned in it.

Let not these observations be misunderstood. They involve no impeachment of the mercantile body, as such. The character of this profession, whether in the city or the country, for general intelligence and probity, is beyond reproach; as is the reputation of the young men, as a class, who are charged with the endless subordinate (or, in one sense, primary) agencies in the world of trade. But no profession is free from unworthy members. And even if there were fewer of this sort than there are, engaged in mercantile pursuits, your situation would still be one to demand for you the restraints and safeguards of true religion. Not that religion would infallibly preserve you either from error or sin. But you would be far safer with it than you can be without it. It would hold you back from many a scene of peril, and blunt the edge of many an enticement to evil. It would come to the help of your good purposes, when borne down by a formidable array of numbers, or giving way under some sudden temptation. It would establish your moral principles on a solid basis, and insure you those Divine succours, without which, all our strength is weakness, and our wisdom, folly.

But there is the still weightier consideration to be pondered by you, already mentioned. The one great alternative demands our care, "Except ye repent, ye shall all likewise perish"—REPENTANCE or PERDITION. Here is a sufficient, an unanswerable argument why you should all "seek the kingdom of God" without delay, viz., that this is the only way in which you can be prepared for death and eternity. Some of you have had this argument presented to you lately with a solemnity and a tenderness which the pulpit cannot emulate. Who that stood by the bed-side of the lamented SLOAN, can forget his testimony! There he lay, his manly form writhing under paroxysms of intense suffering, and his generous nature pierced with the deeper anguish of a reclaiming conscience, and an anticipated judgment—there he lay, lamenting with bitter sorrow that he had postponed his preparation for death until the hand of death was upon him. It is not for us to draw aside the curtain, and learn whether those anxious prayers for mercy which engaged so large a portion of the last forty-eight hours of his life, received a gracious answer. We may hope that they did. We may cherish the alleviating thought that the confidence he expressed was well grounded, a confidence reposing not on his own works or merits, which he so emphatically disclaimed, but wholly on the true foundation, the righteousness of Christ. This will not abate the force of his admissions, or the urgency of his appeals. It was his dying testimony, that it is most unwise to neglect the claims of religion in the season of health. It was his earnest and affectionate admonition to some of his kind and sympathizing friends, "See that you do not defer your preparation, as I have done, until you are laid upon a death-bed." What can I add to this? If we could revoke him from yonder cemetery, if we could call back his immortal spirit from the unseen world, and he could stand for a brief space where I stand, and you could hear again the tones of that familiar voice, think you he would cancel the confessions and expostulations of his death-scene? You cannot believe this. You cannot doubt that with the experience he has now had of the eternal world, he would plead with you, trumpet-tongued, to be reconciled to God; that he would warn you against all delays; and entreat you with tears to "seek first the kingdom of God." Do you not owe it to his memory, as well as to yourselves, to heed this counsel?

"Smitten friends
Are angels sent on errands full of love;
For us they languish, and for us they die:
And shall they languish, shall they die, in vain?
Ungrateful, shall we grieve their hovering shades,
Which wait the revolution in our hearts?
Shall we disdain their silent, soft address;
Their posthumous advice and pious prayer;
Senseless, as herds that graze their hallow'd graves,
Tread under foot their agonies and groans;
Frustrate their anguish, and destroy their deaths?"

Under any circumstances, an appeal from an individual who is just passing into eternity, must be regarded with seriousness. But in this case it derives great force and solemnity from the character of the man. It is no barren, posthumous compliment, when it is stated, that he was a man of generous impulses and untarnished honour, one who scorned all meanness and chicanery, and who would rather do no business at all, than not do it on principles of straightforward honesty.* Here, in the judgment of very many intelligent persons, he had a foundation upon which he might have rested with safety: "If virtues like these do not insure salvation, who can hope to be

* Mr. Sloan's disposition may be inferred from an anecdote which I have received on the best authority. Before he came to this city to reside, he had been in business in Tennessee. His property was entirely absorbed in discharging the liabilities contracted by the firm of which he was a member. He went out several months since to collect some money from a person who was largely in debt to him, and returned without it. "Why did you not get your money?" said a friend to him. "Because," he replied, "I went to the house, and found them all packed up, just about removing to Texas. And when I looked at his wife and little children, and considered that if I insisted upon my claim, it might be taking the bread out of their mouths, and breaking up their plans, I couldn't do it. I chose rather to lose the money myself; and so I turned about, and came back, without even mentioning the subject to him."

saved?" And yet, when the hour of trial came, SLOAN did not feel that he could trust to this foundation. He well knew that his character was about to be subjected to the scrutiny of that immaculate Being in whose sight the very heavens are not clean, and that the graceful qualities which had procured him the esteem of his fellow-men, might prove a very insufficient equipment to fit him for the presence of a holy God. His testimony on this vital point, corroborated as it is by the whole tenor of Scripture, may well put you upon a careful examination of your principles. If he could not trust to his morality, can you? If, when the icy fingers of death came to grasp his hope, it shrivelled and vanished, what will become of yours? If he found it needful to fly to the blood of sprinkling and the righteousness of Christ for pardon, how can YOU escape if you neglect this great salvation? May that Almighty Spirit whose succour he so anxiously implored, seal upon your hearts his dying counsels, and lead you all to the Lamb of God, who taketh away the sin of the world!

THE END.

www.ingramcontent.com/pod-product-compliance
Lightning Source LLC
LaVergne TN
LVHW020058110826
845151LV00001B/12

* 9 7 8 1 4 2 5 5 4 5 2 4 6 *